The *Sams Teach Yourself in 24 Hours* Series

Sams Teach Yourself in 24 Hours books provide quick and e[...]
answers in a proven step-by-step approach that works for y[...]
In just 24 sessions of one hour or less, you will tackle every task
you need to get the results you want. Let our experienced
authors present the most accurate information to get you reliable
answers—fast!

File Operation Keys

KEY COMBINATION	FUNCTION
Ctrl+O	Opens a new file
Ctrl+B	Backs up a file
Ctrl+P	Prints (register, list, and so on)
Shift+Delete	Cuts the selected data and places it on the Clipboard
Ctrl+Insert	Copies the selected data and places it on the Clipboard
Shift+Insert	Pastes cut or copied data from the Clipboard to a new location
F1	Opens Quicken Help for the current window

Navigation Shortcut Keys

KEY COMBINATION	FUNCTION
Alt+left arrow	Moves to the previous window
Alt+right arrow	Moves to the next window
Alt+Home	Opens the Quicken Home Page
Tab	Moves to the next field or column
Shift+Tab	Moves to the previous field or column
Home	Moves to the beginning of the field
Home twice	Moves to the first field in a transaction or window or the first row in a report
Home three times	Moves to the first transaction in a window
Home four times	Moves to the first transaction in a register
Ctrl+Home	Moves to the first transaction or the upper-left section of a report
End	Moves to the end of a field
End twice	Moves to the last field in a transaction or window or to the last row in a report
End three times	Moves to the last transaction in a window
End four times	Moves to the last transaction in a register
Ctrl+End	Moves to the last transaction or lower-right section of a report
PgDn	Moves to the next window or check
PgUp	Moves to the previous window or check
Up arrow	Moves up one row
Down arrow	Moves down one row

Teach Yourself Quicken® Deluxe 99 in 24 Hours

List and Window Shortcut Keys

KEY COMBINATION	FUNCTION
Ctrl+A	Opens the Account List
Ctrl+C	Opens the Category/Transfer List
Ctrl+H	Opens the View Loans window
Ctrl+J	Opens the Scheduled Transaction List
Ctrl+K	Opens the Financial Calendar
Ctrl+L	Opens the Class List
Ctrl+Q	Opens the Currency List
Ctrl+R	Opens the register
Ctrl+T	Opens the Memorized Transaction List
Ctrl+U	Opens Portfolio view
Ctrl+W	Opens the Write Checks window
Ctrl+Y	Opens the Security List

Register Shortcut Keys

KEY COMBINATION	FUNCTION
Ctrl+E	Edits transaction
Ctrl+D	Deletes transaction
Ctrl+I	Inserts new transaction
Ctrl+M	Memorizes transaction
Ctrl+N	Creates new transaction
Ctrl+S	Opens Split Transaction Window
Ctrl+V	Voids selected transaction
Ctrl+X	Goes to transfer
Ctrl+F	Opens Quicken Find dialog box
Ctrl+Enter	Closes Split Transaction Window
Shift+Ctrl+F	Finds next match

Register Date Shortcut Keys

KEY COMBINATION	FUNCTION
t	Enters today's date
m	Enters the first day of the current month
h	Enters the last day of the current month
y	Enters the first day of the current year
r	Enters the last day of the current year
Ctrl+G	Opens the Go To Date dialog box
Ctrl+PgDn	Moves to the next month
Ctrl+PgUp	Moves to the previous month

SAMS

Patrice-Anne Rutledge

SAMS
Teach Yourself
Quicken® Deluxe 99
in 24 Hours

SAMS

A Division of Macmillan Computer Publishing
201 West 103rd St., Indianapolis, Indiana, 46290 USA

Sams Teach Yourself Quicken® Deluxe 99 in 24 Hours

Copyright © 1999 by Sams Publishing

FIRST EDITION

International Standard Book Number: 0-672-31358-8

Library of Congress Catalog Card Number: 98-85314

Printed in the United States of America

First Printing: 1999

00 99   4   3   2

Trademarks

EXECUTIVE EDITOR
Angela Wethington

ACQUISITIONS EDITOR
Jamie Milazzo

DEVELOPMENT EDITOR
Brian Kent-Proffitt

MANAGING EDITOR
Thomas F. Hayes

PROJECT EDITOR
Lori A. Lyons

COPY EDITORS
Andy Saff
Shanon Martin

INDEXER
Chris Wilcox

TECHNICAL EDITOR
Jo Ann Schiller

PROOOFREADER
Lynne Miles-Morillo

PRODUCTION
Lisa England

Overview

Contents

Dedication

To my family—thanks for your love and support.

Acknowledgments

I'd like to thank everyone who contributed to the creation of *Sams Teach Yourself Quicken Deluxe 99 in 24 Hours*: Jamie Milazzo, for suggesting I write this book and providing enthusiasm and support throughout the project; Dave Karlins, for contributing several great chapters; Brian Kent-Proffitt, for his many organizational and editorial contributions; and Jo Ann Schiller, for her attention to detail.

And special thanks to my mom, Phyllis Rutledge, for both her editorial expertise and her encouragement throughout the creation of this book.

About the Author

PATRICE-ANNE RUTLEDGE is the author or contributing author of 15 computer and business books by leading publishers, including *Using Microsoft Office 97 Bestseller Edition*, also published by Macmillan. As both an independent consultant and manager at leading international technology firms, Patrice has been involved in many aspects of computing: developing financial applications, managing technical communications programs, and localizing software. Patrice began her career as a technical translator, but quickly discovered new opportunities in the computer industry. She is a graduate of the University of California with a degree in French Linguistics and has been using Quicken to manage her home and business finances for the past five years. When Patrice isn't busy writing, she enjoys traveling, foreign films, good music, and trying the many ethnic restaurants in the San Francisco bay area where she resides. You can reach her at patrice_rutledge@compuserve.com.

Tell Us What You Think!

As the reader of this book, *you* are our most important critic and commentator. We value your opinion and want to know what we're doing right, what we could do better, what areas you'd like to see us publish in, and any other words of wisdom you're willing to pass our way.

As the Executive Editor for the General Desktop Applications team at Macmillan Computer Publishing, I welcome your comments. You can fax, email, or write me directly to let me know what you did or didn't like about this book—as well as what we can do to make our books stronger.

Please note that I cannot help you with technical problems related to the topic of this book, and that due to the high volume of mail I receive, I might not be able to reply to every message.

When you write, please be sure to include this book's title and author as well as your name and phone or fax number. I will carefully review your comments and share them with the author and editors who worked on the book.

Fax: 317-581-4663
E-mail: office@mcp.com
Mail: Executive Editor
         General Desktop Applications
         Macmillan Computer Publishing
         201 West 103rd Street
         Indianapolis, IN 46290 USA

Introduction

Quicken is one of the most popular personal finance software programs available today. Quicken Deluxe 99, the latest version of this program, enables you to easily track your income and expenses, analyze your investments, and create a budget—among other things. It also offers time-saving Internet features that enable you to download stock quotes, access bank and credit card account information, and pay bills online. Quicken Home & Business 99 provides added features for small business owners, such as the ability to track payables and receivables as well as create invoices.

Before you get started learning Quicken, take a few minutes to understand how this book is organized and the common conventions it uses.

What This Book Will Do for You

If you've never used Quicken before or only have a basic familiarity with it, then this book is for you. In 24 lessons of one hour or less, you'll learn the basics of how to use this powerful program in clear, easy-to-understand steps. *Sams Teach Yourself Quicken Deluxe 99 in 24 Hours* covers everything you need to know to use Quicken—from installation to transaction entry to reporting and analysis. It provides comprehensive coverage of all basic Quicken features, but in a way that's easy for beginners to follow. Each chapter, referred to as an "hour" in this book, teaches you how to perform an essential Quicken task. The hours progress from the basics to more advanced tasks, such as downloading information from the Internet and analyzing your investment portfolio.

Sams Teach Yourself Quicken Deluxe 99 in 24 Hours focuses on the Quicken Deluxe 99 version but is also useful if you purchased Quicken Home & Business 99. This book includes an appendix especially for Home & Business users that provides a quick overview of the business features of this related product.

Conventions Used in This Book

Sams Teach Yourself Quicken Deluxe 99 in 24 Hours uses a number of conventions that are consistent throughout the entire book:

- Menu commands are separated by a comma. For example, if you need to select the Banking option from the Features menu, you'll see Features, Banking.
- Internet addresses and text you type appear in `monospaced type`.
- Every hour ends with common questions and answers.

In addition to these conventions, each hour also includes the following elements:

Notes provide additional information and material related to the topic of discussion.

Tips offer alternate or time-saving ways to do things.

Cautions warn you about potential pitfalls and tell you how to avoid them.

NEW TERM   New terms that might be confusing are explained separately.

PART I
Getting Started

Hour

HOUR 1

Getting Acquainted with Quicken

This hour introduces you to Quicken Deluxe 99, the powerful, versatile financial tracking and planning software from Intuit. After you install Quicken for the first time, you want to spend some time familiarizing yourself with its features and how to navigate the Quicken desktop. If you're upgrading from a previous version, Quicken automatically upgrades your files as you open them. In addition, Quicken Deluxe 99 provides several enhancements to its online help functionality to make using the program even easier.

The highlights of this hour include

- What Quicken can do for you
- How to start Quicken
- What are the best ways to navigate Quicken
- Where to find online help
- How to use Quicken's calculator
- How to exit Quicken

Exploring What Quicken Can Do for You

Quicken Deluxe 99 is a powerful, yet easy-to-use software program for tracking and planning your finances. You can use Quicken to do the following:

- Track your bank accounts, credit cards, and cash.
- Track your investments and analyze how they are performing.
- Track your loans, including mortgages and car loans.
- Plan for taxes, retirement, college expenses, and savings.
- Create reports and graphs that calculate and analyze your financial performance.
- Set up budgets and forecasts.
- Track your household inventory and emergency records.
- Pay your bills, access account information, and download stock quotes online.

Quicken may seem complicated at first, but you can break down the tasks you need to perform into three main steps. First, you set up accounts to track your bank accounts, credit cards, cash, investments, loans, and other assets. Next, you record transactions in these accounts. And finally, you use Quicken's reporting and analytical tools to view both the big picture and individual details of your financial progress.

Exploring Quicken's New Features

If you used a previous version of Quicken, you find many of its new features make handling your finances even easier. Some of Quicken Deluxe 99's most time-saving new features include the following:

- *QuickEntry*. Quicken now includes a separate application called QuickEntry that lets you quickly record register data. This can save you time by directly accessing just your registers rather then the entire Quicken program. It also enables you to let other people perform data entry in your Quicken accounts without letting them view previously entered data or any of your other Quicken information.
- *Quicken financial activity centers*. Quicken has greatly expanded what it previously called Snapshots into a new feature called a Financial Activity Center. Centers combine Snapshots with reports and Web links on a particular topic. Quicken Deluxe 99 includes several centers on topics such as banking, planning, and investing.
- *One Step Update*. You can now download stock quotes and news, update your Web portfolio, and access online account information in one step rather than connecting to the Internet separately to download this information.

- *Multicurrency support.* If you spend time overseas and make purchases using other currencies, you can now record these directly in Quicken. Multicurrency support lets you enter a transaction in one currency, automatically convert it to your home currency, and update exchange rates.

Starting Quicken

To start Quicken, double-click the Quicken Deluxe 99 icon that is placed on your Windows desktop when you installed the program (see Figure 1.1).

FIGURE 1.1

Click this desktop icon to start Quicken.

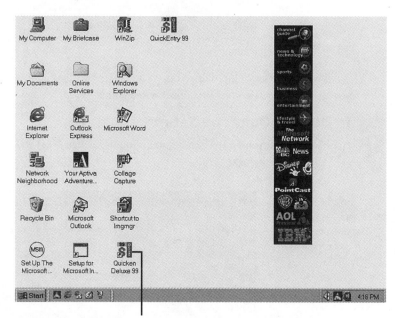

Double-click to start Quicken

Using Quicken for the First Time

When you install Quicken for the first time, the Quicken New User Setup dialog box greets you as soon as you finish the installation procedure. Figure 1.2 displays this dialog box.

 Be sure to have your latest checking account statement on hand before you start this procedure.

FIGURE 1.2

Quicken New User Setup guides you through creating your first account.

Quicken New User Setup helps you set up categories that apply to your financial situation as well as create your first checking account.

To Do: Use Quicken's Setup

To Do

1. In the Quicken New User Setup dialog box, click Next to continue. Figure 1.3 illustrates the next step.

FIGURE 1.3

Answer some basic questions to determine which categories you need.

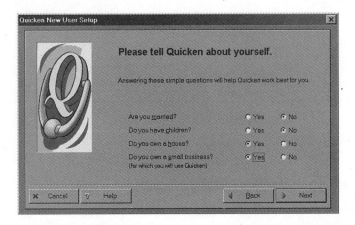

2. Answer basic questions about your marital status, children, home ownership, and small business requirements and click Next (see Figure 1.4).

FIGURE 1.4

*Your first account
should be a checking
account.*

3. Quicken sets up a checking account for you. Enter an Account Name and click
   Next (see Figure 1.5).

FIGURE 1.5

*Let Quicken know if
you have your check-
ing account statement.*

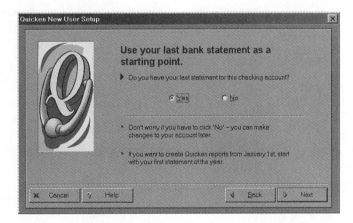

4. Click Yes if you have your latest checking account statement and then click Next
   to continue. Figure 1.6 displays the next step.

FIGURE **1.6**

Enter information based on your latest checking account statement.

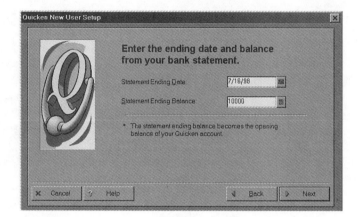

5. Enter the Statement Ending Date and Ending Balance for this account and click Next. Figure 1.7 illustrates this final step.

FIGURE **1.7**

Verify that your data is accurate in this summary step.

6. Verify that this information is correct, modify if necessary, and click Done.

You now have a basic Quicken file that includes a checking account. Quicken calls this file QDATA. From here you can continue setting up other accounts that you need (bank accounts, credit card accounts, investment accounts, loans, and so on).

> Hour 2, "Working with Data Files and Accounts," shows you how to set up additional accounts.

Upgrading to Quicken Deluxe 99

If you are upgrading from a previous version, Quicken recognizes this and automatically converts your old Quicken data file to a Quicken Deluxe 99 format when you open it. Quicken doesn't delete your old files, but rather saves them in a special folder, such as \Q98FILES, in case you ever need to use them again.

Navigating the Quicken Desktop

Quicken offers several options for navigating its system and finding the features you want. Quicken menus are the most basic form of navigational assistance and something that almost all users should be familiar with. Figure 1.8 displays Quicken menus.

FIGURE 1.8

Use menus to navigate Quicken.

Quicken menus

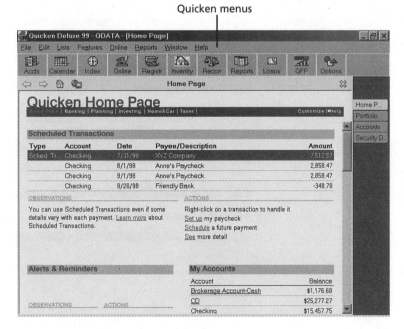

With these menus you can access all parts of the Quicken system. Before you start using the program, be sure to familiarize yourself with these menus and their submenus. Quicken menus and their most important functions include the following:

- *File.* Provides access to file activities such as backing up, setting passwords, and printing.
- *Edit.* Provides access to the Quicken calculator and Quicken customization options.

- *Lists.* Lets you display and edit lists of accounts, transactions, categories, classes, and securities.
- *Features.* Offers a gateway to Quicken's main features for banking, bill payment, investing, financial planning, and tax planning.
- *Online.* Provides a gateway to Quicken's online account access, investment information retrieval, and bill paying features.
- *Reports.* Provides access to Quicken reporting and graphing features.
- *Window.* Enables you to quickly set navigation options such as QuickTabs, the Iconbar, and Activity bar as well as to reopen the last few windows you used.
- *Help.* Offers several options for getting online help.

Using the Iconbar

You can use the Iconbar to immediately reach the most common areas of Quicken. Figure 1.9 illustrates the icons that display by default, but you can adjust this if you want, adding or deleting icons to reflect the Quicken features you use most.

Iconbar

FIGURE 1.9

The Iconbar is another navigational tool.

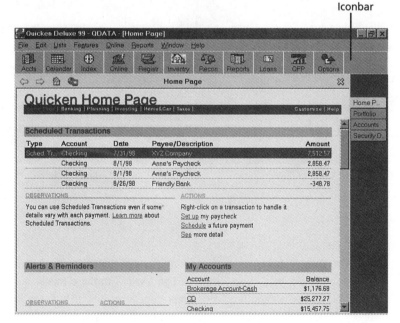

Select Edit, Options, Iconbar to customize the Iconbar. Hour 11, "Customizing Quicken," shows you how to do this.

 Select Window, Show Top Iconbar to toggle the Iconbar on and off. A check mark before the menu option indicates that the Iconbar displays.

Using the Activity Bar

If you're new to Quicken, you may prefer to navigate the system through a list of functional tasks. The Activity bar provides this type of navigational support. To activate it, select Window, Show Activity Bar.

Quicken now displays the Activity bar at the bottom of the screen, shown in Figure 1.10.

FIGURE 1.10

The activity bar provides functional navigation assistance.

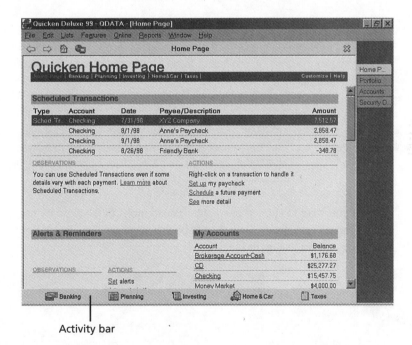

Activity bar

The Activity bar includes five icons covering different functional areas of Quicken: Banking, Planning, Investing, Home & Car, and Taxes. Click an icon to display a list of tasks you can perform (see Figure 1.11).

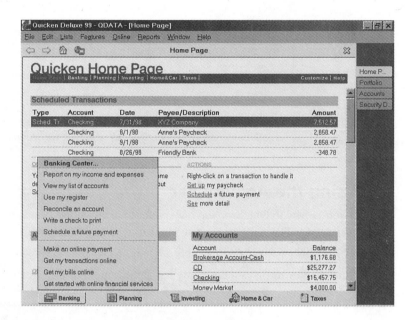

FIGURE **1.11**

*The Activity bar dis-
plays a list of tasks.*

Select the task you want and Quicken opens the appropriate window or dialog box for
you. For example, if you select View My Portfolio from the Investing icon menu,
Quicken opens Portfolio view.

Depending on your Windows screen settings, you may no longer be able to
see the Iconbar if you activate the Activity bar. To reactive the Iconbar (hid-
ing the Activity bar), select Window, Show Top Iconbar.

If you want to shorten the display descriptions in the Activity bar, you can do so in the
General Options dialog box. Select Edit, Options, Quicken Program to display this dialog
box, shown in Figure 1.12.

FIGURE **1.12**

*Set up the Activity bar
in this dialog box.*

Select the Use Short Commands on Activity Bar Menus check box if you want the Activity bar to display short descriptions rather than the default detailed descriptions. Click OK.

Using QuickTabs

After you open an account in Quicken, a corresponding QuickTab displays on the right side of the screen. Figure 1.13 illustrates several QuickTabs.

QuickTabs

FIGURE 1.13

Use QuickTabs to quickly move between accounts.

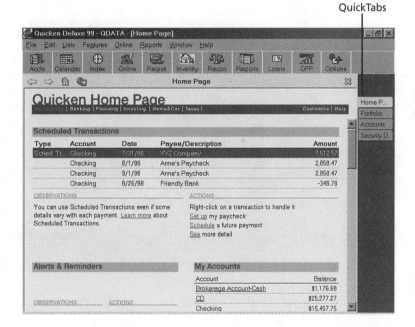

You can select these tabs to quickly move from one account to another.

To move the QuickTabs to the left side of the screen, select Window, QuickTabs on Right. The check mark next to this menu option is removed and the QuickTabs move to the left.

To deactivate QuickTabs, select Window, Show QuickTabs. Again, the check mark is removed and the QuickTabs no longer display.

Getting Help

Quicken provides several ways for you to get help when you have a question or problem, including detailed online help and a user's guide with numerous examples. You can also use Quicken Audio to get voice-over help on using specific features if you don't want to see written help. And with the How Do I button in most Quicken windows, you can view a list of frequently asked questions and their answers.

Using Online Help

To access Quicken online help, select Help, Index, which displays the Help Topics: Quicken Help dialog box, shown in Figure 1.14.

FIGURE 1.14

Search for the topic on which you need help.

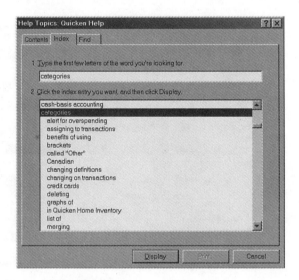

From the Index tab, you can search for information on a variety of topics. For example, if you want to learn how to use Quicken categories, enter the word categories and you get a long list of subtopics from which to choose.

Select the topic you want to see and click Display. Quicken either opens the help topic or opens another dialog box with additional subtopics. Select the topic you want to see in the Topics Found dialog box and click Display. Figure 1.15 illustrates a Quicken help topic.

To perform an even more specific search by looking for exact words rather than a concept, click the Find tab. After setting up Quicken's find feature, you can perform complex searches in online help.

FIGURE 1.15

Quicken displays help on the topic you selected.

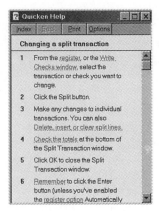

 To get help on the current window, select Help, Current Window. Quicken directly opens the help topic for this window.

To print a topic, click the Print button. The Print dialog box displays (see Figure 1.16). Click OK to print.

FIGURE 1.16

You can print online help topics.

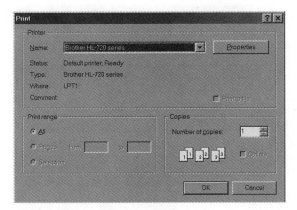

Using the Quicken User's Guide

Quicken includes a User's Guide that offers advice on the best ways to use Quicken. To access this guide, select Help, Index and click the Contents tab, shown in Figure 1.17.

FIGURE 1.17

Select Quicken User's Guide from the Contents tab.

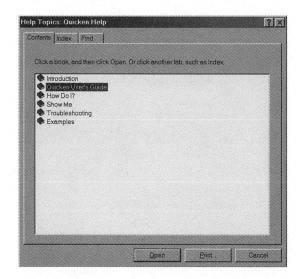

Select the Quicken User's Guide and click Open. Quicken displays a series of dialog boxes similar to the Index tab. Use these to navigate to the information you want, which displays as illustrated in Figure 1.18.

FIGURE 1.18

The Online User's Guide provides advice on using Quicken.

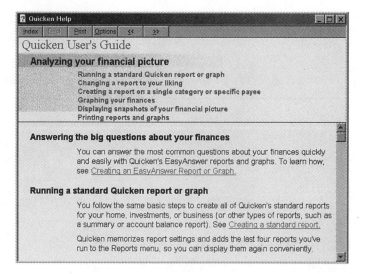

The Contents tab also includes an introduction to Quicken, a troubleshooting guide, and several examples.

Using Quicken Audio

Quicken Audio provides voice-over help on how to perform many Quicken tasks. The first time you attempt to do something in Quicken, the Quicken Audio dialog box appears (see Figure 1.19) and starts to play audio help on that feature.

FIGURE 1.19

You can listen to audio help if you want.

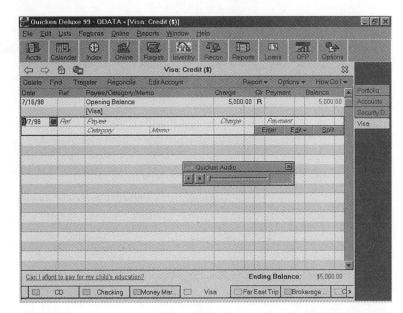

Use the Stop button to stop the audio help and the Play button to play it again. Click the X button to close the audio help.

To activate Quicken Audio later on, select Help, Quicken Audio. A check mark appears next to this menu option. If you don't want to use this feature, be sure that it isn't selected.

Using the How Do I Button

In most Quicken windows a How Do I button is located on the right side of the toolbar. Click the button to display a list of possible questions you could have on using the open window. Figure 1.20 illustrates this list in the Category & Transfer List window.

FIGURE 1.20

Select How Do I to see a list of frequently asked questions.

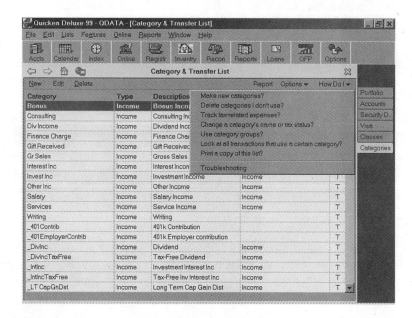

In this example, you find answers to common questions such as: How do I make new categories, delete categories I don't use, and track tax-related expenses? Select the option you want to see and Quicken displays a help topic to answer the question.

Using the Quicken Calculator

Quicken's calculator is a useful tool to have, especially when you need to perform calculations in conjunction with your Quicken activities. You can access the calculator by selecting Edit, Use Calculator. Figure 1.21 displays the Quicken Calculator.

FIGURE 1.21

Use the Quicken calculator to quickly make calculations.

This calculator functions much the same as any regular calculator. You can also access the calculator from other locations in Quicken in which you need to enter numbers. For example, in a Quicken checking account register you need to record payments and deposits. Next to those fields Quicken includes a small calculator icon. Click this icon to display the Quicken calculator. Figure 1.22 illustrates an example of this.

FIGURE 1.22

You can also access the calculator from the register.

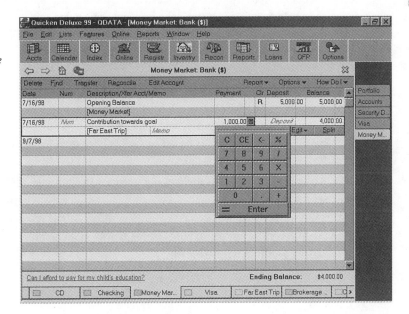

Exiting Quicken

To exit Quicken, select File, Exit. You can also exit by clicking the X button in the upper-right portion of your Quicken window.

 Quicken may display the Backup dialog box when you exit. Specify how often you want Quicken to prompt you to back up by selecting Edit, Options, Quicken Program and choosing the General tab.

Summary

This hour introduced you to Quicken Deluxe 99 and its many features. Whether you're new to Quicken or upgrading, its automated assistance can have you up and running quickly. To navigate the Quicken desktop, you can use a variety of navigational tools—menus, Iconbar, Activity bar, and QuickTabs. Quicken also includes extensive online and voice-over help to guide you through your first days using this program.

Q&A

Q What's the best way to navigate Quicken?

A There is no one best way—a lot depends on how you personally want to use the software. If you're brand new to Quicken, however, the Activity bar provides navigational assistance that is based on tasks rather than features and is usually easier for beginners to understand.

Q After I set up my initial checking account in Quicken, which account should I set up next?

A There is no exact order you must follow to set up Quicken, but one approach you might take is to set up all bank accounts first, then credits cards, cash, loans, assets, 401(k), and finally investments.

HOUR 2

Working with Data Files and Accounts

This hour shows you how to create additional data files and accounts when you start using Quicken. Although one data file is enough to keep an entire set of financial records, Quicken provides the flexibility of supporting multiple data files. A data file contains multiple accounts; each Quicken account provides an easy way to track a financial asset, such as a bank account, credit card, investment, or other asset.

The highlights of this hour include

- Why you might want to create an additional data file
- What types of Quicken accounts you should use
- How to set up a basic account
- How to view an Account List
- How to edit, delete, and hide accounts

Creating a New Data File

Quicken automatically creates a data file when you set up the program for the first time. This data file is called Qdata by default.

NEW TERM A *data file* is a collection of accounts, categories, classes, memorized transactions, and so on. A data file contains multiple accounts.

One data file should be enough for most people, but for some situations you might need more than one. For example, if you track your small business finances separately from your personal finances or if individual members of your household keep separate financial accounts, you may need more than one data file.

To Do: Create a Data File

1. Select File, New to open the Creating New File dialog box, shown in Figure 2.1.

2. Specify that you want to create a new Quicken file and click OK. The Create Quicken File dialog box appears (see Figure 2.2).

FIGURE 2.1

You can create new Quicken files and accounts from this dialog box.

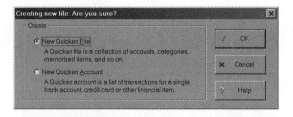

FIGURE 2.2

Choose a meaningful name for your Quicken data files.

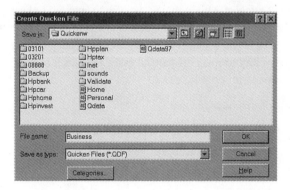

3. In the File Name text box, enter a filename for this data file. Be sure to choose a filename that appropriately identifies what the file contains (Business, Personal, or so on).

When naming a file, remember that you can't use commas, quotation marks, slashes, brackets, braces, periods, plus signs, or minus signs in your filename.

4. Click the Categories button to open the Quicken Categories dialog box, illustrated in Figure 2.3.

FIGURE 2.3

Quicken automatically creates categories based on your personal financial situation.

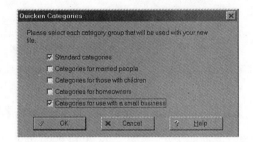

5. Select the categories you want to include in this file. Choices are:

   - Standard categories
   - Categories for married people
   - Categories for those with children
   - Categories for homeowners
   - Categories for use with a small business

6. Click OK to return to the previous dialog box.

Quicken creates investment categories the first time you set up an investment account.

7. If you want to save this data file in a folder other than the current one, enter this location in the Save In field.

8. Click OK to create the data file.

   Quicken creates the new file and displays the Create New Account dialog box (see Figure 2.4) so that you can create the first account for this data file.

FIGURE 2.4

After you create a data file, Quicken prompts you to create an account.

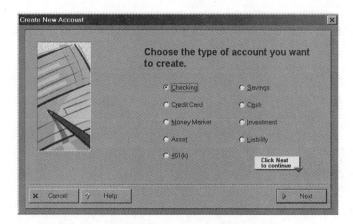

Determining Which Account Type to Use

Quicken offers eight different account types. You don't need to create all eight, but you'll probably want to create most. You will definitely want a checking account, because this is the main account upon which your Quicken financial activity is based. When you set up Quicken for the first time, the program automatically guides you through the creation of a basic checking account. From there, you can add additional accounts based on your personal financial situation. Table 2.1 illustrates the eight main Quicken account types and when to use them.

TABLE 2.1. QUICKEN ACCOUNT TYPES.

Account Type	Description
Checking	Tracks funds and transactions in a checking account. If you have a debit card, you can track those expenses here as well, rather than in a credit card account.
Credit card	Tracks credit card transactions.
Money market	Tracks funds in a money market account.
Asset	Tracks an asset you own, such as your home.
401(k)	Tracks investments (usually mutual funds) you hold in a company-sponsored 401(k) plan. Differs from a regular investment account in that you don't need to know the amount of shares you own or their purchase price to track performance.
Savings	Tracks funds in a savings account.
Cash	Tracks cash expenses, such as an emergency fund or petty cash fund.

Account Type	Description
Investment	Tracks investments you hold with brokerage or mutual funds firms. You need one account for each firm with which you have an account. You do *not* need an individual account for each stock, bond, or mutual fund that you own.
Liability	Tracks a debt you owe, such as a mortgage or car loan.

This hour covers the basics of setting up an account, focusing on checking, savings, money market, credit card, and cash accounts. The other account types are covered in later hours.

Quicken Home & Business includes two additional account types—
Invoices/Receivables and Bills/Payables. The appendix covers Quicken Home
& Business and these account types in more detail.

Creating a New Account

You create a new account in the Create New Account dialog box. You can open this dialog box by

- Creating a new data file. The Create New Account dialog box displays automatically after Quicken completes the data file.
- Selecting File, New and choosing the New Quicken Account option in the Creating New File dialog box.
- Selecting the Accts icon on the iconbar and clicking the New button in the Account List that displays.

In the Create New Account dialog box, you can choose the kind of account you want to create from the eight available options. The dialog box then guides you through the creation of this account type. Setting up an account is similar for all account types, but there are a few differences as well.

Before you set up an account, be sure to have any related statements on
hand so you'll have all the information you need to complete the account
setup.

In the following example, you'll create a savings account to complement the checking account Quicken automatically created for you. Setting up a savings account is nearly identical to setting up checking and money market accounts.

To Do: Create a New Savings Account

1. Select Savings in the Create New Account dialog box (see Figure 2.5) and click OK.

   The Savings Account Setup dialog box appears, as shown in Figure 2.6.

   In this dialog box, you can set up a new savings account with step-by-step EasyStep guidance or use the Summary tab to expedite the setup.

FIGURE 2.5

You can set up nine different types of Quicken accounts.

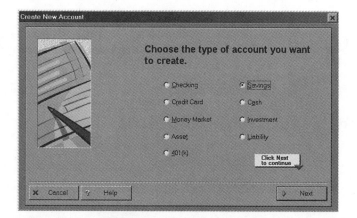

FIGURE 2.6

Quicken can provide step-by-step guidance for setting up an account or enable you to set up an account on your own.

2. On the EasyStep tab, enter an account name and description for this account.

3. Click the Summary tab to continue. Figure 2.7 illustrates this tab.

FIGURE 2.7

Use your latest account statement to determine your current balance.

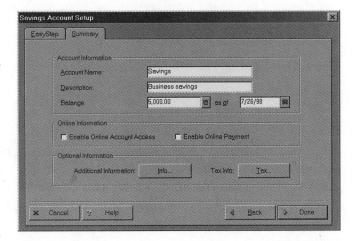

4. In the Balance and As Of fields, enter the account balance and the date of your last statement, respectively.

5. Select Enable Online Account Access if you want to be able to retrieve online statements for this account.

6. Select Enable Online Payment if you want to be able to pay bills online from this account. You must link this account to a checking account to choose this option.

 Enabling online services is described later this hour.

7. Optionally, click the Info button to display the Additional Account Information dialog box, shown in Figure 2.8. You can enter more detailed information about your financial institution in this dialog box.

FIGURE 2.8

Enter the address and other information if you want.

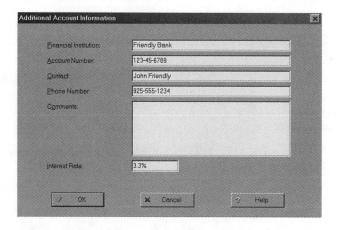

8. Click OK to return to the previous dialog box.

9. Optionally, click the Tax button to display the Tax Schedule Information dialog box, shown in Figure 2.9.

FIGURE 2.9

Specify tax information in this dialog box.

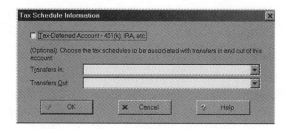

10. Specify whether this is a Tax-Deferred Account such as a 401(k) or IRA, select optional Transfers In and Transfers Out accounts, and click OK.

> If you want to set up a 401(k), you should use the 401(k) Setup dialog box to set up an account specifically designed to handle 401(k) investment tracking.

11. If you don't choose to enable online services, the Done button appears. Click this button to complete the setup and display the register for this savings account (see Figure 2.10).

FIGURE 2.10

Quicken displays the register for your new savings account.

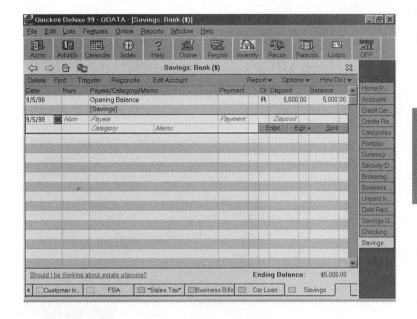

Setting Up a Credit Card

The Credit Card Setup Account dialog box is similar to the dialog box you use to set up bank accounts, but there are a few small differences on the Summary tab, illustrated in Figure 2.11.

FIGURE 2.11

You can access credit card account information from the Internet.

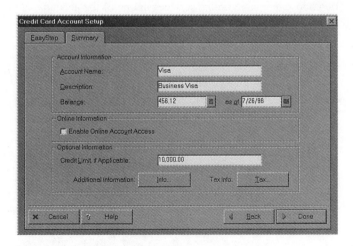

Instead of offering online investment or payment, a credit card account gives you online account access. You can also specify the card's credit limit if one exists.

Setting Up a Cash Account

Because you can't enable online access to a cash account, this option doesn't display on the Summary tab of the Cash Account Setup dialog box, shown in Figure 2.12.

FIGURE 2.12

A cash account enables you to track your household cash expenditures or petty cash for a small business.

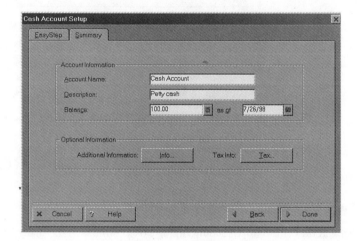

Setting Up an Account with Online Services Enabled

If you choose to enable online services in one of the account setup dialog boxes (see Figure 2.13), Quicken provides several steps to help you set up this feature.

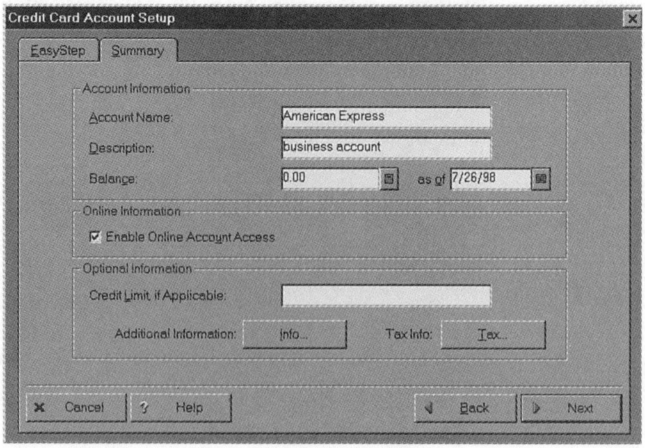

FIGURE 2.13

If you enable online services, Quicken prompts you for more information.

You can also set up online services later by selecting Online, Online Financial Services Setup.

In the next step, select the appropriate financial institution from the drop-down list (see Figure 2.14) and click Next.

2

FIGURE 2.14

If you have already set up your financial institution, you can select it from the drop-down list.

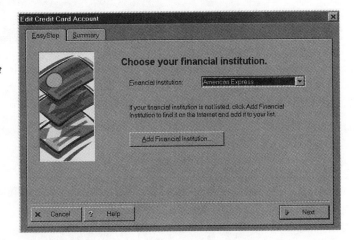

If you haven't set up a financial institution for online services yet, click the Add Financial Institution button; Quicken then connects to the Internet to set up this institution. Hour 23, "Using Online Financial Services," provides more detail about setting up Quicken's online services.

Depending on the type of account, Quicken then asks a series of questions regarding account, customer, and routing numbers.

You must already have these numbers to complete the online services setup in this dialog box. If you don't have this information, set up online services after you receive the necessary access numbers from your financial institution.

When you reach the final step, click Done to complete the account setup.

Viewing the Account List

After you create several Quicken accounts, you will probably want to view a list of your accounts. To do so, select Lists, Account to open the Account List, shown in Figure 2.15.

FIGURE 2.15

The Account List enables you to view and manage your accounts in one location.

Account	Type		Description	Trans	Balance	Checks
Brokerage Account-Cash	Bank	⚡	Linked Checking Account	2	$5,086.67	
CD	Bank			3	$25,277.27	
Checking	Bank			10	$15,556.98	
Money Market	Bank			2	$4,000.00	
Savings	Bank			1	$5,000.00	
Credit Card	Credit			1	$0.00	
Visa	Credit			2	-$4,750.00	
Customer Invoices	Asset			4	$110.00	
Far East Trip	Asset		Savings goal account	2	$1,000.00	
FSA	Asset			2	$50.00	
Sales Tax	Liability			1	$0.00	
Business Bills	Liability			3	-$100.00	
Car Loan	Liability			2	-$16,771.64	
401(k)	401(k)		Anne's 401(k)	10	$18,598.35	
Brokerage Account	Invest	⚡	Anne's Brokerage Acco...	0	$0.00	

Balance Total: $53,057.63

You can also click the Accts icon on the iconbar to open the Account List.

The Account List details the account type, description, number of entered transactions, and balance, and indicates whether there are any checks to print for each account.

The lightning icon next to an account indicates that it's enabled to work with online financial services.

To open the register for an account, select it in the list and then click Open.

By default, Quicken displays all accounts, but you can choose to limit your view to specific account types. To do so, select Options and then choose from the submenu the type of account you want to view. Options include displaying only bank, credit card, investment, or other accounts.

Editing an Account

To edit an existing account, select it in the Account List and click Edit. The Edit dialog box for that type of account opens. Figure 2.16 shows the Edit Bank Account dialog box.

FIGURE 2.16

You can edit an account you previously set up.

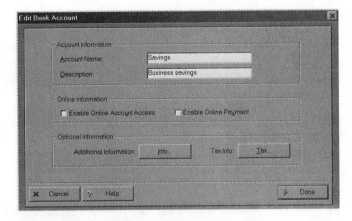

Make any necessary changes in the dialog box and then click Done.

> Click New to create a new account from within the Account List window. The Create New Account dialog box displays.

Deleting an Account

If you no longer need an account, you can delete it. To delete an account, select it and click Delete. Quicken displays a warning dialog box, shown in Figure 2.17, that asks you to type the word *YES* to confirm you want to delete the selected account.

FIGURE 2.17

Quicken verifies that you want to delete the selected account.

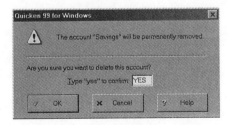

Click OK to complete the deletion.

Remember that if you delete an account, you delete all its related transactions as well.

Hiding Accounts

If you no longer need to enter transactions in an account, you can hide the account. That way, it doesn't display automatically in your Account List or appear on reports, but the data and transactions the account contains still reside in your Quicken file for historical tracking.

To hide an account, select it and click Hide. The account disappears from the Account List, but is not deleted. To view hidden accounts in the list, select Options, View Hidden Accounts. The account displays on the list again, with a small hand icon next to the account name to identify that the account is hidden.

FIGURE 2.18

You can hide, but not delete, accounts.

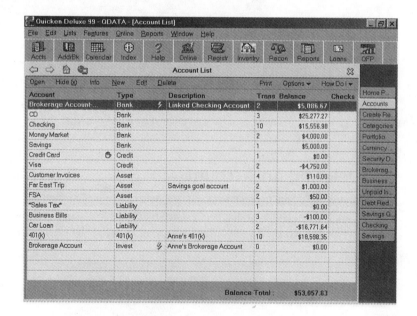

When you create Quicken reports and graphs later on, you can choose whether to include these hidden accounts.

Entering Additional Account Information

If you want to enter additional information about a selected account, click Info to display
the Additional Account Information dialog box (see Figure 2.19).

FIGURE 2.19

*You can provide more
detail about your
accounts if you want.*

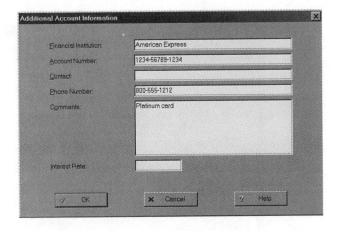

This is the same information you view from the setup dialog boxes. Enter any necessary
details and click OK to return to the Account List.

To Do: Print the Account List

1. Select Print to open the Print dialog box, shown in Figure 2.20.

2. Specify in the Print To panel the printer you want to use.

3. In the Orientation panel, select either a portrait or landscape page orientation.

FIGURE 2.20

*You can set print para-
meters in the Print
dialog box.*

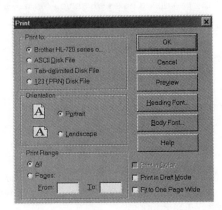

4. Select All in the Print Range panel to print all pages of your Account List if there are more than one (which is rather unlikely).

5. To preview what your category list will look like when printed, select the Preview button. Quicken previews the list, as shown in Figure 2.21.

FIGURE 2.21

Preview your document to see what it will look like on paper.

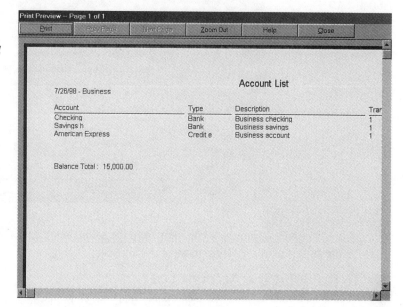

If you want to modify the report fonts, select the Heading Font or Body Font buttons to open dialog boxes where you can make modifications.

6. Click OK to print.

Be sure to turn on your printer before clicking OK.

If you want to include the details you entered in the Additional Account Information dialog box in your printed copy, select Options, Include Additional Info When Printing.

Summary

This hour showed you how to create additional data files and accounts to design a Quicken system that works for you. You can create a second, or even third, data file to track a separate small business or the finances of another member of your household. You can also set up nine different types of accounts that enable you to track bank accounts, credit cards, cash, and other assets.

In Hour 3, "Categorizing and Classifying Transactions," you'll learn how to set up categories, subcategories, and classes to track more precisely the information you'll enter in these accounts.

2

Q&A

Q Should I enable online services when I set up an account, or should I do it later?

A You can do either with Quicken, but remember that you must already have a number to use for online transactions from your financial institution before you can enable online services such as online account access or payment. If you don't already have this number when you set up your account, you can always enable online services later.

Q I closed a bank account. Should I delete it or hide it?

A When you delete an account, you delete all the information it contains. If you have used the account in the past and it's just no longer active, such as a bank account you closed or credit card you canceled, it's better to hide the account than delete it. That way you retain all its transaction information for historical tracking.

HOUR 3

Categorizing and Classifying Transactions

This hour introduces you to the concept of categories, category groups, and classes in Quicken. These organizational units provide maximum flexibility in how you design and set up your Quicken system. They also provide a way to specifically track, analyze, and evaluate your income and expenses based on your own personal financial situation.

The highlights of this hour include

- Why you should use categories, category groups, and classes
- How to set up and use categories and subcategories
- Why you might want to create category groups
- How to set up and use classes

Understanding Categories and Classes

Quicken provides several ways for you to organize your transactions and data. When you first begin using Quicken, it's important to design and use a logical organization system for handling your financial transactions, so that you can properly track and analyze this data for budget, tax, and other purposes.

The most commonly used Quicken organizational unit is the category. Quicken includes many default categories that you can use as a starting point for organizing your transactions. Quicken's default categories fall into six groups: standard, married, homeowner, business, children, and investment. When you first set up Quicken and answer questions about your family status, homeownership, and so on, Quicken creates categories of income and expense based on your response. Examples of categories include Salary, Interest Income, Groceries, and Home Repair.

Categories can be further broken down into subcategories. For example, you might want to divide a large category such as Auto into subcategories of Fuel, Insurance, and Service.

In addition to dividing categories into smaller groups, you can also createcategory groups that contain multiple categories. Income, Mandatory Expense, and Discretionary Expense are examples of category groups.

Finally, you can also create classes that further organize your Quicken data. Classes aren't categories, but rather an optional organizational layer. For example, you can set up classes for Home, Work, and Business to separately track your income and expenses for each. Or if you have several businesses or own several rental properties, you can create a class for each. Later you can create and print reports based on these specific classes to view and analyze only transactions that pertain to the selected class.

Before you start entering data in Quicken, it's a good idea to look at the defaults the program contains and determine the right organizational structure for your personal financial situation using a combination of categories, subcategories, category groups, and classes.

> You assign categories, subcategories, and classes to transactions when you enter them in the register.

Working with Categories and Subcategories

To display the Category & Transfer List, select Lists, Category/Transfer (see Figure 3.1).

FIGURE 3.1

The Category & Transfer List provides detailed information on all the categories you can use.

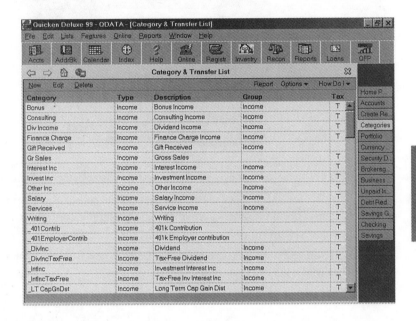

This list displays the type, description, group, and tax status for each default category that Quicken includes.

> If the tax status column is hidden from view, scroll to the right to see it.

To Do: Create a New Category

1. Click New to open the Set Up Category dialog box shown in Figure 3.2.

2. In the Name and Description fields, enter a name and description for this category.

3. Select a category group from the Group drop-down list, which includes Quicken's default category groups as well those you add.

4. Specify the type of category in the Type group box. Choices include Income, Expense, and Subcategory.

5. If you select Expense, the Spending Is Not Discretionary check box appears. If the expense is mandatory, such as a loan payment, select this box.

FIGURE 3.2

*You can easily create
your own categories.*

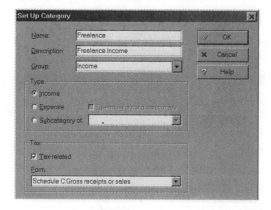

6. If you select Subcategory Of, choose the master category from the drop-down list.

7. Select the Tax-Related check box if you want to link this category to a tax line item schedule. Doing so provides a more useful record of tax-related transactions when it's time to prepare your income taxes for the year.

8. If you select the Tax-Related check box, choose from the drop-down list the form to which the category should link.

> To assign tax line items all at once rather than individually by category, select Options, Assign Tax Items to open the Tax Link Assistant. Hour 14, "Planning for Taxes," provides details on how to use the Tax Link Assistant as well as more information on using Quicken to organize and, hopefully, minimize your taxes.

> If you're not sure which tax form to link to each category, refer to Quicken's extensive online help or to your own tax forms.

9. Click OK to return to the Category & Transfer List.

Editing an Existing Category

To edit an existing category, click Edit to open the Edit Category dialog box, shown in Figure 3.3.

FIGURE 3.3

Use the Edit Category dialog box to modify an existing category.

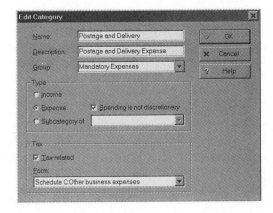

This dialog box is identical to the Set Up Category dialog box. You can modify the current category information and click OK to return to the Category & Transfer List.

Deleting a Category

To delete a category you don't need, select it and click the Delete button. Figure 3.4 illustrates the Delete Category dialog box that opens.

FIGURE 3.4

You can delete categories you don't need, but be sure to think of the consequences first.

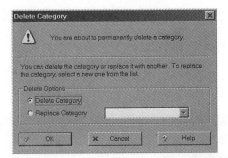

In this dialog box, you can either choose to delete the category or replace it with an alternative category you select from the drop-down list. Click OK to complete the deletion or alteration and return to the Category & Transfer List.

If you delete a subcategory, Quicken reassigns any related transactions to the master category. Quicken doesn't let you delete a category that contains subcategories, however. If you choose to replace one category with another, Quicken reassigns to the new replacement all transactions related to the original category.

A category deletion is permanent, so be sure to consider the consequences of deleting a category before you do so. If you haven't assigned any transactions to the category, you can delete it without the potential for problems. However, if you delete a category to which you assigned many transactions, then the category assignment is also deleted and the transactions are no longer assigned to any category.

Adding a Category from Quicken's Default Category List

Quicken creates default categories based on your answers to several questions when you set up the program. If your situation changes and you later want to add default categories you didn't initially receive, you can do so. For example, if you purchase your first house, have a child, or start a business, you can add categories you'll probably need.

Quicken automatically adds investment categories as soon as you create your first investment account. You can easily identify investment categories because they begin with an underscore, as in _DivInc.

To Do: Add a Category

1. Select Options, Add Categories to open the Add Categories dialog box, shown in Figure 3.5.

FIGURE 3.5

Add Quicken default categories you didn't receive when you first installed the program.

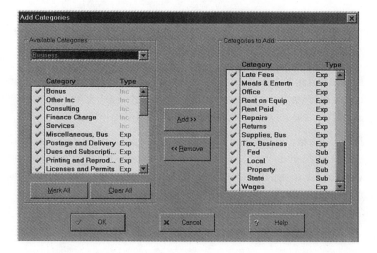

2. Select the type of default categories from the Available Categories drop-down list. Choices include Standard, Married, Homeowner, Business, Children, and Investment.

3. Select the categories you want to add from the list that displays. A green check mark appears before each selected category.

4. When you finish selecting categories, click the Add button to move your selections to the Categories to Add List.

> To save time, you can select all listed categories by clicking the Mark All button. You can also use the Clear All and Remove buttons to delete your selections.

5. When you finish making selections, click OK to return to the Category & Transfer List.

▲ Your newly added categories appear on the list.

Printing a Category List

You can print this list for reference. To do so, select File, Print List, which opens the Print dialog box. Before printing, you can preview the list by selecting Preview. Figure 3.6 displays the Print List window.

FIGURE 3.6

Print a list of your Quicken categories for easy reference.

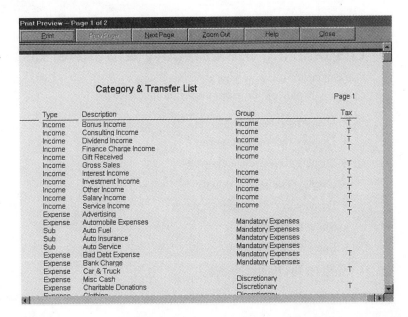

Specify the print parameters and click OK. You can use this list to determine the Quicken default categories you want to keep, modify, or delete as well as the categories you need to add.

You can also print a list of transactions based on a selected category by clicking the Report button. Quicken displays a Category Report for the chosen category, as shown in Figure 3.7.

FIGURE 3.7

Get a detailed report on transactions relating to a selected category.

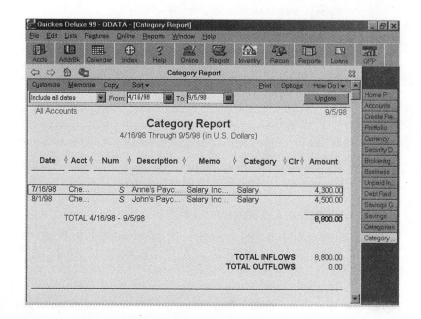

Customizing the Category & Transfer List

You can customize how you view the Category & Transfer List. Select Options and choose a display option from the menu that appears:

- Display All Categories
- Display Income Categories
- Display Expense Categories
- Display Transfer Accounts
- Display Tax-Related Categories
- Show Descriptions
- Show Category Group
- Show Tax Item

Assigning Category Groups

If you want to assign specific category groups to categories, follow the steps in the following To Do section.

To Do: Assign Category Groups

1. Select Options, Assign Category Group to open the Assign Category Groups dialog box illustrated in Figure 3.8.

FIGURE 3.8

Category groups provide a way to organize a large number of individual categories.

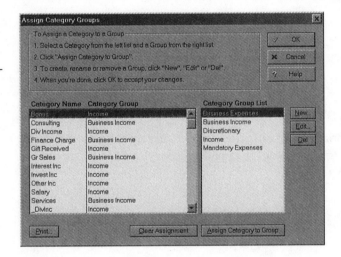

2. Choose a category name from the list on the left side of the dialog box.

3. Choose a corresponding category group from the list on the right side of the dialog box.

4. Click the Assign Category to Group button.

5. Continue assigning categories to the category group and click OK when you finish.

Modifying Category Groups

You can create, edit, or delete category groups to define and organize your categories more clearly. To add a new category group, click the New button in the Assign Category Groups dialog box. The Create Category Group dialog box appears, as shown in Figure 3.9.

FIGURE 3.9

You can create your own category groups in addition to the defaults.

To create a new category enter a group name for the category group on the Create Category Group dialog box and click OK.

To rename a category click the Edit button on the Assign Category Groups dialog box to display the Edit Category Group dialog box, which is identical to the Create Category Group dialog box. Enter a new name and click OK.

Finally, to delete a category group, click the Del button.

Printing a List of Category Groups

To print a list of categories and the category groups to which they are assigned, click the Print button. In the Print dialog box that displays, specify your print parameters and click OK.

Working with Classes

To display the Class List, select Lists, Class (see Figure 3.10).

FIGURE 3.10

Classes provide another way to organize your Quicken data.

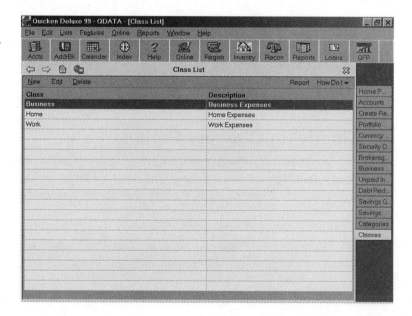

This list displays each class and its description. If you haven't entered any previous classes, the list is empty.

To Do: Create a New Class

1. Click New to open the Set Up Class dialog box, illustrated in Figure 3.11.

FIGURE 3.11

You can create a variety of classes for different needs.

2. Enter a name and description for this category.

3. Enter an optional copy number if desired. A copy number is useful, for example, if you have more than one job or business and need to file multiple Schedule C forms or receive multiple W-2 forms.

 4. Click OK to return to the Class List.

Editing an Existing Class

To edit an existing class, click Edit to open the Edit Class dialog box, shown in Figure 3.12.

FIGURE 3.12

Modify an existing class in the Edit Class dialog box.

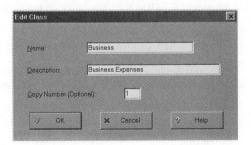

This dialog box is identical to the Set Up Class dialog box. You can modify the current class information and then click OK to return to the Class List.

3

Deleting a Class

To delete a category you don't need, select it and click the Delete button. Quicken warns you that you are about to delete a class permanently. Click OK to continue with the deletion.

 If you have already assigned to existing transactions the class you want to delete, Quicken removes this class assignment. It does not, however, remove the transaction itself.

Summary

This hour introduced you to the concept of categories, category groups, and classes. Use categories to define how to organize your basic income and expenses down to the subcategory level. Use category groups to create larger organizational units that contain multiple categories that are particularly useful for budgeting. And finally, you can use classes to track separately the financial activity of your home and business or of different members of your household.

As you'll learn in Hour 4, "Entering Transactions in the Register," you can see the benefit of using these organizational units once you begin entering data in the register.

Q&A

Q I own two rental properties. What's a good way to track them?

A You can use classes to differentiate income and expenses for each property. By specifying the class to use when you run reports, you can get an exact view of the finances of each individual property.

Q Do I have to use categories, subcategories, category groups, and classes?

A You don't have to, but you'll at least want to use categories to categorize your basic transactions. Without categories, it will be difficult to get a meaningful view of your financial picture.

HOUR 4

Entering Transactions in the Register

This hour shows you how to record transactions in a Quicken register. Quicken makes using the register easier with features such as QuickFill to reduce data entry, paycheck setup to automate the creation of paycheck transactions, and QuickEntry to enable others to enter data but not have access to confidential Quicken information. You can also customize how you use and view the register and record transactions in multiple currencies.

The highlights of this hour include:

- How to record transactions in Quicken registers
- Why you should take advantage of QuickFill, split transactions, and paycheck setup
- Where to customize the Quicken register
- How to search for register transactions
- How to set up multicurrency support
- How to use QuickEntry

Making a Basic Register Entry

In Quicken you record account transactions in a register. Each account has its own register, but all Quicken registers have a similar appearance. Figure 4.1 illustrates a sample register for a checking account.

FIGURE 4.1

Enter your account transactions in the register.

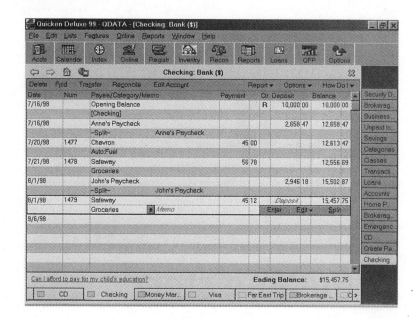

In a Quicken register you record three main types of transactions—payments, deposits, and transfers.

Banking, credit card, and cash accounts all use these same three transaction types. An investment account, however, records securities, security actions, price, and shares.

To open the register for a particular account, click the Accts icon on the Iconbar and double-click the account you want to open in the Accounts List.

To Do: Enter a Basic Transaction

1. Modify the Date field if necessary. The default is today's date.

2. In the Num field, select the type of transaction. Options include the following:

   - *Next Check Num.* Records the next check number in sequence.

   - *ATM.* Records an ATM withdrawal.

   - *Deposit.* Records a deposit and automatically moves you to the Deposit field from the Payee field.

   - *Print check.* Records a check that you want to print.

   - *Transfer.* Records a transfer of funds from this account to another.

   - *EFT.* Records an electronic funds transfer such as an online transaction.

3. Next, enter the Payee—the organization or person you are paying. In the case of a deposit, this is the organization/person who is paying you.

4. Enter either the Payment or Deposit amount. Quicken moves to the correct field based on your entry in the Num field.

> Quicken skips the Clr field that you use later to indicate the transaction's cleared status during reconciliation. Hour 6, "Reconciling Accounts," covers this topic in more detail.

5. Select a Category that reflects the nature of this transaction from the drop-down list.

> If you want to add a category to the list, click the Add Cat button.

6. You can enter an optional class in the category field as well by separating the category and class with a backslash (\)—for example, Auto:Gas\Home.

> Hour 3, "Categorizing and Classifying Transactions," provides more details on how to set up and use categories and classes in Quicken.

7. Enter an optional Memo.

> You can change the order of the Category and Memo fields in the Register Options dialog box. From the register select Options, Register Options and toggle the Show Memo Before Category to change the order.

▲ 8. Click Enter to save this transaction.

Using QuickFill

When you first start using Quicken you have to enter register transactions manually, but after you have entered a number of transactions your data entry work can be minimized. Quicken achieves this through the process of memorizing transactions—saving each transaction you enter and letting you recall it at a later date. So for example, if you pay $29.95 monthly for cable TV, you can enter this transaction once and then recall it every month when you pay this bill. If all the transaction information is the same except for the amount (such as in the case of weekly grocery expenses at the same store), you can recall the basic transaction and then just adjust the amount. This process is called QuickFill.

QuickFill works when you begin to enter a payee. Quicken recalls the list of memorized transactions and starts looking for matches as you type. Figure 4.2 illustrates this.

FIGURE 4.2

Using QuickFill can expedite data entry.

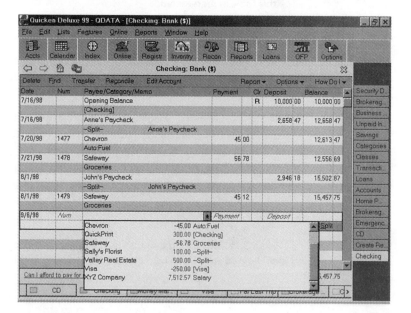

Hour 8, "Memorizing Transactions," provides more details on the best way
to use memorized transactions in Quicken.

Transferring Between Accounts

You can also transfer funds between accounts in the register. For example, you might
transfer extra money in your checking account to a higher interest money market
account. Or you might use money in your checking account to fund additional security
purchases in a brokerage account.

To Do: Transfer Funds Between Accounts

1. Click the Transfer button. Quicken displays the Transfer dialog box, shown in
   Figure 4.3.

FIGURE 4.3

*Transfer money to and
from accounts in this
dialog box.*

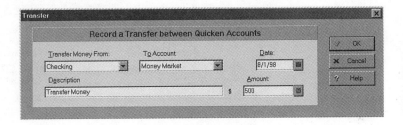

2. Select the account you want to Transfer Money From.

3. In the To Account field, enter the account to which you want to transfer these
   funds.

4. Select a Date for this transfer.

5. Enter a Description if desired.

6. Finally, enter the Amount of this transfer.

▲ 7. Click OK to record the transaction and return to the register.

Creating Split Transactions

If you want to allocate a transaction to more than one category, you can create a split
transaction. For example, you went shopping at a large department store and purchased
clothes, a VCR, and some personal items. You might want to assign these items to three
different categories.

To Do: Assign Items to Different Categories

1. Click the Split button that displays when you click the Category drop-down list (see Figure 4.4).

FIGURE 4.4

The Split button opens the Split Transaction Window.

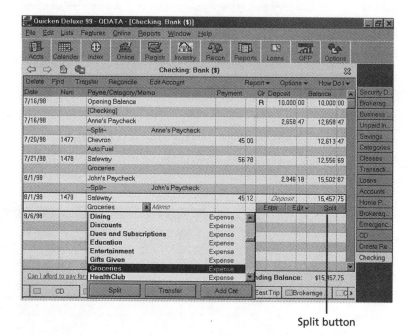

Split button

Figure 4.5 illustrates the Split Transaction Window.

FIGURE 4.5

You can split one transaction among several categories.

▼

▼ 2. Select the Category from the drop-down list, including an optional class if desired.

3. Enter an optional Memo.

4. Enter the Amount of this particular portion of the transaction.

5. Continue entering categories until you itemize all your purchases.

6. Click Adjust to verify that the total adds up properly.

7. Click OK to return to the register.

Figure 4.6 illustrates a completed split transaction.

FIGURE 4.6

This split transaction divides the total amount among three different categories.

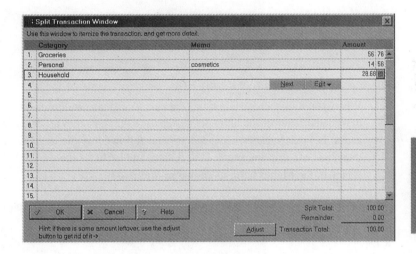

▲

Making Register Entries in Multiple Currencies

Quicken now offers the capability to enter register transactions in more than one currency as well as to create reports in multiple currencies.

The ability to track multiple currencies is a new Quicken Deluxe 99 feature that reduces manual currency conversions for users who need to record transactions in more than one currency.

For example, if you travel overseas and make cash and credit card payments in other currencies such as the franc, mark, or pound, you can enter the transaction in the currency in which you paid and let Quicken convert this amount to your local currency (the U.S. dollar by default).

First, though, you need to activate multicurrency support. To do so, select Edit,
Options, Quicken Program. On the Settings tab of the General Options dialog box
(see Figure 4.7), select the Multicurrency Support check box and click OK.

FIGURE 4.7

*Set up Quicken to
support multiple
currencies.*

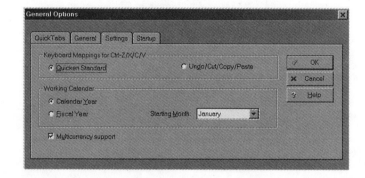

When you make a register entry, you can specify an amount followed by a special key (a
designated letter of the alphabet assigned to that currency). For example, to enter a transaction in French francs, enter the amount followed by the letter F, such as 500F. Quicken
then converts this amount to U.S. dollars and includes the original amount in French
francs in the Memo field, as shown in Figure 4.8.

FIGURE 4.8

*You can enter a trans-
action in one currency
and convert it to
another.*

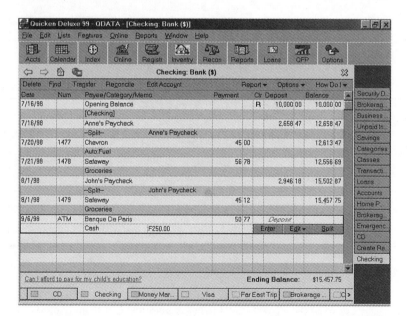

Tracking Currencies

To specify the currencies you want to be able to use, their conversion rates, and the key to enter in the register, you need to go to the Currency List (see Figure 4.9).

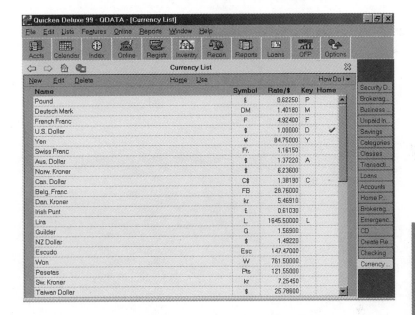

This list includes commonly used currencies, with their symbol, rate of exchange, and key. Quicken indicates your home currency with a green check mark in the Home column. If you want to change your home currency, select the new currency and click Home. Quicken verifies that you want to change.

To Do: Add a Currency

1. Select the New button that opens the Set Up New Currency dialog box, illustrated in Figure 4.10.

FIGURE 4.10

You can add additional currencies if needed.

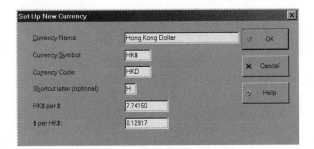

▼   2. Enter a new Currency Name, its appropriate Symbol, and Code.

     3. Enter an optional Shortcut Letter if you want to be able to enter transactions in this currency in the register. Quicken displays this shortcut in the Key column of the Currency List.

     4. In the Amt per $ field, indicate the value of one U.S. dollar in the target currency.

     5. In the $ per Amt field, enter the value in U.S. dollars of one unit of the target currency.

▲   6. Click OK to return to the Currency List.

To edit an existing currency, select it and click Edit. The Edit Currency dialog box displays, shown in Figure 4.11.

FIGURE 4.11

Edit a currency in this dialog box.

This dialog box is almost identical to the Set Up New Currency dialog box. Make any necessary changes and click OK.

To delete a currency, select it and click Delete. Quicken verifies that you want to delete and proceeds with the deletion.

Before you delete a currency, be sure that you've never recorded a transaction in it.

Changing Transactions

If you make a mistake when recording a transaction, you can easily correct it by making changes directly in the register. For example, if you enter the wrong amount you can overwrite this field with the correct number. You can also make changes to payees, categories, classes, and so on.

If you try to change a reconciled transaction, Quicken displays a warning dialog box asking whether you really want to modify a transaction that you reconciled.

You can delete a transaction as well. To do so, select the transaction, click the Edit button on the Transaction toolbar, and choose Delete Transaction from the menu that displays. Quicken confirms you want to delete.

You can also void a transaction if you want to maintain it, but not record the amount. Select the transaction you want to void, click the Edit button on the Transaction toolbar, and choose Void Transaction. Figure 4.12 displays a voided transaction.

FIGURE 4.12

Quicken clearly indicates voided transactions.

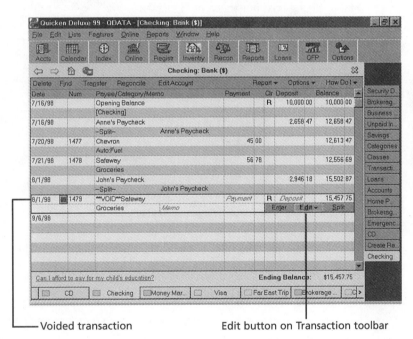

Voided transaction   Edit button on Transaction toolbar

Viewing the Register

You can customize how you view the register to make it work best for you. By default the register displays transactions sorted by date and amount. You can also display the register by choosing any of the following sort options:

- Amount (largest first)
- Amount (smallest first)
- Check Number
- Payee
- Order Entered
- Date/Order Entered
- Cleared Status

To specify the register's sort order, select Options and the order you want from the menu that displays.

To set additional register options, select Options, Register Options to open the Register Options dialog box, illustrated in Figure 4.13.

FIGURE 4.13

Set options for QuickFill and basic register display.

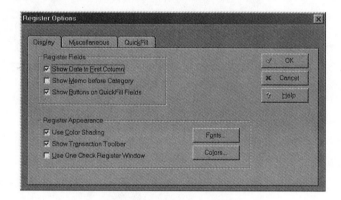

This dialog box includes three tabs—Display, Miscellaneous, and QuickFill—that let you specify exactly how you want the register to look and behave.

Locating Transactions

If you want to find a specific transaction in a large register, use Quicken's find feature to locate it quickly.

To Do: Locate a Transaction

1. Click the Find button to open the Quicken Find dialog box, illustrated in Figure 4.14.

2. First select the type of field you want to Search from the drop-down list. Options include: All Fields, Amount, Cleared Status, Memo, Date, Category/Class, Check Number, or Payee.

FIGURE 4.14

You can search through thousands of records to find the right one.

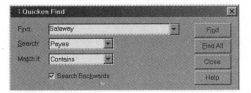

3. Enter the exact criteria in the Find field. What displays in the drop-down list depends on what you entered in the Search field.

4. Set specific Match If parameters such as Greater Than or Less Than for numeric fields or Contains or Exact for text fields. For example, if you search on a payee named XYZ, Exact would only match payees with this exact name, whereas Contains would also match on payees named XYZ Company or XYZ Industries.

5. If you want to Search Backward, select this check box. Searching backward locates the most recent transactions first.

6. Click Find to locate the first matching record in the register.

7. Click Find All to display a report listing all matches, as shown in Figure 4.15.

FIGURE 4.15

You can create a report based on your search findings.

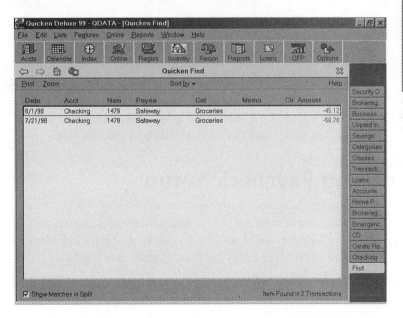

8. Click Close when you're done searching.

Using One-Line Display

If you want to enter transactions in the register using a one-line display rather than the default two-line display, select Options, One-Line Display. Figure 4.16 illustrates a register using one-line display.

FIGURE 4.16

You can display transactions on either one line or two.

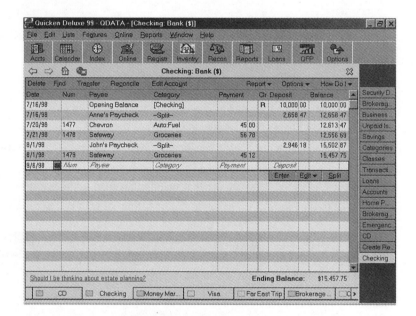

When you enter transactions on only one line, Quicken eliminates the Memo field and decreases the amount of available space in the other fields.

Using Paycheck Setup

Quicken includes an automated feature to help you set up your paycheck and properly categorize your income and deductions into split transactions. Quicken memorizes the paycheck transaction, so after you set up your paycheck you won't need to categorize these items again unless you want to make modifications.

To set up your paycheck using Quicken's automated EasyStep approach, select Features, Banking, Set Up Paycheck to open the Paycheck Setup dialog box, illustrated in Figure 4.17.

This first dialog box provides an overview of the paycheck setup tool. Click Next to continue (see Figure 4.18).

FIGURE 4.17

This dialog box introduces paycheck setup.

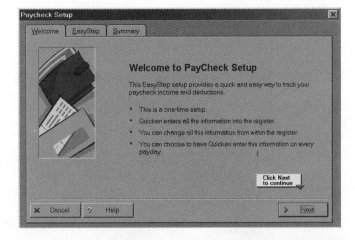

FIGURE 4.18

Specify the items you want to track in your paycheck.

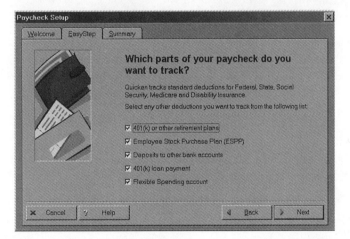

You must use the EasyStep process to set up a paycheck; you can't skip to the Summary tab to enter your information.

Select any additional items you want Quicken to track and categorize and click Next. Options include the following:

- 401(k) or other retirement plans.
- Employee Stock Purchase Plan (ESPP)
- Deposits to other bank accounts

- 401(k) loan payment
- Flexible Spending account

The remaining steps ask you to specify basic information about your pay—amount, frequency, and so on—as well as detailed information about the additional items you want to track.

When you reach the final step, the Summary tab appears, shown in Figure 4.19.

FIGURE 4.19

Make any final adjustments on the Summary tab.

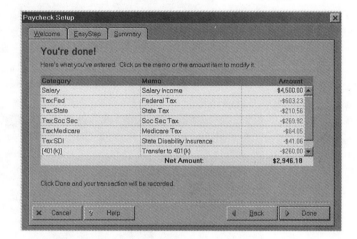

On this tab you can see a summary of everything you entered and can make any final changes if necessary.

Later, you can edit the itemized categories you entered while setting up your paycheck. To do so, select Features, Banking, Set Up Paycheck.

Figure 4.20 displays the Manage Paycheck dialog box that appears.

FIGURE 4.20

After you set up a paycheck, you can modify it.

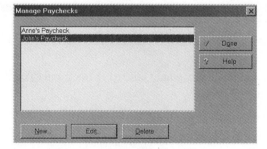

This dialog box only appears if you already set up a paycheck. If you haven't, the Set Up Paycheck dialog box appears.

Select the paycheck you want to edit and click the Edit button. The Editing Paycheck dialog box appears. Click Next to open the Split Transaction Window in which you can make modifications. Figure 4.21 illustrates this window.

FIGURE 4.21

You can make changes to your paycheck later in this window.

Category		Memo	Amount	
1.	Salary	Salary Income	4,500	00
2.	Tax:Fed	Federal Tax	-603	23
3.	Tax:State	State Tax	-210	56
4.	Tax:Soc Sec	Soc Sec Tax	-269	92
5.	Tax:Medicare	Medicare Tax	-64	05
6.	Tax:SDI	State Disability Insurance	-41	06
7.	[401(k)]	Transfer to 401(k)	-260	00
8.	[401(k)]		-105	00
9.				
10.				
11.				
12.				
13.				
14.				
15.				

Split Transaction Window

Use this window to itemize the transaction, and get more detail.

✓ OK   ✗ Cancel   ? Help

Split Total: 2,946.18
Remainder: 0.00

Hint: if there is some amount leftover, use the adjust button to get rid of it ->

Adjust   Transaction Total: 2,946.18

Click OK when you finish. Quicken memorizes the new paycheck transaction with adjusted category splits.

Click Delete to delete a paycheck transaction you no longer need, such as one for a former job.

Using QuickEntry

Quicken's new QuickEntry feature lets you quickly record transactions for your banking, cash, and credit card accounts without displaying Quicken's full set of features. QuickEntry essentially displays the register and nothing else. This feature is also useful if you want someone to handle your transaction data entry without access to other detailed financial information.

> QuickEntry is a new Quicken Deluxe 99 feature that both simplifies and provides greater control over register data entry.

To use QuickEntry, double-click the QuickEntry 99 icon on the Windows desktop. Figure 4.22 displays the QuickEntry register view, which appears.

FIGURE 4.22

QuickEntry simplifies register data entry.

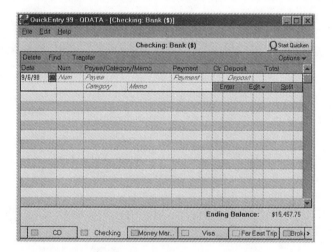

You use the QuickEntry register as you would any other register. To change to different account registers, select the account you want to use by clicking the tabs at the bottom of the screen. QuickEntry also includes the sort, display, and search options that are part of the full product.

After you finish adding data in QuickEntry, exit the application by choosing File, Exit. When you return to Quicken, the Accept Transactions dialog box appears, shown in Figure 4.23.

FIGURE 4.23

You can accept transactions someone else entered in QuickEntry.

Accept Transactions displays all the transactions recorded in QuickEntry. From this dialog box, you can select the following options:

- *Accept All.* Accepts all listed entries and records them in the appropriate Quicken accounts.

- *Accept.* Accepts the selected entry, but not other entries.

- *Edit.* Displays the Create Register Transaction dialog box in which you can modify the selected transaction before accepting it.

- *Delete.* Deletes the selected transaction.

- *Finish Later.* Closes the Accept Transaction dialog box without recording these transaction to the Quicken registers. You can open this dialog box later by choosing Features, Banking, Accept Transactions.

 You can show transaction history in QuickEntry by selecting this option on the Register Options dialog box Miscellaneous tab. Open this dialog box by selecting Edit, Options, Register.

4

Summary

This hour showed you how to use Quicken registers to record your financial transactions. Use the QuickFill feature to automate data entry tasks as much as possible and split transactions to make your entries more precise. Use the Paycheck Setup tool to simplify one of the most complicated transactions you have to enter. Use QuickEntry to both simplify and provide more control over register entries.

Q&A

Q When should I use QuickEntry rather than a regular Quicken register.

A One of the main advantages of QuickEntry is that it gives someone the ability to enter data in your Quicken registers without access to your Quicken data. QuickEntry can also provide you an alternate way to open account registers directly to record transactions.

Q Why should I bother taking the time to record split transactions?

A Using split transactions can help you track your income and expenses more precisely. For example, most people make purchases that should be divided into several categories (such as buying clothes, food, small appliances, personal items, and so on all at one superstore). If you don't split these transactions into separate categories, you won't have accurate information for budget and other expense tracking purposes. Setting up a paycheck with several categories is another example. If you don't split the transactions, you won't have accurate records at tax time.

PART II
Managing Your Accounts

Hour

Hour 5

Creating and Printing Checks

You can use Quicken to print checks directly to your printer. When you do, you save time and work, and you also connect your check printing to Quicken's budget features.

In the first part of this hour, you learn how you can use Quicken to help you keep your account balances healthy as you print checks. Then, you learn how to get great looking checks out of your printer that align perfectly with the text you add.

The highlights of this hour include

- Understanding how check writing works in Quicken
- How to write a check from your checking account in Quicken
- How to set check alerts to warn you if you exceed your budget
- How to set check alerts to warn you if you exceed a defined minimum or maximum balance
- How to print checks on your printer

Understanding Quicken Checks

You may be aware that you can use Quicken to print checks on your printer. But did you know that when you use Quicken to print checks, you can get help managing your budget? As you print checks, Quicken can also alert you when the following occur:

- Your account drops below a minimum balance that you define when you print your check
- Your checking account balance goes above a limit you define
- It is time to reorder printed check forms
- Monthly expenses exceed your budget

By printing your checks in Quicken, you not only save the time and hassle of writing checks, but you allow Quicken to serve as your financial advisor, alerting you if you are breaking any of your self-imposed rules for managing your checking account.

> Before you experiment with printing checks, it might be helpful to make a list of alerts you want to define for your checking account. Use the questions below to create an alert list that you can use when you begin to print checks.

Following are some questions to ask yourself as you prepare to set up Quicken for check printing:

- *What minimum balance do you want to define?* Quicken alerts you if a check you print lowers your balance below this amount?
- *What maximum balance do you want to define for your checking account?* For example, you might decide that you want to transfer any balance over $2000 to a money market account, rather than have it sit in your checking account.
- *For which items in your household budget do you want to define monthly spending limits?* For example, do you have a recreation budget you are trying to stick to? Or a clothing budget? A dining out limit? Make a list of these items, and Quicken helps you stick to your budget as you print checks.

Writing a Check

The first step in writing checks in Quicken is to enter them into your checking account. In Hour 4, you learned to enter transactions. Here, we quickly review how to enter a check, and then explore check printing options.

To Do: Enter a Check in Your Checking Account

1. From the Quicken Home Page, click your checking account in the My Accounts area. Figure 5.1 shows a checking account.

2. At the end of the check register, enter a date in the Date column (or leave today's date, which is set by default). Press the tab key, or click in the next column to enter a check number, *but don't enter a check number*. If you are going to be printing checks, check numbers are assigned automatically.

FIGURE 5.1

The first step in printing a check is to enter a transaction in your checking account.

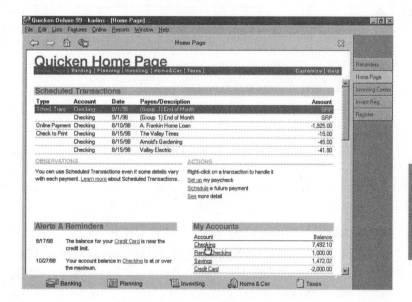

3. Click the drop-down menu arrow in the Num column, and select Print Check, as shown in Figure 5.2.

4. Enter a Payee and a Payment amount in the Checking ledger. Now you're ready to tell Quicken which check printing options you want to use.

FIGURE 5.2

When you print checks, numbers are assigned automatically.

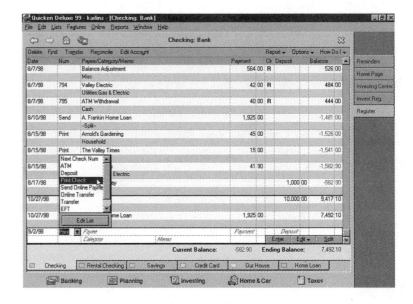

▲

Setting Check Options

You need to have some checks ready to print before you can define check options. So, if you've generated at least one check, you're ready to go.

After you have entered at least one check, select File, Print Checks from the Quicken menu. The Select Checks to Print dialog box opens. The first set of check printing options let you tell Quicken which checks you want to print, what numbering sequence you are using, and how your checks should look.

To Do: Define Check Printing Options

▼To Do

1. With checks entered into your checking account, select File, Print Checks from the Quicken menu. The Select Checks to Print dialog box opens.

2. In the First Check Number field, enter the number of the first check you will print. For example, if you have previously been using checks you fill out by hand, and your last hand-written check was number 780, you should assign check number 781 here if you want to maintain continuous check numbering. Figure 5.3 shows a sequence of printed checks starting at 781.

3. In the Print area, select one radio button to print All Checks, Checks Dated Through..., or Selected Checks.

   If you select All Checks, every check in your checkbook that has not yet been printed prints. If you select Checks Dated Through..., you are prompted to enter a date. And, if you click the Selected Checks radio button, the Choose button becomes active, and the Select Checks to Print dialog box opens.

▼

FIGURE 5.3

The first time you print checks you assign a starting check number.

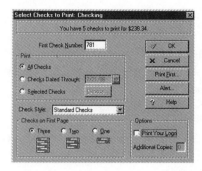

As a general rule, you should only set the First Check Number once. After that, Quicken assigns new check numbers sequentially. Tampering with the First Check Number after you've initially printed a check can cause you to end up with nonsequentially numbered checks.

You can remove a check from the list of those to be printed by clicking it (the check mark disappears). Then, click the Done button in the dialog box. Figure 5.4 shows two checks deselected from a list of checks to print.

4. After you've selected which checks to print and assigned an initial check number, you can use the Check Style drop-down menu to choose your check style. You learn how to order checks a bit later in this chapter, but if you have checks already, you can select a style here. If you select Wallet or Standard style checks, you can use the Three, Two, or One radio buttons to define how many checks are printed on a page.

5. If you are using Standard or Voucher checks, you can use the Print Logo check box to include a Bitmap (*.bmp) format graphic image on your checks.

FIGURE 5.4

You can elect to not print some of your unpaid checks.

Print	Date	Payee	Category	Amount
✓	7/21/98	Arnold's Gardening	Household	45.00
✓	7/21/98	The Valley Times	Subscriptions	15.00
✓	7/21/98	Valley Electric	Utilities:Gas & Electric	107.11
	7/21/98	The Valley Times	Subscriptions	15.00
	7/21/98	Valley Electric	Utilities:Gas & Electric	56.23

5

▼ 6. If you are printing Voucher style checks, you can use the Additional Copies field to
      print duplicate or multiple copies of each printed check.

   7. After you have finished defining your checks, you can click the Print First button
      to print the check with the earliest check number, or you can click the OK Button
▲   to print all your checks.

> Before you actually print real checks, you want to review the section at the
> end of this hour on setting up your printer for check printing.

Setting Check Alerts

There are additional features that can be connected to check printing to help manage your
budget. These features are available in the Print Checks dialog box.

Here's where you can tell Quicken to warn you if your checking account balance is
too high or too low. And this is where you tell Quicken to warn you if you exceed
your budget.

To Do: Define Checking Account Limits

   1. Select File, Print Checks (unless you are already in the Select Checks to Print
      dialog box).

   2. Click the Alert button in the dialog box.

   3. Click the Account Max Balances check box, and enter a maximum account limit.
      Figure 5.5 shows a defined maximum balance of $2000.

FIGURE 5.5

*Defining a maximum
balance—anything
over this, and Quicken
displays a warning.*

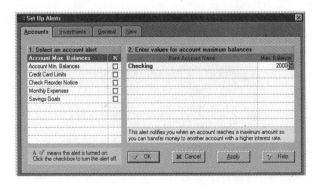

   4. Click the Account Min. Balances check box and enter a minimum balance for your
      account. If you print a check that brings your balance below this amount, you see
▼   the warning shown in Figure 5.6.

FIGURE 5.6

Warning! Checks have been printed that reduced the balance below the defined minimum for this account.

5. When you have defined your alerts, click the OK button in the Set Up Alerts dialog box. You can then print checks or close the dialog box. The alerts you define remain in effect for all checks you print, unless you change them.

You can also define budget limits for any category of expense. Quicken issues a warning when you print a check that exceeds the limits for these expenses.

To Do: Define Budget Warnings

1. Select File, Print Checks (unless you are already in the Select Checks to Print dialog box).

2. Click the Alert button in the dialog box.

3. Click the Monthly Expenses check box in the Set Up Alerts dialog box.

4. In the area on the right side of the dialog box, click a category (or subcategory) of expense, and enter the spending limit per month for that category. Figure 5.7 shows a $50/month limit for spending on subscriptions.

FIGURE 5.7

Budget alerts trigger a warning if you write a check that exceeds the limit.

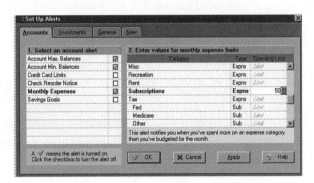

5. You can enter budget limits for as many expense categories as you want. When you finish, click the OK button in the Set Up Alerts dialog box.

You can now print checks, secure in the knowledge that if you exceed your budget for any defined category, Quicken warns you that you're over budget.

5

Understanding the Check Print Process

Now that you've learned to control the way checks are printed, you can send your checks to the printer. But what if you don't have checks?

Well, as you might expect, the good folks at Intuit, who publish Quicken, make it easy for you to order checks. And as you also would expect, those checks work very well with Quicken's check printing feature.

You can see the whole catalog for Intuit checks at their Web site. You can get to the Quicken catalog by selecting Online, Quicken on the Web, Quicken Store from the Quicken 99 menu.

If you haven't defined your Internet connection for Quicken yet, you are prompted to do so when you go to the online store. A pretty straightforward wizard will ask you about your Internet hookup, and after that, connecting will be automatic when you go to the store.

> For a full explanation of how to connect to the Internet through Quicken, see Hour 23, "Using Online Financial Services."

The Quicken site is periodically updated, but it's always easy to find the page with supplies. Figure 5.8 shows a section of the online catalog describing the three types of Quicken checks: Standard, Voucher, and Wallet style.

If you don't have an Internet connection, you can use the ordering materials that came with Quicken to order checks.

Other options include purchasing printed checks from other vendors or ordering custom printed checks from your bank or a printer. Regular checkbook style tear-out checks do not, of course, fit in your printer. But many banks now offer printed sheets of checks for computerized check writing.

Setting Up Your Printer

If you use Quicken checks with Quicken, you find the checks print pretty smoothly. If you have custom printed checks, you may need to do more experimenting to get your checks to print right.

The challenge in either case is to get the printed information to align just right so that the payee name, the date, the check number, and so on are in the right place when your check prints. As you set up your check printing attributes, you can also choose a font for your text.

FIGURE 5.8

Quicken sells checks at its Web site.

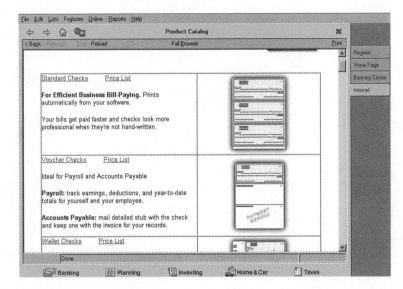

You should experiment before you waste your valuable printed checks (and mess up your check numbering) by printing a bunch of misaligned checks.

To Do: Adjust Printing Setup

1. Select File, Printer Setup, For Printing Checks from the Quicken menu.

2. Select the printer to which checks are to be printed from the Printer drop-down menu.

3. Click the Page-oriented radio button for sheet-fed printers, or the Continuous radio button for continuous roll paper printers.

4. From the Check Style drop-down menu, select the type of Quicken checks you are using. If you are using custom checks from your own printer, you have to experiment and adjust, starting with the style closest to the one you're using. Figure 5.9 shows Standard checks being selected.

5. Choose from one of the three Partial Page Printing Style options—normally you use Portrait.

6. In the drop-down menus at the bottom of the dialog box, you can select manual or automatic feed for your paper.

To Do

5

FIGURE 5.9

Define your check style.

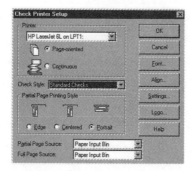

7. Use the Font button to open the Font dialog box. Here you can select a font size and style for all the text in your check.

8. The Align button serves two functions—one now, one later. You can click the Align button and select any of the three check settings to adjust the location of checks on a page. Even before you start tinkering with text alignment, click the Print Sample button in the Fine Alignment dialog box. This button prints a sample of your check text, and you should just put a blank piece of paper in your printer to do this. Then, hold your paper and your check, together, up to a light and see how the print is aligned.

9. If your check text doesn't align with your check, entering a positive value of 1 in the vertical spin box moves text up 1/100th of an inch on the check, and entering a positive value in the Horizontal spin box moves the check to the right in increments of 1/100th of an inch. You can use these spin boxes to micro-tune the location of your check text on the check. Figure 5.10, shows text being moved 1/10th (10/100ths—same thing) of an inch up the page.

FIGURE 5.10

You can fine-tune your text so that it fits perfectly on your printed check

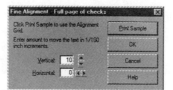

10. The Settings button opens a dialog box associated with your selected printer.

11. The Logo button allows you to select any *.bmp format bitmap image on your computer to insert in your checks. Figure 5.11 shows a picture being added to personalize Quicken checks.

FIGURE 5.11

Printed checks can be personalized with images.

After you have experimented with printing checks on blank paper, you're ready to put your real check sheets in your printer and pay some bills.

Reprinting Checks

After you send checks to the printer, Quicken displays a dialog box asking you whether all the checks printed okay. The Did Check(s) Print OK? dialog box appears, as shown in Figure 5.12.

If your checks didn't print right, either because you entered wrong information or because your printer let you down, type the check number of the first misprinted check in the First Incorrectly Printed Check area of the dialog box. Then, click the OK button. You return to the Select Checks to Print dialog box. You can try printing again or cancel the print job.

FIGURE 5.12

If your check(s) misprint, you can try again.

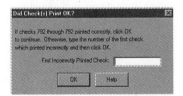

If you canceled the print job because you didn't issue the check, you can void that check in the Checking view by right-clicking the check and selecting Void Transaction from the context menu.

Summary

There are two big advantages to printing checks in Quicken. One is the convenience of not wearing your fingers out writing bunches of checks. The other is that when you print checks with Quicken, you utilize all the budgeting power of Quicken 99 to help you keep on top of your expenses.

Q&A

Q Where do you get checks to print in Quicken?

A Quicken sells checks. You can order them online or use materials that came with Quicken 99.

Q How much of a hassle is it to align your checks?

A It's a bit of a hassle at first, until you print your first check right. After that, it's simple.

HOUR 6

Reconciling Accounts

You've religiously entered every check, every savings account deposit and withdrawal, and every investment transaction in your Quicken accounts. Then you get a monthly statement from your friendly financial institution and guess what? The balance doesn't always match Quicken's balance.

One possibility is that it's wrong. Another possibility is that you've missed one of those service charges your financial institution slips into your balance each month. Or, you might have made a data entry error in your Quicken accounts.

Actually, your Quicken account balance hardly ever matches the balance on your monthly statements, even if you and the bank are on the exact same wavelength on charges and fees. That's because your Quicken account reflects your current balance, whereas your bank statement only reflects checks and deposits that have cleared.

There are many possible explanations for why your monthly statements might not match your Quicken account balances. But all those reasons are good reasons to reconcile each monthly statement with your Quicken accounts. If you reconcile your accounts monthly, Quicken provides an accurate picture of your financial state.

The highlights of this hour include

- How you can reconcile your Quicken balance with the balance on your bank statement

- How to reconcile your credit card statements with the balance for your Quicken credit accounts

- How to adjust your Quicken balances to bring them in line with your monthly account statements

- How to print a reconciliation report to document discrepancies between your Quicken account balances and your bank balances

Reconciling a Checking or Savings Account

If you use Quicken to keep your checkbook records, you should reconcile your Quicken checking account with your statement each time it comes in the mail. This is basically the same process as reconciling your old-fashioned checkbook with your statement.

Savings accounts are likely to have less activity than checking accounts, so balancing them might be a simple process. However, because savings accounts pay interest, that has to be added to your Quicken account each month.

Reconciling Your Checking Account

The first step in reconciling your checking account is to open the account. If you have been paying checks by hand, make sure you've entered all your checks into the Quicken register. If you've been printing Quicken checks, all your checks are already entered into your account ledger.

To Do: Balance Your Checking Account

1. View your checking account (you can click your account in the Quicken Home Page).

2. Click the Reconcile button at the top of the account view. The Reconcile Bank Statement dialog box opens as shown in Figure 6.1.

3. Enter the opening balance listed on your bank statement in the Opening Balance field of the dialog box.

4. Enter the closing balance listed on your statement in the Ending Balance field.

5. If you know of any other expenses assigned to your account, enter them in the Service Charge field.

FIGURE 6.1

*Starting to reconcile
your bank statement
and Quicken balance.*

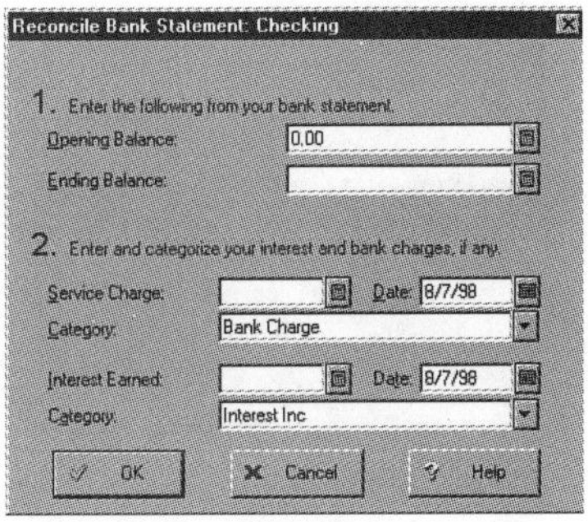

▼

6. After you enter your opening and closing statement balances and fees, click the
   OK button in the Reconcile Bank Statement dialog box. You see a new window
   where you mark cleared checks and deposits, as shown in Figure 6.2.

FIGURE 6.2

*Quicken's checkbook
reconciliation window
looks just like your
checkbook.*

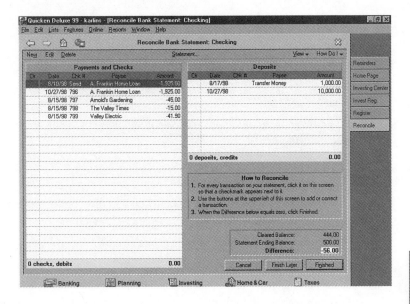

6

7. Now you can click deposits and checks to clear them. If the checks (and deposits)
   are marked as cleared on your statement, click them here. In Figure 6.3, all the
   checks and deposits are cleared, except for one check.

8. After you have clicked all the checks and deposits that have cleared your bank, your
   statement may still not match your Quicken balance. In Figure 6.3, the balance was

▼

▼ off by $48.63. The next step is to reconcile your account balance and your statement balance.

FIGURE 6.3

Clearing checks.

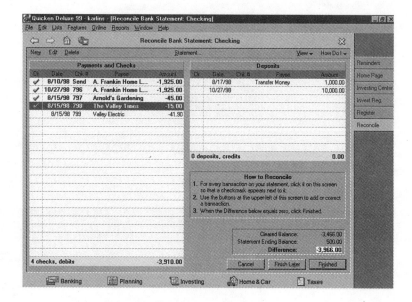

▲

If your checking account balance does not match your bank statements, following are some things to check:

- Did you enter every withdrawal, including ATM withdrawals? (Remember that night you needed to raid the ATM for an emergency $40?)

- Have you cleared a check in Quicken that didn't clear the bank? (Or has a check cleared the bank that you didn't mark as cleared?).

- Did you enter any deposits or debits twice?

If you find credits or debits in your account that you neglected to enter into Quicken, you can do that next. If that doesn't reconcile your account, you are at least able to identify the difference and raise it to your financial institution.

> When you mark checks or deposits as cleared (see Figure 6.3), they appear in your account view with an "R" in the Clr (cleared) column. You should *not* delete checks that have been reconciled from your account, or your Quicken account can not reflect an accurate account balance.

Reconcile Differences Between Quicken and Your Checking Statement

If you can identify missing charges or deposits, you can enter them and see whether those changes reconcile your Quicken balance and your account statement.

To Do: Reconcile Your Balances

1. If you discovered a withdrawal or check that you didn't enter in your checking account, you can do that from the Reconcile window by clicking the New button in the upper-left corner of the Reconcile window. This toggles you back to the checking Account view.

2. Add missing transactions in the Account view.

3. After you add new transactions, click the Return to Reconcile button in the lower-right corner of the window.

4. Clear your newly entered transaction (if it has cleared the bank) in the Reconcile Bank Statement window. If your balance still does not match the bank balance, it's back to the drawing board. Are there other deposits or expenses you neglected to enter?

5. If your account balances still do not match, check to see whether you've entered correct amounts for your cleared activity. If you find an error, click the Edit button in the upper-left corner of the Reconcile window and change the transaction.

6. If after all your work, your account balances are just slightly off, you can let Quicken create an expense (or deposit) category that covers the discrepancy. Click the Finished button in the Reconcile window and select Adjust when prompted. Quicken creates debit or credit items in your account to cover the discrepancy between your accounts.

7. If you do let Quicken adjust your account balance, you are prompted to create a reconciliation report, as shown in Figure 6.4. If you click the Yes button in the Reconciliation Complete dialog box, you are prompted to name and save the report.

FIGURE 6.4

You can let Quicken create a report documenting discrepancies between your account balance and your statement.

Reconciling a Savings Account

Reconciling Quicken balances and bank statements is similar for both checking and savings accounts. The main difference is that most checking accounts do not pay interest, whereas most savings accounts do.

Quicken does not calculate accumulated interest, but you can enter interest as an income item in your savings account. Figure 6.5 shows a savings account being reconciled, with two interest payments marked as cleared.

FIGURE 6.5

Balancing a savings account.

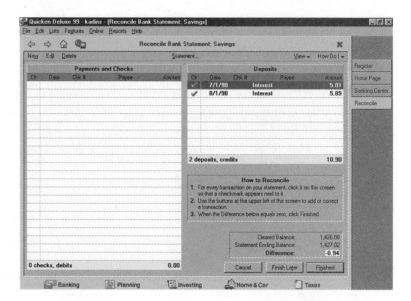

Just as with balancing a checking account, if your savings account balance is within pennies of your bank statement, you can elect to let Quicken create a transaction line of "Balance Adjustment." In Figure 6.6, a line has been added to the savings account with an adjustment of 94 cents.

Reconciling a Credit Card Account

When your credit card statement arrives in the mail, you can and should reconcile that statement with the balance in your Quicken account. Even more so than with a checking or savings account, it's likely that you have debits on your card that you didn't record. These might include the following:

FIGURE 6.6

You can let Quicken adjust your balances with a special transaction line.

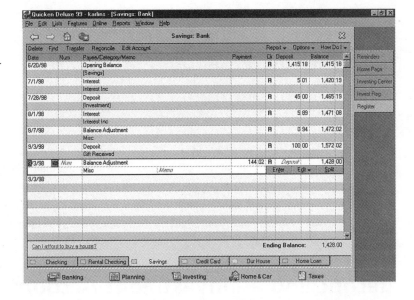

- Monthly charges assigned to your credit card such as gym memberships, online services, or other bills.
- Cash advances.
- Charges that you did not record in your account.

When you get your credit card statement, the first step, even before you start to reconcile, is to go through it carefully and look for expenses (and payments) not recorded in your account. Add these transactions to your credit card account. Then, you can reconcile your balances.

To Do: Reconcile Your Credit Card Balance

1. View your credit card account, if you're not looking at it.
2. Click the Reconcile button at the top of the Credit Card view.
3. In the Credit Card Statement Information dialog box, enter Charges, Payments, and the Ending Balance on your statement in the top three fields in the dialog box.
4. In the Finance Charges field, enter the amount of interest you paid.
5. When you have finished entering finance charges and clearing all payments and charges, click the Finished button in the Reconcile window. If your balances do not match, you see the Adjusting Register to Agree with Statement dialog box, shown in Figure 6.7.

▲ To Do

▼

6

FIGURE 6.7

Quicken identifies balance discrepancies in your credit card statement.

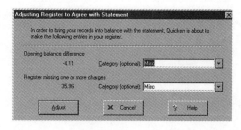

6. You can either let Quicken adjust your account with a miscellaneous charge (or credit), or you can click the Cancel button in the dialog box, return to the Reconcile window, and continue to look for missing credits and expenses or mistakes in your transactions.

7. After you reconcile your credit card balance, you are prompted to generate a payment to that account, if you have a balance.

Reconciling an Investment Account

When you get a statement from your investment institution, you can reconcile that statement with the balance in an investment account.

To Do: Balance an Investment Account Balance

1. View your investment account (you can click a link at the Quicken Home Page).

2. Select Features, Investing, Reconcile from the Quicken menu.

3. If you have more than one investment, you see the Choose Reconcile Account dialog box. Use the drop-down menu to select your investment account. Then click the OK button.

4. In the Reconcile Mutual Fund dialog box, enter your starting share balance in the first field.

5. Enter the Ending Share Balance—this is the value of your shares as reflected in your printed statement.

6. Enter the ending price per share in the last field in the dialog box. If you don't know the ending price, you can leave this field blank. When you have filled in all four fields in the Reconcile Mutual Fund Account, as shown in Figure 6.8, click the OK button.

7. When you click the Finish button, if the balance in your account does not match that in your statement, you are prompted with a dialog box with an Adjust button. You can click that button to create a new transaction in your register reconciling your statements.

FIGURE **6.8**

*Letting Quicken
calculate your
investment balance.*

▲

Printing Reconciliation Reports

Each time you reconcile an account, you can print a reconciliation report for your
records.

To Do: Print a Reconciliation Report

1. View the account from which you will print a reconciliation report.

2. From the Quicken menu, select Reports, Banking, Reconciliation. The
   Reconciliation Report Setup dialog box appears, as shown in Figure 6.9.

FIGURE **6.9**

*Preparing a recon-
ciliation report.*

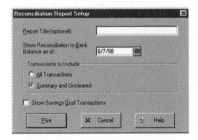

3. You can enter an optional report title in the setup dialog box. Other fields vary
   depending on what type of account you are printing a report from. But all reports
   allow you to select a date from which to balance the account.

4. After you fill in the fields in the Reconciliation Report Balance dialog box, click
   the Print button. You see the Print dialog box.

5. In the Print dialog box, you can click the Preview button to see your report before
   you send it to the printer. Figure 6.10 shows a savings account reconciliation

▼   report ready to print.

6

FIGURE 6.10

*You can print a
reconciliation report
to show the balance
in any account.*

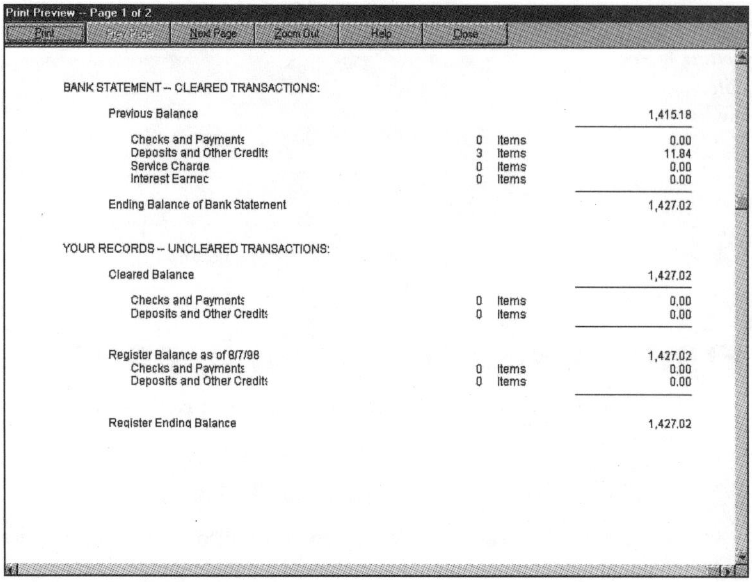

Summary

Reconciliation between your Quicken accounts and the statements you get from your financial institution is essential to maintaining the accuracy and validity of your Quicken balances.

Reconciliation is an opportunity to check both your statement and your Quicken balance for accuracy. Depending on the type of account you are reconciling, you likely have additional debits and credits to enter as you reconcile your report.

If you are unable to completely reconcile your Quicken balance and your statement balance, you can elect to let Quicken create a new transaction in your account to cover the difference between the two balances.

Q&A

Q If your checking account balance doesn't match that on your statement, where do you start to reconcile the balances?

A The first thing to do is to reconcile the accounts, and mark all cleared transactions.

Q I can balance a checkbook, will it be hard for me to balance a Quicken checking account?

A Balancing your Quicken account works just like balancing your checkbook.

Hour 7

Scheduling and Tracking Financial Activity

One of the most useful and powerful things about Quicken is the way it automates regular financial activity. You can schedule transactions that occur regularly, such as your rent, house payment, or utility bills. And you can schedule regular income transactions such as your paycheck.

Quicken allows you to see an overview of your financial picture in calendar form, and prompts you to enter these regularly scheduled transactions.

The highlights of this hour include

- Schedule repeating bill payments
- Schedule regular income transactions
- Use Quicken to organize contact information for your financial affairs
- Manage your scheduled transactions
- Using Quicken as a date book

Using the Financial Calendar

The Financial Calendar displays your scheduled financial transactions in Calendar view. You can add transactions to the Calendar view and get a picture of your upcoming bills and income.

In this hour, you first learn to use the Financial Calendar to get a visual picture of your income and expenses. Then, you learn to add scheduled transactions and manage them on a monthly basis.

Viewing the Calendar

You can see your transactions for any month in calendar form. You can elect to see either *scheduled* transactions, *recorded* transactions, or both. Scheduled transactions are bills you expect to pay, or income you expect to receive. Recorded transactions are bills you've paid or income you've received (and recorded).

There are a number of easy ways to schedule transactions, but before you explore them, you learn to view and organize the Financial Calendar itself.

To Do: View Your Financial Calendar

1. Select Features, Reminders, Financial Calendar from the Quicken menu. The Calendar appears as shown in Figure 7.1.

FIGURE 7.1

Viewing your Financial Calendar.

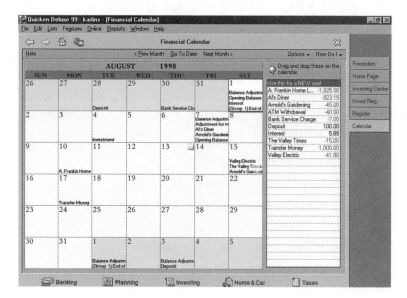

▼ 2. You can see the previous month's calendar by clicking the <Prev Month button at the top of the Calendar, or the next month by clicking the Next Month> button. If you click the Go to Date button, you can enter any date in the Go To Date dialog box to jump right to that day on the Calendar.

3. You can see a detailed breakdown of all scheduled transactions by double-clicking a date in the Financial Calendar. Figure 7.2 shows all transactions scheduled for August 7th.

FIGURE 7.2

Viewing scheduled transactions for a date in Calendar view.

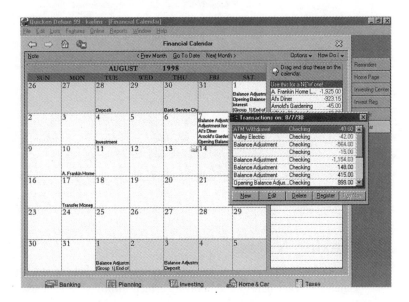

4. The buttons at the bottom of the Transactions Due dialog box allow you to add a new transaction or edit an existing one. The New button allows you to schedule a new transaction for the selected date. The other buttons apply to the specific transaction selected from the list of scheduled transactions for the day. The Edit button opens the Edit Register Transaction dialog box, where you can change the selected transaction amount or other details. The Delete button deletes the selected transaction, and the Register button enters the transaction as registered.

Remember, if you want to edit, delete, or register a transaction, you must first click that specific transaction in the Transactions Due list.

7

▼

▼ 5. You can also view your account balances in graph form. To do this, click the Options button at the top of the Financial Calendar and select Show Account Graph from the menu, as shown in Figure 7.3.

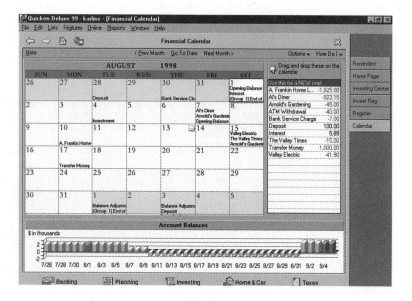

FIGURE 7.3

Displaying account balances as a chart.

▲

Making Notes

You've just seen how you can view, and even edit and register transactions from the Calendar. You can also add notes, in effect turning your Calendar into a date book.

To Do: Add Notes to the Calendar

1. Select a date in the Calendar.

2. Right-click the date and select Note. The Note dialog box appears, as shown in Figure 7.4.

FIGURE 7.4

Creating a reminder note.

▼

▼   3. Select a background color for the note from the Note Color drop-down menu.

4. Type a message, as shown in Figure 7.4.

5. When you complete your note, click the Save button in the Note dialog box.

After you define a note, a small colored icon appears in the upper-right corner of the assigned date. You can view notes by clicking this icon. If you no longer need the note,
▲   you can click the Delete Note button in the Note dialog box.

Setting Calendar Options

You can elect to view the following types of transactions in the Calendar:

- Recorded Transactions
- Scheduled Transactions
- The Account Graph
- Memorized Transactions
- Calendar Accounts

You can select any or all these categories of transactions by clicking the Options menu at the top of the Financial Calendar, and clicking a category. A check mark next to the category means that type of transaction displays in the Financial Calendar.

Recorded transactions are transactions that you entered as completed. You learned to record transactions in Hour 4, "Entering Transactions in the Register." Scheduled Transactions are regularly occurring expenses or sources of income. You learn to define these and use them to save time in the next section of this hour. You visited the Account Graph earlier in this hour.

Memorized Transactions are explored in the next hour of this book, "Memorizing Transactions." For now, you can simply note that they can be viewed in the Financial Calendar.

Finally, the Calendar Accounts option in the Options menu opens a dialog box from which you can select the accounts to be displayed on the Financial Calendar. For example, you might elect not to include your investment account in the Calendar.

Figure 7.5 shows the Options menu, with Scheduled Transactions, Recorded Transactions, and the Account Graph selected for display.

7

FIGURE 7.5

Customizing your Financial Calendar display.

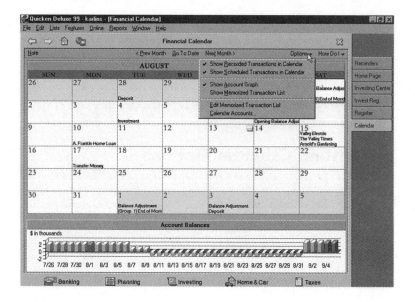

Scheduling Transactions

One of the handiest things about Quicken is its capability to schedule your bills for you. Quicken can't anticipate every random bill you have to pay, but if you have bills that come each week, each month, each quarter, or on another regular schedule, you can ask Quicken to prompt you to pay them.

What if those bills are for different amounts each month? For example, your electric bill is due the same time each month, but it may be different each month. Quicken can ask you to fill in an amount each time these bills are due.

Quicken also allows you to group bills, so rather than being prompted to pay bills on the exact day the are due, you can print or write several checks at once.

In this section you learn to define and group scheduled transactions.

Creating a Scheduled Transaction

You can define a scheduled transaction in the Scheduled Transactions list. After you do, that transaction appears on your Calendar.

To Do: Create a Scheduled Transaction

1. Select Lists, Scheduled Transactions from the main Quicken menu.

2. Click the New button at the top of the Scheduled Transaction list. The Create Scheduled Transaction dialog box appears.

3. Click the Account to Use drop-down arrow to see a list of your existing accounts. Select one for your scheduled transaction.

4. Select a Type of Transaction from the drop-down menu.

5. Enter a Payee and a Category (for expenses). If you have already defined the payee, or your expense is assigned to an existing category, you can select them using the drop-down menus. If you want Quicken to print checks for you, you can click the Address button in the dialog box and enter the payee address.

6. The Memo field is for miscellaneous information, such as a reminder that an account should be canceled on a certain date.

7. Enter the date that the next payment is due in the Next Date field, and enter the amount of the payment in the Amount field.

8. If your expense is split between different categories, you can click the Split button and define the amount of the expense you want to assign to different categories.

9. In the How Often field, select the frequency of the bill from the drop-down menu. If the bill is the same amount each month, select Automatically Enter from the Record in Register drop-down menu. If the bill is for a different amount each month, select Prompt Before Enter, as shown in Figure 7.6.

FIGURE 7.6

Some regularly scheduled bills are for different amounts each month.

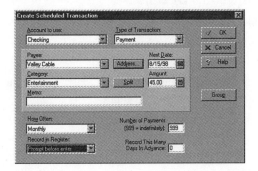

10. When you have completed the Create Scheduled Transaction dialog box, click the OK button. You see a dialog box verifying that you've defined a scheduled transaction. Click the OK button, and your transaction appears in the Scheduled Transaction List, as shown in Figure 7.7.

FIGURE 7.7

Scheduled Transaction List.

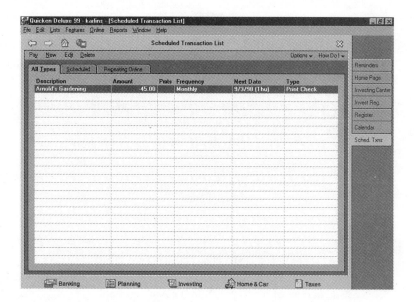

Grouping Scheduled Transactions

If you want to pay a bunch of bills at the same time, you can include them in a group. You can have up to 12 different groups of bills. So, for example, you can assign some bills to a mid-month payment and others to an end of the month payment. That way, all your scheduled bills can be paid in a couple batches, instead of trickling in every day.

To Do: Create a Group of Bills

1. In the Scheduled Transaction List, click one of your scheduled transactions.

2. Click the Edit button, and in the Edit Scheduled Transaction dialog box, click the Group button.

3. In the Create Transaction Group dialog box, enter a group name in the Group Name field—for example, "End of Month."

4. Click the OK button. The Assign Transactions to Group dialog box appears. Your first group is called Group 1, your second group is called Group 2, and so on, up to a maximum of 12 groups.

5. In the Grp column, double-click in the row of each transaction you want to include in this group. Figure 7.8 shows three transactions assigned to Group 1.

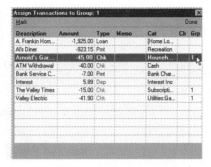

FIGURE 7.8

Grouping transactions for easy payment.

▲

Scheduling One-Time Payments

You can add an existing transaction to your Financial Calendar, or create a new transaction directly in the Financial Calendar.

To create a new transaction in the Calendar, first select the Calendar tab to see the Financial Calendar, and then right-click a date. Select Transactions from the context menu, and click the New button.

Use the New Transactions dialog box to enter a new transaction. Select Once Only from the How Often drop-down menu if this not a regularly scheduled payment.

Figure 7.9 shows a one-time payment being assigned to a date. On the scheduled date, you are prompted to make this payment.

FIGURE 7.9

Scheduling a one-time payment.

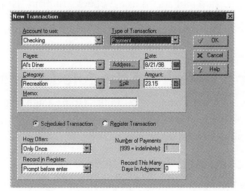

Recording or Skipping a Scheduled Transaction

After you schedule payments, your payments due appear in the Quicken Home Page when you start a new Quicken session.

7

You can right-click a scheduled transaction in the Home Page and select Enter This Scheduled Transaction as shown in Figure 7.10.

FIGURE 7.10

Entering scheduled transactions.

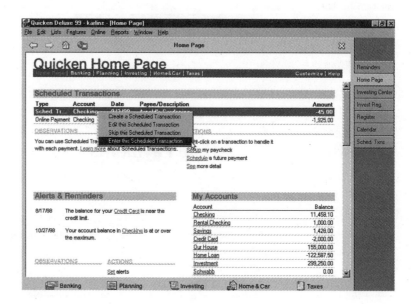

After you enter a scheduled transaction, you hear the "cha-ching" sound of your transactions being registered. If you have scheduled this (or these) transactions to be paid by checks, checks are generated and added to the checks to print list on your Home Page.

You can review Hour 5, "Creating and Printing Checks" for a complete discussion of printing checks.

Modifying and Deleting Scheduled Transactions

You can right-click a scheduled transaction in the Home Page to modify it. For example, you may have scheduled a payment to a restaurant, but the bill turned out to be a different amount than the amount you scheduled.

To Do: Edit a Scheduled Transaction

1. Right-click a scheduled transaction in the Home Page.

2. Select Edit this Scheduled Transaction from the context menu.

3. The Record Scheduled Transaction dialog box appears. You can make changes to any field in the dialog box, and then click the Record button in the dialog box to register the revised transaction.

▲

You can also skip a transaction by right-clicking a scheduled transaction in the Home Page and selecting Skip this Scheduled Transaction from the context menu.

Using Reminders

In addition to seeing reminders of scheduled transactions in the Quicken Home Page, you can also see a list of reminders in the Reminders view. To do that, select Features, Reminders, Reminders from the main Quicken menu. Figure 7.11 shows scheduled reminders.

FIGURE 7.11

Viewing a list of scheduled financial activity.

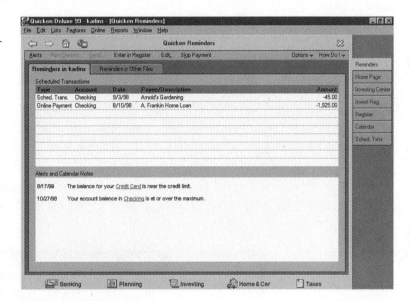

You can control the display of reminders by clicking the Options button at the top of the Reminders view, and then clicking Reminders. You can select Show Reminders When Starting Quicken to display a list of scheduled transactions in the Home Page. And, you can also select Show Reminders From Other Files if you have multiple Quicken files on your computer.

The third option in this menu, Days Shown, opens the Days Shown dialog box. Here, you can define how many days in advance you wish to display reminders. Figure 7.12 shows the dialog box being set to display reminders 14 days in advance, and notes 30 days in advance.

7

FIGURE 7.12

Customizing reminder options.

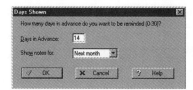

Using Alerts

In Hour 5 of this book, you learned to attach Alerts to your checking account. Alerts can be assigned, for example, to warn you when balances get too low, or when you spend too much on a category.

You can also define Alerts independent of your checking account.

To Do: Define Alerts

1. Select Features, Reminders, Alerts from the main Quicken menu.

2. In the left side of the dialog box, select an account to which you want to assign an alert.

3. Click in the check box to activate the alert.

4. In the right side of the dialog box, edit the alert criteria. For example, Figure 7.13 shows the Credit Card Alert being defined to warn me when my credit card balance reaches $3,000.

FIGURE 7.13

Defining an alert for credit card balance.

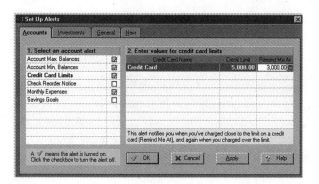

After you define alerts, you can select Features, Reminders, Reminders to see Alerts in the bottom half of the view.

Using the Financial Address Book

Quicken Deluxe 99 comes with its own address book, the Quicken Financial Address Book.

To start this program, click the Start button in Windows and select the Financial Address Book from the Quicken group. You see a blank address book, as shown in Figure 7.14.

FIGURE 7.14

Opening the Financial Address Book.

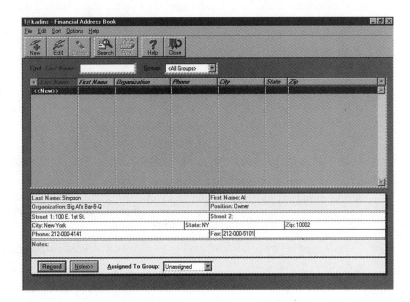

You can add and edit addresses in this address book, and use it to look up addresses as you need them.

Adding Addresses

As soon as you open your Financial Address Book, you're ready to enter a new record.

To Do: Enter a New Record

1. Enter last and first name, organization, addresses, and phone numbers in the fields in the form at the bottom of the Financial Address Book.

2. You can assign a record to a group (Quicken, Family, Friends, or Work) by selecting a group from the Assigned to Group drop-down menu at the bottom of the form.

3. You can add notes about this record by clicking the Notes button at the bottom of the form and entering memos in the large, white Notes area. You can toggle back out of the Notes field by clicking the Notes button again.

7

▲

4. When you complete entering your record, click the Record button at the bottom of the form. Your new record appears in the list at the top of the window.

Editing and Deleting Addresses

To edit a record in your Financial Address Book, click the record in the top (list) section of the Address book. Your record appears in the bottom half of the window. You can click in any field in a record to change the entry.

You can delete a record by selecting it and clicking the Delete button in the Iconbar at the very top of the Financial Address Book (below the menu).

You can print any selected record(s) by clicking the Print button in the Iconbar. (You can select more than one record by holding down the Shift key as you click records in the list).

Sorting and Searching Through Addresses

You can sort your records by Last Name, First Name, Organization, or City. Or, you can define another field (for example, zip code).

To Do: Sort Your Address List

To Do

1. With the Financial Address Book open, and at least two records entered, select the Sort menu.

2. Click By Last Name. Your records are now listed in alphabetical order by last name (A-Z).

3. Select the Sort menu again and click By.

4. In the Financial Address Book—Sort By dialog box, click Zip, as shown in Figure 7.15. Then click the OK button in the dialog box. Your records are sorted by zip code.

FIGURE 7.15

Sorting addresses by zip code.

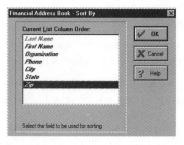

▲

The Financial Address book makes it easy to look at your records. You can filter your address list by selecting a group from the Group drop-down menu under the Iconbar.

You can look up a record by typing a last name in the Find Last Name field at the top of the list. As you type, the Financial Address book looks up the letters you type, so it is not usually necessary to type the entire name. If you click a different column heading (for example, Organization), you can enter letters in the Find field to look up a record using another field.

Printing an Address List

To print your records, simply click the Print icon. In the Print dialog box, click the On drop-down menu to choose between printing in any of the following formats:

- Address book (Addresses in record form)
- Phone book (only names and phone numbers print)
- Labels (select a label style from the On drop-down menu)
- Rolodex cards (select a card style from the On drop-down menu)
- Envelopes (select an envelope size from the On drop-down menu)

If you have sorted or filtered your list (by group), only selected records print.

Summary

Quicken does many things to make it easy to pay your bills. You can schedule regularly occurring bills, and Quicken prompts you to pay them right from the Quicken Home Page. You can add bills to your Calendar to remind yourself to pay them.

Quicken's Calendar shows you a graphical picture of your upcoming transactions. And the Financial Address Book makes it easy to print envelopes, labels, or address books.

Q&A

Q Can transactions be scheduled if you don't know the amount of the transaction?

A Yes, you can have Quicken prompt you to supply an amount for a regularly scheduled transaction.

Q How do I know whether I have scheduled transactions to deal with?

A Scheduled transactions are displayed in the Quicken Home Page. Or, you can see a list of scheduled transactions by viewing the Scheduled Transactions List.

7

HOUR **8**

Memorizing Transactions

This hour introduces the concept of memorized transactions, a Quicken feature that can help you save time and maintain consistency in your data entry. Quicken enables you to memorize, or save, the details of a transaction so that you can use it over and over again. You can view and print lists of transactions you've memorized as well as edit and delete them. Finally, you can lock a transaction to prevent it from changing.

The highlights of this hour include

- Why you'll want to memorize transactions
- How to view and print a list of memorized transactions
- Why you might want to delete some memorized transactions
- How to lock transactions
- How to add a memorized transaction to the iconbar

Understanding Memorized Transactions

By default, Quicken memorizes all your register entries. Then when you begin to enter another transaction for that same payee, Quicken recognizes that payee and automatically enters the remaining transaction information for you (amount, memo, category, and class) using QuickFill. Memorized transactions and QuickFill are very useful features that you'll most likely want to use, but you can also deactivate them if you want.

To view the options for using memorized transactions and QuickFill, select Edit, Options, Register to open the Register Options dialog box shown in Figure 8.1.

FIGURE 8.1

You can choose whether Quicken automatically memorizes transactions.

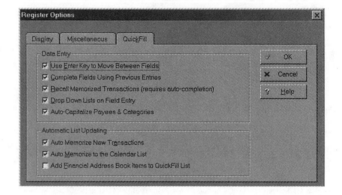

On the QuickFill tab, you'll find the following options that determine how Quicken handles memorized transactions and QuickFill:

- *Auto Memorize New Transactions.* Tells Quicken to automatically save every register entry and place it in the memorized transaction list for future use.

- *Auto Memorize to the Calendar List.* Tells Quicken to save every register entry automatically to the Financial Calendar list for future use.

- *Complete Fields Using Previous Entries.* Enables QuickFill to save time in making register entries by completing entries as you begin to type.

- *Recall Memorized Transaction (requires auto-completion).* This option is available only if you select Complete Fields Using Previous Entries. Enables Quicken to refer to the Memorized Transaction List when using QuickFill.

Viewing a List of Memorized Transactions

To view a list of memorized transactions, select Lists, Memorized Transaction. Figure 8.2 displays the Memorized Transaction List.

FIGURE 8.2

You can view the transactions you've previously memorized.

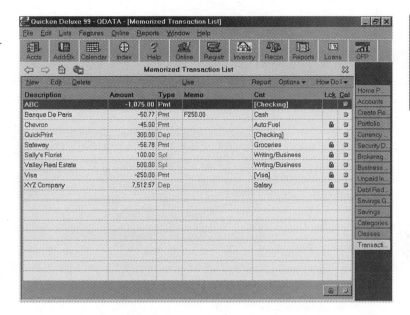

The list includes all transactions you've memorized including the description, amount, type, memo, category, locked status, and calendar status.

To view a long list more easily, you can sort it in several different ways—by description, amount, type, memo, or category. To choose the sort order you want, click the Options button and select the preferred order.

Adding a Memorized Transaction Manually

Although you'll usually add memorized transactions to the list automatically, you can also add a transaction manually.

To Do: Add a Memorized Transaction

1. Click the New button to open the Create Memorized Transaction dialog box, as shown in Figure 8.3.

FIGURE 8.3

Memorizing transactions manually provides added flexibility.

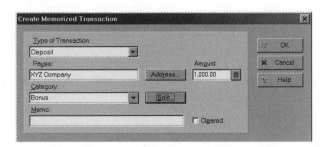

▼ 2. Select a type of transaction: Payment, Deposit, Print Check, or Online Pmt
      (payment).

   3. Enter the payee's name in the Payee field.

   4. If you select Print Check as the transaction type, click the Address button to open
      the Printed Check Information dialog box, illustrated in Figure 8.4.

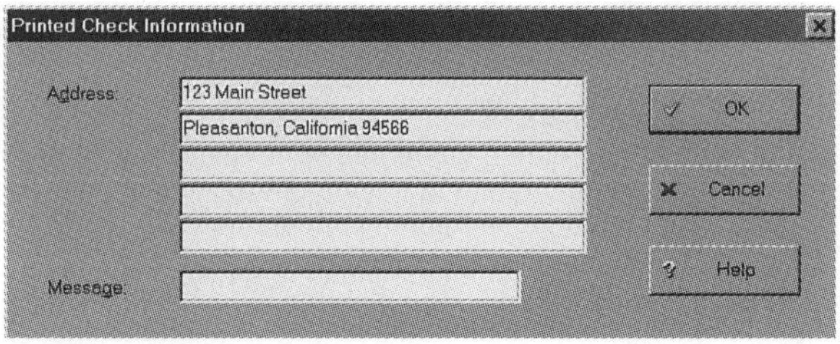

FIGURE 8.4

*You can add address
information if the
transaction is for a
printed check.*

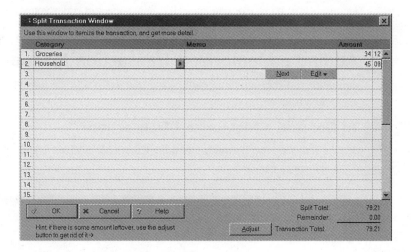

   5. Enter an address and message in the dialog box and click OK to return to the
      Create Memorized Transaction dialog box.

   6. Enter an amount for the transaction.

   7. Select a category from the drop-down list.

   8. Click the Split button if you are entering a split transaction. The Split Transaction
      Window appears (see Figure 8.5).

FIGURE 8.5

*You can also memorize
split transactions.*

▼

8

▼ 9. Select a category in the first column, add a memo in the second column if desired, and enter in the last column an amount for each split line.

10. Click the Adjust button to adjust the entries properly.

11. Click OK to return to the previous dialog box.

12. Add a memo if desired.

13. Click the Cleared check box if you want to indicate the transaction has cleared.

▲ 14. Click OK to close the Create Memorized Transaction dialog box and return to the Memorized Transaction List.

Editing and Deleting Memorized Transactions

To edit an existing transaction, select it in the Memorized Transaction List and then click the Edit button. Figure 8.6 displays the Edit Memorized Transaction dialog box, which is almost identical to the Create Memorized Transaction dialog box.

FIGURE 8.6

Edit transactions you've already memorized in this dialog box.

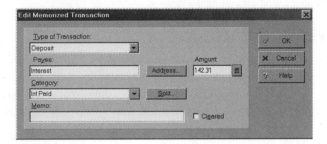

Use this dialog box to make any necessary adjustments to a memorized transaction. For example, you might want to change an assigned category or add a memo field for more information.

To delete a transaction, select it and click the Delete button. Quicken verifies you want to delete the transaction and then performs the deletion.

For example, you might want to delete memorized transactions that you

- Haven't used for a long time
- Have used only once and will never use again (such as vacations, business travel, or one-time expenses)
- Have stopped using (due to relocation, a lifestyle change, a company that went out of business, and so on)

In addition to deleting memorized transactions manually, you can also have Quicken automatically remove memorized transactions you haven't used in a specified number of months. To do this, select Edit, Options, Quicken Program to open the General Options dialog box, shown in Figure 8.7.

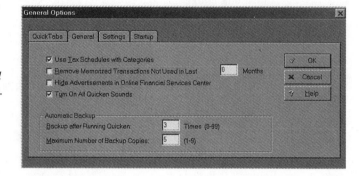

On the General tab, select the Remove Memorized Transactions Not Used in Last x Months check box and enter the desired number of months.

Locking Transactions

When Quicken recognizes a memorized transaction, it automatically finishes entering the transaction for you. In some cases you may want the entire transaction to remain identi- cal, but in others you may want to change this data. When you modify transaction data, Quicken memorizes the transaction again with the latest information.

For example, suppose that you enter a transaction for Valley Cleaners for the first time on July 17th for $15.95. Quicken memorizes this transaction. Two weeks later, you go back to Valley Cleaners, but spend only $6.95. When you enter this second transaction, Quicken recalls the memorized transaction, but you adjust it to reflect the new amount. Quicken then memorizes Valley Cleaners with an amount of $6.95. So any time you adjust a memorized transaction, Quicken overwrites your original memorization with the most recent information.

To avoid such overwriting, you can lock a memorized transaction. When you do so, the information you store in a memorized transaction stays the same, no matter how many times you update it, and Quicken won't overwrite your original memorization.

To lock a transaction, select the Lck (lock) column for that transaction in the Memorized Transaction List window. A lock icon appears in the column, telling you the transaction is locked. To remove a lock, select the Lck column again. Figure 8.8 displays a Memorized Transaction List with several locked transactions.

FIGURE 8.8

Lock a transaction to prevent making any changes to it.

8

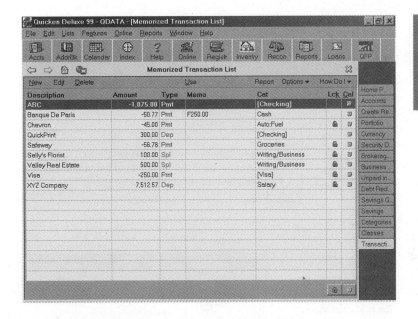

Using a Memorized Transaction on the Financial Calendar

To use a memorized transaction on the Financial Calendar, you must select the Cal (calendar) column for that transaction in the Memorized Transaction List (see Figure 8.9).

FIGURE 8.9

Determine whether you want to list certain memorized transactions on the Financial Calendar.

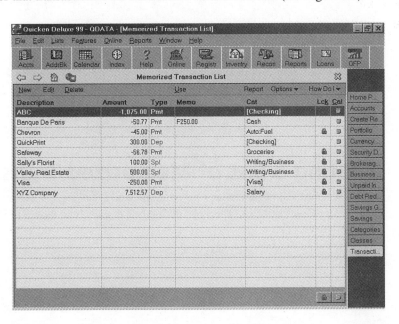

A small calendar icon appears next to selected transactions. If you don't want to display the transaction in the Financial Calendar, deselect the Cal column. Only selected transactions appear on the Financial Calendar, as illustrated in Figure 8.10.

Hour 7, "Scheduling and Tracking Financial Activity," covers in more detail how to use these memorized transactions on the Financial Calendar.

> If you use Quicken Home & Business, you'll notice two additional columns—Cus (customer) and Vdr (vendor)—that you use to associate memorized transactions with customers and vendors.

FIGURE 8.10

You can easily drag transactions from the list to the calendar.

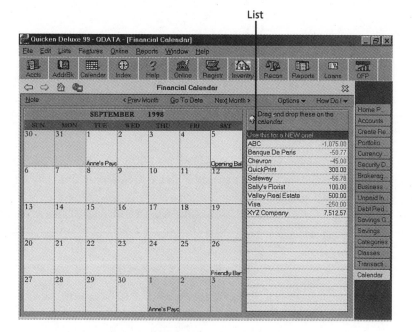

Printing a List of Memorized Transactions

To print a list of memorized transactions while viewing the Memorized Transaction List, select File, Print List. The Print dialog box displays, as shown in Figure 8.11.

FIGURE 8.11

You can print a list of your memorized transactions for easy reference.

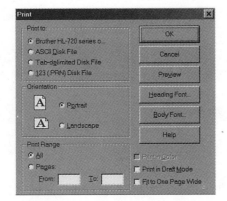

Select the designated printer and other parameters and click OK to print.

Adding a Memorized Transaction to the Iconbar

If you use the same memorized transaction over and over again, you can add it to the iconbar to make entering it even easier.

For example, you might make the following transactions on a regular basis:

- $40 ATM withdrawal
- $5.95 for a buffet lunch
- $8.00 for a round-trip subway or train fare

To Do: Create an Icon for a Memorized Transaction

1. Select Edit, Options, Iconbar to open the Customize Iconbar dialog box, shown in Figure 8.12.

FIGURE 8.12

Adding a memorized transaction to the iconbar makes data entry even easier.

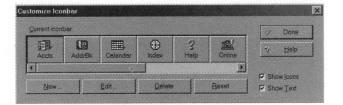

FIGURE 8.13

Select the icon action that uses a specific memorized transaction.

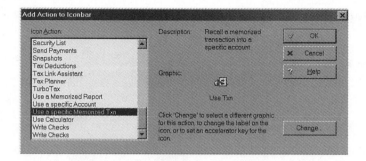

2. Click New to open the Add Action to Iconbar dialog box (see Figure 8.13).

3. Select Use a Specific Memorized Txn (transaction) from the Icon Action list.

> If you want to customize the icon graphic or text, click the Change button to display the Change Iconbar Item dialog box. Quicken includes a number of graphics possibilities for icons.

4. Click OK to display the Assign Memorized Transaction to Icon dialog box, illustrated in Figure 8.14.

FIGURE 8.14

Specify where to record the memorized transaction.

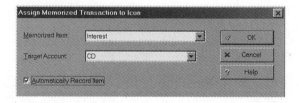

5. Select the memorized item and target account from the drop-down lists.

6. Choose the Automatically Record Item check box to specify that Quicken automatically enter the transaction in the register when you select the icon.

7. Click OK to return to the Customize Iconbar dialog box.

8. Click Done to return to Quicken.

8

Summary

This hour provided more details on how to manage memorized transactions successfully in Quicken. Using memorized transactions and QuickFill can automate data-entry tasks and help save you time. You can view and print a list of memorized transactions as well as edit, customize, and delete them. If you want to memorize a transaction once and never alter it, you can lock the transaction. You can also use memorized transactions on the Financial Calendar and add them to the iconbar for even easier access.

Hour 9, "Managing Loans," introduces you to Quicken's loan setup and tracking capabilities.

Q&A

Q Quicken isn't memorizing my transactions. What should I do?

A Be sure that you select Auto Memorize New Transactions in the Register Options dialog box's QuickFill tab; otherwise, Quicken doesn't memorize transactions. Select Edit, Options, Register to access this dialog box.

Q Is it a good idea to keep all my memorized transactions, or should I delete some of them?

A If you know you'll never use a memorized transaction again, then you should delete it. Having too many memorized transactions makes it harder for QuickFill to find an exact match, so you'll end up typing more information manually.

HOUR 9

Managing Loans

This hour shows you how to set up loans to track the money you borrow to purchase a house, car, boat, or other item. When you set up a loan, Quicken automatically creates a liability account for that loan. You can later modify, view, and analyze your loans as well as automate payments and make extra payments if necessary.

The highlights of this hour include:

- How to set up a loan
- How to set up a loan payment
- How to modify loans and loan details
- Where to view loan schedules, reports, and graphs

Setting Up a Loan

You'll want to create a liability account for every loan you currently have, such as a mortgage, car loan, or home equity loan. Quicken provides a loan setup dialog box to make setting up a loan an easy process. Once you finish this procedure, Quicken creates a liability account for this loan.

You can also tie an asset account to a liability. For example, you may want to track your mortgage as a liability and your house as an asset to follow its market value. Hour 17, "Tracking Real Estate," provides more details on how to use Quicken accounts to track real estate properties.

> Have your loan paperwork on-hand so that you can easily answer all questions in the loan setup dialog box.

To Do: Set Up a Loan

1. Select Features, Bills, Loans to open the View Loans window. If this is the first loan you are setting up in Quicken, the window appears empty, as shown in Figure 9.1.

FIGURE 9.1

You can set up and track loans from the View Loans window.

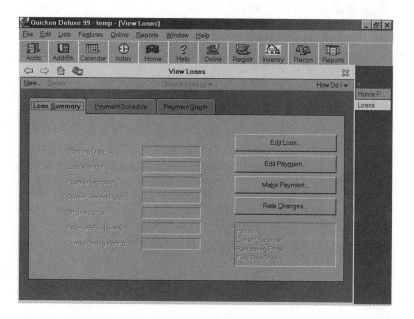

> You can also open an existing loan by selecting Choose Loan or delete a loan by selecting Delete.

▼ 2. Click the New button to display the Loan Setup dialog box, illustrated in Figure 9.2.

FIGURE 9.2

Use the Loan Setup dialog box to set up your first loan.

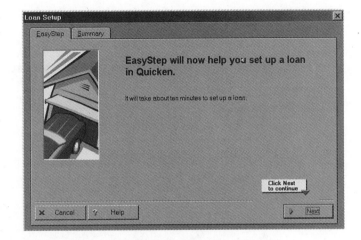

3. Click the Summary tab to expedite loan setup. Figure 9.3 displays this tab.

FIGURE 9.3

The Summary tab simplifies loan setup.

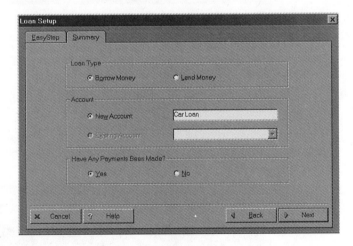

If you need more step-by-step guidance for setting up a loan, click Next from the EasyStep tab.

4. Specify whether you want to borrow or lend money.

5. If you are setting up a new account, select New Account and enter an account name. If you are setting up an existing account, select the account from the drop-down list.

▼   6. Indicate whether or not you've already made payments on this loan, by choosing
           Yes or No. Then click Next to continue (see Figure 9.4).

FIGURE 9.4

Specify exact informa-
tion about your loan to
track it properly.

7. Enter the opening date, original balance, and original length of the loan.

8. Select a compounding period. Choices available in the Compounding Period
    drop-down list include Daily, Monthly, and Semi-Annually.

9. If you pay this loan at standard intervals, select the interval from the Standard
    Period drop-down list. The list includes eight options—from daily to annually.

10. If you have another form of payment plan, select Other Period and enter the pay-
    ments per year, then click Next to continue. Figure 9.5 illustrates the following step.

FIGURE 9.5

Quicken can calculate
your payments for you.

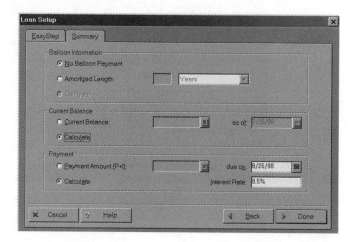

▼

▼ 11. If you don't have a balloon payment, select No Balloon Payment.

12. If you do have a balloon payment, you can either enter its amortized length or select the Calculate option to tell Quicken to calculate the length for you.

13. If you indicated that you made previous payments on this loan, the Current Balance group box appears. Enter the current balance as of a specified date or select the Calculate option to tell Quicken to calculate the balance for you based on the other information you provide.

14. Next, enter your payment amount (the payment plus interest) and the date on which it's due, or choose the Calculate option to tell Quicken to calculate these items.

15. Enter the interest rate of this loan and click Done. If you asked Quicken to calculate any amounts for you, it redisplays this step with the new calculated amounts (see Figure 9.6).

FIGURE 9.6

Quicken redisplays any calculated amounts for your approval.

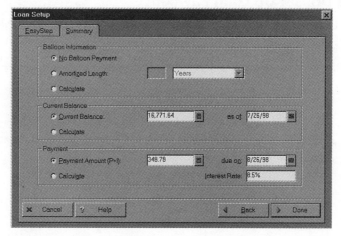

16. Click Done to continue to the Setup Loan Payment dialog box, shown in Figure 9.7.

▼ Quicken displays the current interest rate and principal and interest payment from your previous entries. If necessary, you can change these here.

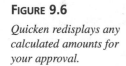

FIGURE 9.7

Setting up loan payments is easy too.

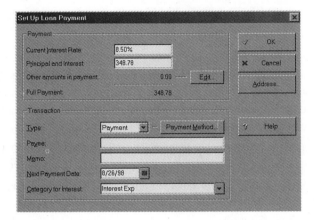

To Do: Set Up Loan Payments

1. If you want to add another amount in the payment, click the Edit button in the Setup Loan Payment dialog box to display the Split Transaction Window (see Figure 9.8).

FIGURE 9.8

Record additional payments, such as mortgage insurance, in the Split Transaction Window.

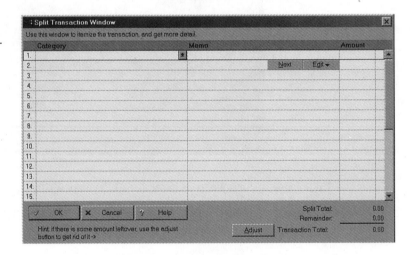

2. Enter a category, optional memo, and amount for each additional item and click OK to return to the previous dialog box. An example of an additional amount you might want to include in your payment is mortgage insurance for a home loan.

3. Select a transaction type—either a Payment or Print Check.

4. Click the Payment Method button to display the Select Payment Method dialog box, shown in Figure 9.9.

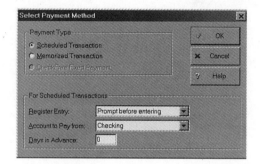

5. Specify whether this is a Scheduled Transaction, Memorized Transaction, or CheckFree Fixed Payment. Selecting Scheduled Transaction activates the For Scheduled Transactions group box.

A scheduled transaction is a transaction that Quicken automatically reminds you to record. A memorized transaction is a transaction that you save and can recall when you record data for the same payee again. A CheckFree fixed payment is a payment you make with CheckFree, an online bill payment service that works with Quicken.

6. In the Register Entry drop-down list, specify how you want to register entries. You can either prompt before entering or automatically enter the payment.

7. Choose an account from which to pay, enter the days in advance you want Quicken to remind you of the transaction, and click OK to return to the Set Up Loan Payment dialog box.

8. Enter the name of the payee (the financial institution providing the loan) as well as an optional memo notation.

9. Enter the next payment date or use the Calendar button to help you determine this date.

10. From the Category for Interest drop-down list, select a category for interest with which you want to track all interest expenses related to this loan. Figure 9.10 illustrates these entries.

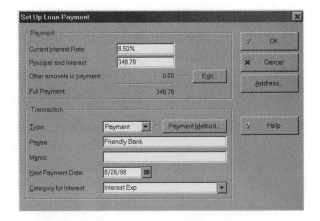

11. If you choose Printed Check as your transaction type, you can click the Address button to open the Printed Check Information dialog box (see Figure 9.11).

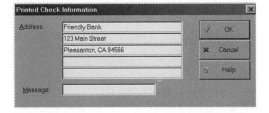

12. Enter address information and an optional message for your printed check and click OK to return to the previous dialog box.

13. Click OK to complete setting up your loan payment. Quicken prompts you with a dialog box asking whether you want to associate an asset with this loan. For exam-ple, you could set up an asset account for your house to complement the mortgage loan account.

If you decide not to set up an asset account, Quicken displays the Loan Summary tab in the View Loans window. Figure 9.12 illustrates this tab, which provides a summary of the loan information you just entered.

FIGURE 9.12

*This tab summarizes
your loan.*

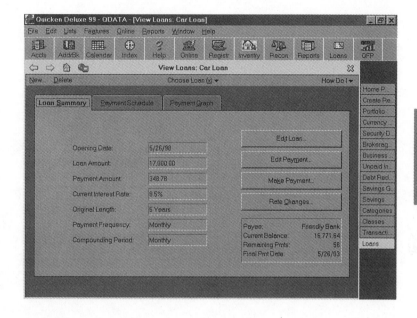

Modifying Loans

From the View Loans window, you can make modifications to an existing loan, make
regular or extra payments, and change loan rates.

Editing Loans

To edit a loan, click the Edit Loan button, which opens the Edit Loan dialog box shown
in Figure 9.13.

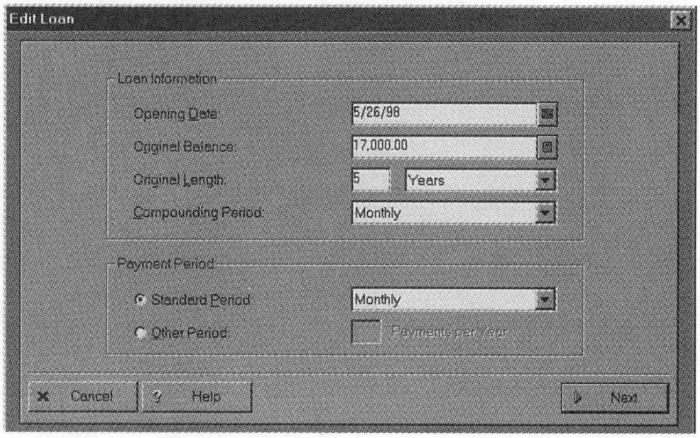

FIGURE 9.13

*You can modify a loan
you already created.*

In this first step, you can modify basic loan information and payment periods that you previously set up in the Loan Setup dialog box.

Click Next to continue to the second editing dialog box (see Figure 9.14).

FIGURE 9.14

You can edit payment information as well.

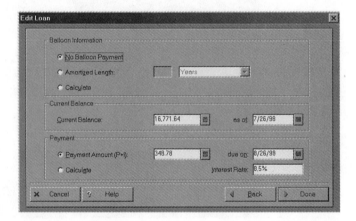

Here you can edit balloon payment, balance, and regular payment information. Click Done to return to the View Loans window.

Editing Payments

To edit a payment, click the Edit Payment button, which displays the Edit Loan Payment dialog box illustrated in Figure 9.15.

FIGURE 9.15

Quicken also enables you to modify loan payments.

This dialog box is very similar to the Set Up Loan Payment dialog box. You can modify your original entries here.

Making Payments

You can also make regular or extra payments from the View Loans window. To do so, click the Make Payment button. Quicken asks whether you want to make a regular or extra payment.

To make a regular payment, click the Regular button, which opens the Make Regular Payment dialog box (see Figure 9.16).

FIGURE 9.16

Record a regular pay-ment transaction from the View Loans window.

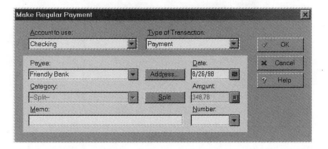

Quicken defaults to the payment information you provided when you set up this account, including the account to use, transaction type, payment amount, and date. Make any nec-essary modifications, then click OK to record the payment.

To make an extra payment, click the Extra button in the prompt to display the Make Extra Payment dialog box, shown in Figure 9.17.

FIGURE 9.17

You can also make extra payments from this window.

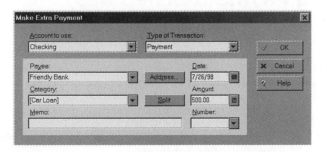

The Make Extra Payment dialog box is nearly identical to the Make Regular Payment dialog box except that you use it to make a different kind of payment. Usually you'll make extra payments to pay off your loan faster, but they aren't required.

Modify any of the default information, verifying the amount you want to pay, and then click OK to record the payment.

Changing the Loan Rate

If you have an adjustable rate loan, you may need to change the loan rate from time to time. To do so, click the Rate Change button, which opens the Loan Rate Changes dialog box illustrated in Figure 9.18.

FIGURE 9.18

Record changes in an adjustable rate loan in this dialog box.

This dialog box tracks changes to your loan rates over time. You can edit the existing rate by clicking the Edit button, add a new loan rate by clicking New, or delete a selected rate by clicking Delete.

Viewing Payment Schedules

To view a payment schedule from the View Loans window, select the Payment Schedule tab, shown in Figure 9.19.

This tab lists each payment numerically, detailing the date it's due, principal, interest, and balance due. Scroll down through the list to see the details for the entire loan period.

To print this payment schedule list, select File, Print Loan and click OK in the Print dialog box that appears.

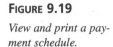

Figure 9.19

View and print a payment schedule.

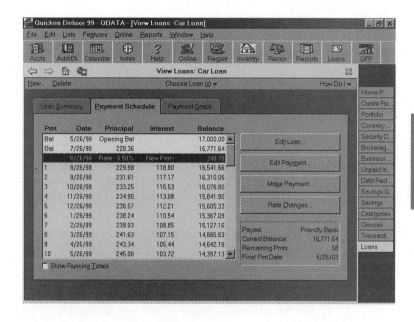

Viewing a Payment Graph

To display your loan payments and balance in a graph, click the Payment Graph tab in the View Loans window. Figure 9.20 displays a sample loan graph.

Figure 9.20

A graph represents your loan progress visually.

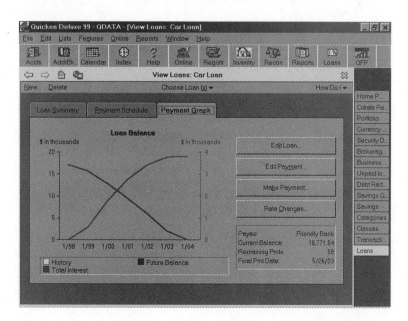

Summary

This hour instructed you on how to set up a loan and its accompanying payments. Use the Set Up Loan and Set Up Loan Payments dialog boxes to automate the creation of a liability account to track a loan. After you create the account, you can modify it, make extra payments, and change the loan rate if necessary. Quicken also provides several reports and graphs to help you evaluate your loans.

Hour 10, "Managing and Protecting Data," moves on to another topic—how to protect the valuable information you enter in Quicken.

Q&A

Q Should I create asset accounts to go with my loan/liability accounts?

A Asset accounts aren't required, but can be useful for viewing your entire financial picture. For example, in the case of a mortgage loan, you will probably want to set up an asset account for your home to track its market value.

Q Is it better to use the EasyStep method for setting up a loan or the Summary tab?

A They both yield the same results, but EasyStep provides more detailed background information on each step and can be useful if this is your first loan setup. Once you are used to the kind of information you need to enter, the Summary tab is faster.

HOUR 10

Managing and Protecting Data

This hour teaches you how to manage and manipulate your Quicken files as well as back up and protect your data. Particularly after you've used Quicken for some time, these are critical skills to master because you want to ensure that months' worth of data are well-maintained and secure.

The highlights of this hour include

- How to copy, delete, rename, and validate a file
- When and how to create a year-end copy
- How to import and export data
- How to back up and restore files
- Why and how to password-protect files and transactions

Managing File Operations

Quicken makes it easy to perform simple file operations such as copying, deleting, renaming, and validating files.

Copying a File

You can copy an existing Quicken file and its contents—partial or entire—to another file. This is useful if you want to create a new file that includes transactions only for a certain date range or you want to create an empty file that includes categories you've already set up, for instance.

 Be sure to distinguish between copying a file and backing it up. Copy a file when you want to specify the transactions to include. Back up a file when you want a complete replica of all your data and transactions in case of file damage or computer problems.

To Do: Copy a File

1. Select File, File Operations, Copy to open the Copy File dialog box (see Figure 10.1).

FIGURE 10.1

You can specify details about the file you want to copy.

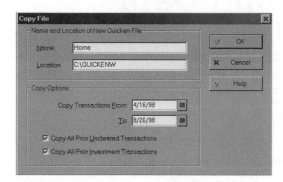

2. In the Name field, enter the name of the new Quicken file.

3. The Location defaults to the current location. Change this if necessary.

4. Select the Copy Transactions To and From dates to indicate the exact date range of transactions you want to copy. The default dates include all existing transactions.

Click the Calendar button next to the date fields for assistance in selecting dates.

If you want to create a new file that includes your existing categories, memorized transactions, and scheduled transactions, but no actual transaction data, enter dates that are later than any transactions in the current file.

5. Select Copy All Prior Uncleared Transactions if you want to include transactions previous to the dates specified that have not been cleared.

6. Select Copy All Prior Investment Transactions if you want to retain all investment activity regardless of date.

7. Click OK to copy the file.

To Do: Delete a File

1. Select File, File Operations, Delete to open the Delete Quicken File dialog box, shown in Figure 10.2.

FIGURE 10.2

Delete files you no longer use or need.

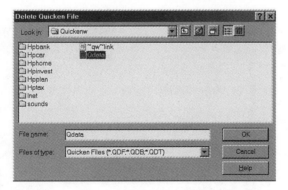

2. In the File Name field, enter the filename of the file you want to delete.

3. Click OK.

4. Quicken asks whether you're sure you want to delete the file (see Figure 10.3). If you are, type YES and click OK. Quicken deletes the selected file.

FIGURE 10.3

Quicken verifies you're deleting the appropriate file before completing the deletion.

If the file you want to delete is password-protected, Quicken prompts you to enter the password.

You can also rename a file. Renaming is useful if you want to create more meaningful names for your files. For example, you may want to create separate Home and Business files or create separate files for individuals in your household if you track your finances separately.

To Do: Rename a File

1. Select File, File Operations, Rename to display the Rename Quicken File dialog box, shown in Figure 10.4.

FIGURE 10.4

Rename a Quicken file to a name that's more meaningful to you.

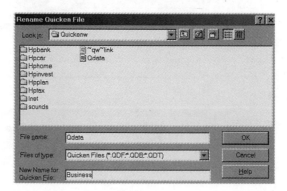

2. In the File Name field, enter the filename of the file you want to rename.

3. If this is a Quicken file, be sure to indicate that in the Files of Type field.

4. In the New Name for Quicken File field, enter the file's new filename.

5. Click OK.

▲ Quicken renames the file.

Validating a File

If you are experiencing problems with a file, you can validate the integrity of its data. Validation checks for common file corruption problems and can often apply a direct fix. To do so, select File, File Operations, Validate. The Validate Quicken File dialog box opens, as shown in Figure 10.5.

FIGURE 10.5

Validate a problem file to ensure its integrity.

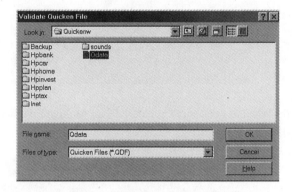

10

Select the file you want to validate and click OK. Quicken validates the file and rebuilds it if necessary.

Creating a Year-End Copy

You can create a year-end copy of your Quicken transactions if you want to archive activity from previous years. There are two ways to do this, and the difference between the two is very important to understand. You can

- *Create an archive*. Selecting this option creates an archive copy of all transactions from previous years. An archive does *not* delete transactions from your current file.

- *Start a new year*. Selecting this option creates an archive copy of your current file and then deletes all transactions previous to the current year. Only investment and uncleared transactions from previous years remain.

> Creating an archive copy of your transactions is not required when you start a new year. This is an optional activity.

To Do: Create an Archive

1. Select File, File Operations, Year-End Copy. The Year-End Copy dialog box displays, shown in Figure 10.6.

FIGURE 10.6

You can either maintain or delete previous transactions when you make a year-end copy.

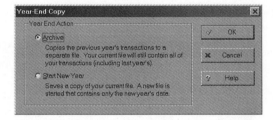

2. Select the Archive option and click OK. The Archive File dialog box opens (see Figure 10.7).

FIGURE 10.7

Specify the exact transactions to include in your archive.

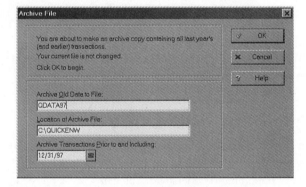

3. Enter the name for the archive in the Archive Old Data to File field.

4. Enter the location of the archive file. The current directory is the default location.

5. In the Archive Transactions Prior to and Including field, enter the last date to include in the archive file.

> Click the Calendar button next to the date fields for assistance in selecting dates.

6. Click OK.

7. Quicken tells you it successfully copied the file and asks whether you want to use the archive or current file (see Figure 10.8).

FIGURE 10.8

*You can continue
working in either the
archived or current
file.*

▲

To Do: Start a New Year

1. Select File, File Operations, Year-End Copy. The Year-End Copy dialog box opens.

2. Select Start New Year and click OK. The Start New Year dialog box appears, as illustrated in Figure 10.9.

FIGURE 10.9

*Specify the dates to
include in your new
year.*

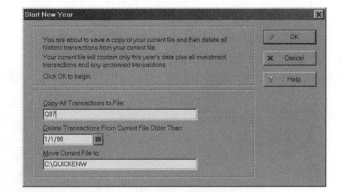

10

3. Enter the name of the archive file in the Copy All Transactions to File field.

4. In the Delete Transactions From Current File Older Than field, enter the first date (such as 1/1/98) you want to include in the new file.

5. In the Move Current File To field, enter the name of the directory to which you want to move the current file.

6. Click OK.

▲

> Starting a new year and deleting all previous years' transactions may cause some of the Quicken online banking features to not work properly. If you use online banking, you shouldn't start a new year.

Exporting and Importing Quicken Data

If you want to copy data from one Quicken file to another, you can export this data to a QIF text file and then import it into the other Quicken file.

For example, you may want to consolidate information from two Quicken files into one or need to reorganize how you've set up your Quicken files.

NEW TERM A *QIF (Quicken Interchange Format)* file is a special kind of text file that you create to export and import data in Quicken.

You can also import the data you just exported into another Quicken file or import data you downloaded or converted from another file format.

To Do: Export Quicken Data

1. Select File, Export to open the QIF Export dialog box, shown in Figure 10.10.

FIGURE 10.10

Export data you want to use in another Quicken file to the QIF format.

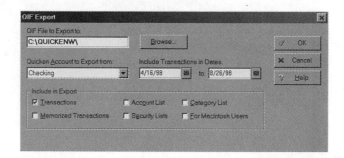

2. In the QIF File to Export To field, enter the name of the file to which you want to export data.

 Click Browse to open the Export to QIF File dialog box, in which you can search for an existing QIF file you want to overwrite.

3. From the Quicken Account to Export From drop-down list of all your accounts, select the account from which you want to export data.

4. In the Include Transactions in Dates field, enter the start and end dates of the transactions you want to export.

5. Select the items you want to include in the export from the Include in Export box: Transactions, Memorized Transactions, Accounts List, Security Lists, Category List, and/or For Macintosh Users (formats for Quicken for Macintosh).

▲ 6. Click OK to export.

To Do: Import Data into Another Quicken File

1. Select File, Import, QIF File to open the QIF Import dialog box, shown in Figure 10.11.

FIGURE 10.11

You can import QIF files into your regular Quicken files.

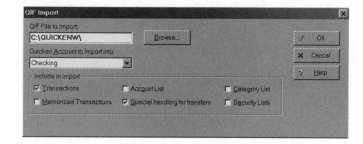

2. In the QIF File to Import field, enter the name of the file into which you want to import data.

> Click Browse to open the Import from QIF File dialog box, in which you can search for an existing QIF file.

3. From the Quicken Account to Import Into drop-down list of all your accounts, select the account into which you want to import data.

4. Select the items you want to include in the import: transactions, memorized transactions, account lists, security lists, category lists, or special handling for transfers.

5. Click OK to import the data.

> You can also import a Web Connect file (data you downloaded from the Internet) by selecting File, Import, Web Connect File.

Backing Up a Quicken File

As you continue to enter transactions and data in Quicken, you'll soon want to start creating backup copies of your files in case of file damage or computer failure. Fortunately, Quicken reminds you to back up by displaying the Automatic Backup reminder every third time you close the program (see Figure 10.12).

10

FIGURE 10.12

Automatic Backup reminds you to back up your Quicken files.

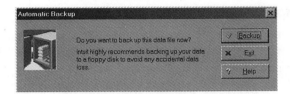

Click Backup to proceed with the backup procedure.

 Be sure to have your backup media (such as a disk) ready when you exit Quicken.

 In the General Options tab, you can specify how often the backup reminder displays. Hour 11, "Customizing Quicken," explains how to set backup options.

To Do: Start a Manual Backup

1. To back up a Quicken file even if you don't receive a reminder, select File, Backup. Figure 10.13 illustrates the dialog box that displays.

FIGURE 10.13

You can back up your Quicken file to an external disk.

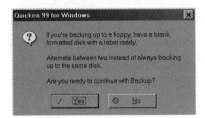

2. This prompt prepares you to back up a Quicken file. It reminds you to have a disk ready to use, suggests that you alternate between two different disks when backing up, and asks whether you're ready to begin. Click Yes to continue.

▼   The Select Backup Drive dialog box displays (see Figure 10.14).

Backing up on two disks or two sets of disks is a good idea in case a disk becomes damaged.

FIGURE 10.14

Select the drive to which you want to back up.

3. Insert a disk in your floppy drive and then, in the Select Backup Drive dialog box, select the backup drive in which you placed the disk.

4. To back up the current file, choose Current File in the File to Back Up group.

5. Click OK. Quicken begins to back up your file and then notifies you when the backup successfully completes.

If your Quicken file is too large for one disk, you may need to use two or more disks.

To back up another Quicken file, choose Select File from List in the File to Back Up group. The Back Up Quicken File dialog box displays (see Figure 10.15).

FIGURE 10.15

Select the file you want to back up in this dialog box.

10

Select the file you want to back up and click OK. Quicken backs up the file.

If your Quicken file becomes damaged or destroyed and you've made a recent backup, you're in luck. Using Quicken's restore utility, you can restore your backed up file and begin using Quicken again.

To Do: Restore a Quicken File

1. Select File, Restore Backup File to display the Select Restore Drive dialog box, shown in Figure 10.16.

FIGURE 10.16

You can restore Quicken data stored on an external disk.

2. Select the drive where the backup is stored and click OK. The Restore Quicken File dialog box displays (see Figure 10.17).

FIGURE 10.17

Restoring a Quicken file is easy if you've backed it up.

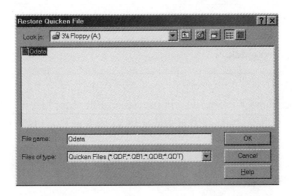

3. Select the file to restore, then click OK.

4. Quicken restores the file, prompting your approval to overwrite the existing file if necessary.

Using Password Protection

You may want to set a password for many reasons. If you share your home computer with other family members, you may want to restrict access to your Quicken file, particularly to children. Or if you use Quicken for a small business, you may want to let only certain employees have access to your records or prohibit them from changing existing transactions.

> Be careful to remember any password you set, because you cannot access your Quicken file without it.

Password-Protecting a File

To set up password protection for a Quicken file for the first time, select File, Passwords, File. The Set Up Password dialog box displays, as shown in Figure 10.18.

FIGURE 10.18

You can enter and con-firm a password for your Quicken files.

Enter the password that you want to use on this file in the Password field and then confirm it in the Confirm Password fields. Then click OK to close the dialog box.

> The password you enter in this dialog box displays as asterisks for privacy reasons. This way, no one can look over your shoulder and read your password as you type.

By entering the password twice, you confirm to Quicken (and to yourself) that you accurately typed the first word you entered. This helps avoid password problems due to mistaken entries.

To Do: Change Your Password

1. Select File, Passwords, File. The Change Password dialog box displays (see Figure 10.19).

FIGURE 10.19

You can create a new password if someone learns your current one.

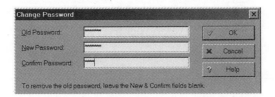

2. Enter your existing password in the Old Password field.
3. Enter the new password in both the New Password and Confirm Password fields.
4. Click OK.

This dialog box displays only if you have already set a password. If you haven't, the Set Up Password dialog box displays.

Removing Your Password

To remove a password, enter your old password in the Change Password dialog box, but leave the New Password and Confirm Password edit boxes blank.

When you remove a password, your file is no longer protected. Anyone can then access your Quicken file.

Opening a Password-Protected File

After you assign a password to your Quicken file, you need to enter it the next time you want to open Quicken. Figure 10.20 shows the dialog box that Quicken displays.

FIGURE 10.20

You can't open a password-protected file without entering the password.

Enter your password to access the protected file, then click OK.

Quicken passwords aren't case-sensitive. *PASSWORD, Password,* and *password* are all treated as the same word.

Password-Protecting Transactions

In some cases, you may also want to password-protect from future changes any transactions you've already entered.

To Do: Set a Transaction Password

1. Select File, Passwords, Transaction. The Password to Modify Existing Transactions dialog box opens, shown in Figure 10.21.

FIGURE 10.21

You can also use a password to protect transactions from future changes.

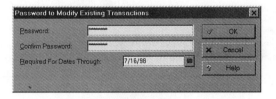

10

2. In the Password field, enter the password you want to use.

3. Enter this password again in the Confirm Password field to verify that you entered it correctly.

4. Enter in the Required for Dates Through field the date through which you want to password-protect transactions.

Click the Calendar button to display a pop-up calendar if you need help in choosing the right date.

When you try to modify a transaction entered on or before the specified date, Quicken prompts you for a password.

To Do: Change Your Transaction Password

1. Select File, Passwords, File. The Change Transaction Password dialog box displays (see Figure 10.22).

FIGURE 10.22

You can modify an existing transaction password.

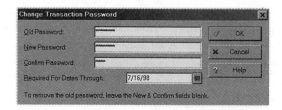

2. Enter your existing password in the Old Password field.

3. Enter the new password in both the New Password and Confirm Password fields.

4. In the Required for Dates Through field, enter the date through which you want to password-protect transactions.

5. Click OK.

This dialog box displays only if you have already set a password. If you haven't, the Password to Modify Existing Transactions dialog box displays.

Removing Your Transaction Password

To remove a password, enter your old password in the Change Password dialog box, but leave the New Password and Confirm Password fields blank.

Modifying a Password-Protected Transaction

When you (or anyone using your Quicken files) try to modify a transaction entered previous to the date you specified, Quicken prompts you for the password when you try to save the modification. Figure 10.23 displays this prompt.

FIGURE 10.23

A transaction password is required to save this transaction.

If you enter the correct password, you can save the modified transaction. If you don't enter the correct password, Quicken displays an error message.

Summary

This hour taught you how to manage and manipulate Quicken files as well as how to protect your valuable data. To copy, delete, rename, and validate files, use Quicken's easy file operation features. To safeguard your files, back them up regularly in case you need to restore them later. And if you share your computer with other users, carefully consider whether to password-protect your Quicken data.

Hour 11, "Customizing Quicken," shows you how to customize both the Quicken interface and many of its common tasks.

Q&A

Q I forgot my password. What can I do?

A If you can't open a password-protected file after numerous attempts, first check whether you have an older version backed up that isn't password-protected. If not, contact Quicken Technical Support for information on its data-recovery procedures.

Q How do I pick a good password?

A If you want to prevent people you know from accessing your files, don't use a password that would be obvious to them. For example, the names of family, friends, and pets aren't good choices. Neither are words that refer to your favorite interests. Instead, choose a password that is meaningful to you and not to anyone else. You might even want to consider making up a word to use as a password. Just be sure to remember what it is when you need to access your data.

Q How do I save my Quicken file?

A Quicken saves automatically, so you don't need to issue a specific command. Saving isn't the same thing as backing up, though, so be sure to back up regularly.

10

HOUR 11

Customizing Quicken

This hour helps you find more ways to make Quicken even easier to use. After you've started to use Quicken, you'll soon want to modify it to fit your needs and the way you use software. Quicken includes many customization options that affect both the way the program looks as well as the way you use it. For example, you can change Quicken's default appearance as well as how you navigate.

The highlights of this hour include

- Why you might want to customize Quicken
- How to customize navigation options such as QuickTabs
- Where to customize backup and memorized transaction options
- How to customize the Quicken desktop and Iconbar

Customizing Quicken Options

You can customize the way Quicken and many of its features look and operate as well as specify the exact default setting you want to use for

- Quicken navigation and data entry
- The register
- Check writing
- Reports and graphs
- Reminders
- Internet and Web connections
- The desktop
- The Iconbar

This hour focuses on the customizations that affect Quicken overall, such as navigation, the Iconbar, and the desktop. Options that affect only a specific Quicken task, such as creating a report or using the register, are covered in the hours that deal with those topics.

There are three ways to customize Quicken options. You can:

- Click the Options icon on the Iconbar to display the Options dialog box, shown in Figure 11.1.

FIGURE 11.1

Quicken includes many customization options.

- Click the appropriate button (General, Checks, Register, Reports, Reminders, or Iconbar) to open the related option dialog box

| If the Options button doesn't display on the Iconbar, you can add it. The section "Customizing the Iconbar" in this hour explains how to do this. |

- Select Edit, Options, then choose from the submenu the option you want to set.
- Click the Options button in Quicken windows, such as the Net Worth Report shown in Figure 11.2, to display the related option dialog box.

FIGURE 11.2

You can determine default reporting options by clicking the Options button.

Options button

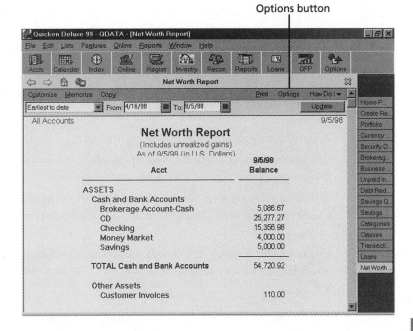

Customizing General Options

You can customize many of Quicken's overall features to create a Quicken configuration that works best for you. To do so, click the Options icon on the Iconbar and select the General button. Figure 11.3 displays the General Options dialog box.

FIGURE 11.3

QuickTabs and the activity bar can help you navigate Quicken.

You can also customize Quicken options by selecting Edit, Options, Quicken Program.

Customizing QuickTabs

On the QuickTabs tab, you can determine when and how to display navigational tools such as QuickTabs, the Activity bar, and flyover help. Options include

- *Show QuickTabs.* You can display QuickTabs on the left or right of your Quicken window.

- *Show Activity Bar.* Select this check box if you want to display the Activity bar at the bottom of the Quicken window. The Activity bar pictorially displays certain groups of tasks and provides easy access to these tasks.

  You can use the standard menu commands on the Activity bar, or shorten them to one or two words by selecting the Use Short Commands on Activity Bar Menus check box.

- *Quicken Color Scheme.* You can choose to keep the default color scheme or change this default to another scheme such as Sand Dune or Autumn.

> You can also select QuickTabs, the Activity bar, and color schemes by clicking the Window menu and making the appropriate selection.

- *Show Flyover Help in Toolbars.* Figure 11.4 illustrates flyover help.

Flyover help

FIGURE 11.4

Flyover help tells you what happens when you select each button.

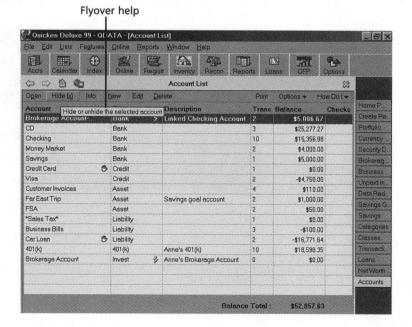

Customizing Backup and Memorized Transactions

On the General tab (shown in Figure 11.5), you can set several other important options.

FIGURE 11.5

Setting backup reminders can help you protect valuable Quicken data.

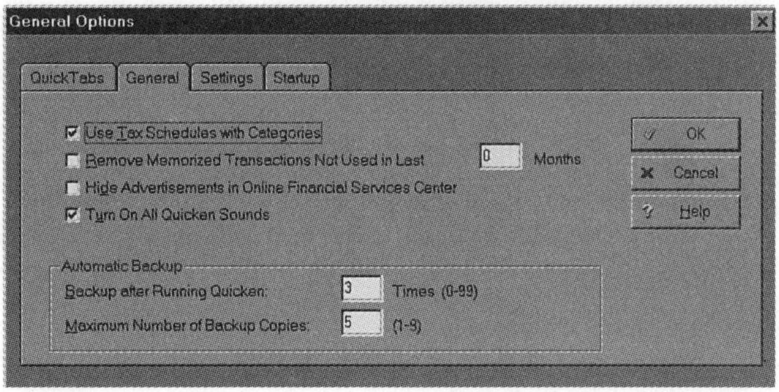

These options include the following:

- *Use Tax Schedules with Categories.* Select this check box if you want to assign a tax schedule to a category.

- *Remove Memorized Transactions Not Used in Last _ Months.* By setting the number of months to retain memorized transactions, you can create a more manageable list of memorized transactions.

   This is particularly important if you have entered a large number of transactions. For example, you may want to remove from the list any memorized transaction that you haven't used in 12 months.

- *Hide Advertisements in Online Financial Services Center.* Select this option if you don't want the Financial Services Center to display ads from associated financial organizations.

- *Turn On All Quicken Sounds.* Select this option if you want sound effects; otherwise, deselect it.

You can also choose Automatic Backup options, such as the following:

- *Backup After Running Quicken _ Times.* You can specify how often you want Quicken to remind you to back up. For example, if you want Quicken to remind you to back up every time you run the program, enter 1. For every third time, enter 3.

- *Maximum Number of Backup Copies.* Enter the maximum backup copies you want Quicken to make, up to 9.

Customizing Settings

On the Settings tab (see Figure 11.6), you can customize keyboard mapping and calendar options.

FIGURE 11.6

You can specify keyboard mappings and working calendars in Quicken.

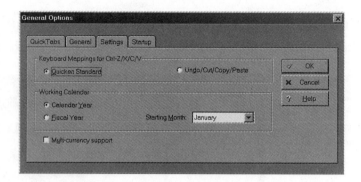

You can set the keyboard mapping for the Ctrl+Z, Ctrl+X, Ctrl+C, and Ctrl+V keystrokes to undo, cut, copy, or paste to or from the Quicken standard keyboard mappings. Table 11.1 describes Quicken's standards for these keyboard commands.

TABLE 11.1. QUICKEN STANDARD KEYBOARD MAPPINGS.

Command	Description
Ctrl+X	Moves to the matching transfer
Ctrl+C	Opens the Category & Transfer List
Ctrl+V	Voids the transaction
Ctrl+Z	QuickZooms to a report amount

You can also set the working calendar to either the calendar year or the fiscal year and establish a specific starting month.

Finally, if you want to activate multicurrency support, select the MultiCurrency Support option. With multicurrency support, you can enter register transactions in one currency and have Quicken automatically covert them to your default currency, such as the U.S. dollar.

Customizing Startup

The Startup tab (see Figure 11.7) offers several choices for determining what you want to see when you start Quicken:

- *At a Glance Page When Starting Quicken.* The Quicken home page displays upon startup.
- *Reminders When Starting Quicken.* Your reminders display upon startup.
- *None.* The last saved desktop displays upon startup.

FIGURE 11.7

Decide what you want to see when you start Quicken.

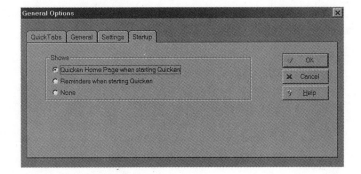

Customizing the Desktop

By default, Quicken saves your desktop (the windows that are open, and so on) every time you exit the program. But you can also customize how you want the Quicken desktop to appear upon startup. To do so, modify your desktop to the appearance you want when you start Quicken. Then select Edit, Options, Desktop. Figure 11.8 shows the Save Desktop dialog box that appears.

FIGURE 11.8

You can set desktop options in the dialog box.

11

Select the Save Current Desktop option and click OK. Your desktop now appears the same way every time you open Quicken.

Customizing the Iconbar

The Iconbar is a useful tool for navigating through Quicken. Use it to access quickly the Quicken windows and dialog boxes you need to perform specific tasks. Figure 11.9 illustrates the Iconbar.

If you have more icons than your screen width can handle, you'll see arrows on the sides of the Iconbar that enable you to scroll to additional icons that are hidden from view. If a hidden icon is one you use regularly, you can move it to a more prominent location on the Iconbar by selecting and dragging the icon to that location.

To customize or activate the Iconbar, select Edit, Options, Iconbar to open the Customize Iconbar dialog box, illustrated in Figure 11.10.

FIGURE 11.9

The iconbar is an easy-to-use navigation tool.

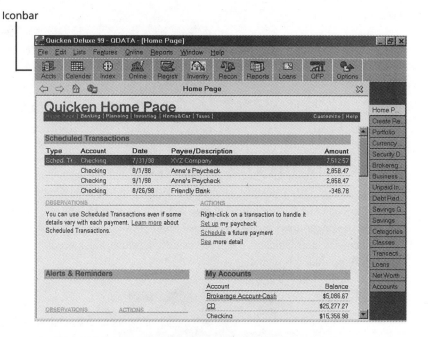

FIGURE 11.10

You can add, edit, or delete icons on the Iconbar.

Select the Edit button on the Customize Iconbar dialog box to modify an existing icon.

If the Iconbar doesn't display, select the Show Icons check box. Select the Show Text check box to display a text description beneath each icon.

The Iconbar provides several icons by default. You can add the Iconbar many other icons to handle tasks you perform regularly. Examples include accessing online banking, opening TurboTax, or preparing a forecast.

To Do: Adding a New Icon

1. Click the New button in the Customize Iconbar dialog box. The Add Action to Iconbar dialog box appears, as shown in Figure 11.11.

FIGURE 11.11

You can add icons that make it easier to per-form common tasks.

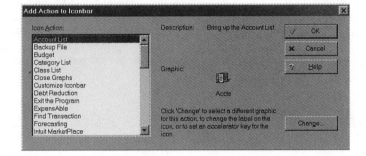

2. Select the task you want from the Icon Action list.

3. Click OK.

> Click the Change button to open the Change Iconbar Item dialog box, where you can select from a variety of other icon images.

11

Deleting Icons

To delete an icon, select the icon in the Customize Iconbar dialog box and then click the Delete button. Quicken asks whether you really want to delete the icon. Click Yes if you do.

> You can always restore a deleted icon later. Deleting an icon doesn't remove it from Quicken, just from the Iconbar.

Resetting the Iconbar

If you've customized the Iconbar and want to return to the default settings, click the Reset button in the Customize Iconbar dialog box. Again, Quicken verifies that you're sure you want to do this.

Summary

This hour covered the basics of customizing Quicken. Quicken's interface is very flexible, and by altering it you can create a program that works the way you do. You can determine how you want to navigate the Quicken system—with Iconbar, Activity bar, and/or QuickTabs. You can specify how often to back up, what you see when you start the program, and how specific keys work.

Hour 12, "Budgeting and Forecasting," starts a new section focusing on using Quicken to plan your financial future.

Q&A

Q What's the best way to navigate Quicken?

A There isn't one easy answer to this question, because it depends on how you best work with software. Try all the different alternatives—the Iconbar, activity bar, and QuickTabs—to see which one you prefer.

Q I chose to display the Activity bar, but now the Iconbar disappeared. What happened?

A If there isn't enough room on your screen for both the Activity bar and the Iconbar, only the last one you added appears. In this case, choose which you prefer and
customize Quicken to display that navigation tool.

Part III
Planning Your Finances

Hour

HOUR 12

Budgeting and Forecasting

This hour shows you how to use Quicken's budget and forecasting tools to manage your finances and preview your financial future. You can use the Budget window to create, modify, and analyze multiple budget scenarios. Quicken offers the added flexibility of automatically creating a budget based on your existing data or letting you create your own budget. Then you can use the Progress Bar to track your progress visually in key budget areas. Finally, the Forecasting window lets you predict your future income and expenses based on past history.

The highlights of this hour include

- Why you should have a budget
- How to create, modify, and customize a budget
- Where to find Quicken budget reports
- How to view and use the Progress Bar
- How to set up, customize, and analyze a forecast

Setting Up a Budget

The ability to create and stick to a budget can have a major impact on your financial future. Quicken's many powerful budgeting features make it easy to create a detailed budget that you can use to manage and modify your spending.

Quicken provides two different ways to create a budget: either automatically or by scratch. Probably the best technique for creating an accurate budget is to combine these two methods. Let Quicken automatically create a budget for you, then modify it to suit your needs. Quicken creates a budget by analyzing your income and expenses over a specified period of time and then sets budget amounts based either on monthly detail or on the average amount per period. Averaging works better for categories such as groceries, for example, than for an expense that comes only at certain times per year such as an insurance payment.

> It's a good idea to have some budget goals in mind, written down on paper, before you start using Quicken's automated budget tools. If you don't have any data in Quicken and are starting from scratch, you'll have to use your own budget estimates. If you already have at least several months' worth of data entered, print a copy of the Cash Flow Report for those months and use that to estimate some budget goals.

> Even though Quicken's budget and forecasting tools can make detailed, complex calculations very quickly, they are only as good as the information you provide. You'll get the most out of these features when you have well-organized, well-categorized data in your Quicken system and a good idea of what you want to achieve from budgeting and forecasting before you begin.

Creating a Budget for the First Time

To create a budget, select Features, Planning, Budgets. If you have never created a budget before, the First Time in Budgets dialog box displays (see Figure 12.1), offering some general advice.

FIGURE 12.1

This dialog box gives you an overview of Quicken's budgeting features.

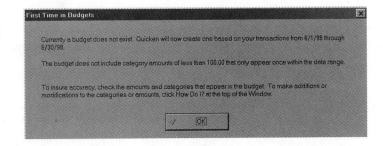

Click OK to continue. Quicken automatically creates a budget based on the last 12 months of data, eliminating category amounts for transactions less than $100 that appear only once during the selected time frame. Note that if you have just started using Quicken and haven't entered any data yet, your budget displays with all zeros (see Figure 12.2).

FIGURE 12.2

Quicken displays an empty budget if you haven't entered any transaction data.

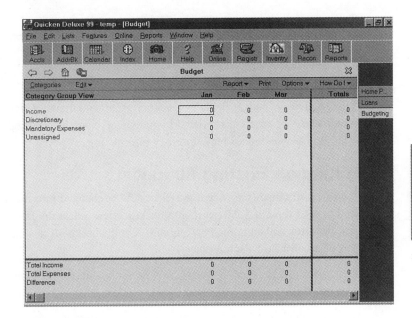

12

Figure 12.3 illustrates a budget created with a year's worth of entered transactions.

FIGURE 12.3

*Basing a budget esti-
mate on existing data
provides a good start
for setting up a budget.*

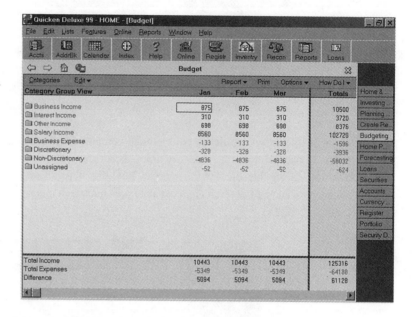

Quicken displays budget fields by category group and month. Click the folder icon next
to each category group to see detail by individual category. The right and lower portions
of the Budget window display summary information.

Editing an Existing Budget

You can easily modify a budget to reflect new or changed information. For example, you
want to set a limit of $350 per month for groceries. Select the January column for the
Groceries row and enter the new amount. If you want to set this amount for every month,
select Edit, Fill Row Right.

In addition, you can clear a specific row or all the data in the budget if you want. To do
so, select Edit and then either Clear Row or Clear All.

You can also choose how you want to display your budget information by selecting
Options and one of the following choices:

- Display Current Month
- Display Current Quarter
- Display Current Year
- Display Months
- Display Quarters

Automatically Creating a Budget

If you want Quicken to create a new budget or update your current one automatically, Quicken makes it easy to do so.

To create a budget automatically, you should have at least several months' worth of data entered in Quicken.

To Do: Create a Budget

1. Select Edit, AutoCreate to open the Automatically Create Budget dialog box, shown in Figure 12.4.

FIGURE 12.4

Automatically creating a budget is the easiest way to get started.

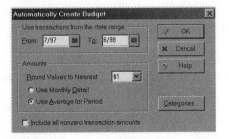

2. Choose a date range in the From and To fields. Usually you'll want to use a year's worth of data to create a budget accurately, but you can choose another date range if you want.

3. In the Round Values to Nearest field, select the rounding option you want to use in your budget. Options include $1, $10, or $100.

4. Next, determine how you want to create amounts. You can choose either of the following options:

   - *Use Monthly Detail*. Quicken uses the actual amount of your income and expenses for the months specified.

   - *Use Average for Period*. Quicken creates monthly averages based on the total amount for the date period specified.

5. By default, Quicken omits single transactions of less than $100. To overwrite this option, select the Use All Nonzero Transaction Amounts check box to include all transactions with a positive amount.

6. To select specific categories to include in a budget, click the Categories button. Figure 12.5 displays the Select Categories to Include dialog box.

12

FIGURE 12.5

*You can include or
exclude specific cate-
gories in a budget.*

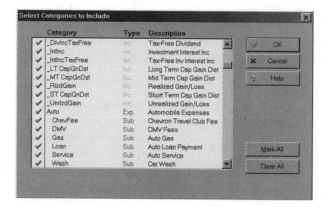

> You can also click the **Categories** button on the Budget window toolbar to
> access this dialog box.

7. The categories included in the existing budget have a green check mark to the left
   of the category name. Click the category to toggle the selection.

> To make selections more quickly, you can click the Mark All button to
> include all categories or the Clear All button to remove all check marks and
> start again.

8. Click OK to close the dialog box and return to the Automatically Create Budget
   dialog box.
9. Click OK to create a new budget.

If the results aren't what you expect, you can restore your previous budget by selecting
Options, Restore Budget.

You can create more than one budget—either for comparative purposes or to track
different income and expenses.

To Do: Create Multiple Budgets

1. Select Options, Other Budgets to open the Manage Budgets dialog box
   (see Figure 12.6).
2. Click Create to display the Create Budget dialog box, shown in Figure 12.7.
3. Enter a name and description and then specify whether you want to:

FIGURE 12.6

You can manage multiple budgets in Quicken.

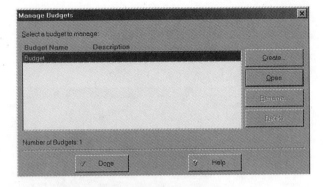

FIGURE 12.7

Determine how to name and create a new budget.

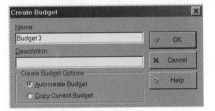

- *AutoCreate Budget.* Quicken displays the Automatically Create Budget dialog box for you to complete.

- *Copy Current Budget.* Quicken copies the current budget and displays a new Budget window with the new budget name.

4. Click OK to complete the new budget.

When you have more than one budget, you can select from the Manage Budgets dialog box the one you want to view. Select Options, Other Budgets, choose the budget name, and click Open.

12

> You can also rename and delete budgets by selecting the Rename or Delete buttons.

To Do: Set Budget Category Groups

If you want to modify the existing category groups to which categories are assigned, follow these steps:

1. Select Options, Category Groups. The Assign Category Groups dialog box appears, as illustrated in Figure 12.8.

2. Select the category name whose category group assignment you want to modify.

3. From the Category Group List on the right, select the appropriate category group.

4. Click the Assign Category to Group button.

5. When you finish assigning category groups, click OK.

FIGURE 12.8

Assigning categories to appropriate category groups helps create a more effective budget.

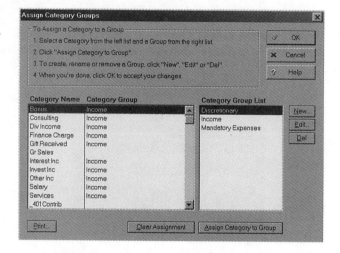

To print a list of your current category group assignments, select the Print button. Specify parameters in the Print dialog box and click OK to print.

Select the Clear Assignment button to remove the category group assignment from the selected category.

You can also add, modify, and remove category groups by selecting the New, Edit, and Del buttons. Hour 3, "Categorizing and Classifying Transactions," contains detailed information on setting up and using category groups.

Printing a Budget

To print the details of the current budget, select Print to open the Print dialog box. Specify print parameters and click OK to print a detailed budget list by category and month. Figure 12.9 previews this list.

FIGURE 12.9

FIGURE 12.9

Once you create a budget, you can create a list of its details.

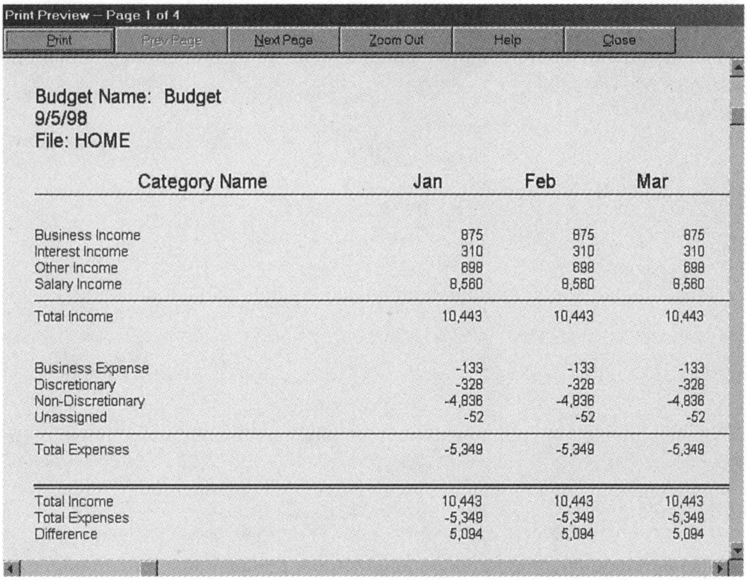

Print Preview -- Page 1 of 4

| Print | Prev Page | Next Page | Zoom Out | Help | Close |

Budget Name: Budget
9/5/98
File: HOME

Category Name	Jan	Feb	Mar
Business Income	875	875	875
Interest Income	310	310	310
Other Income	698	698	698
Salary Income	8,560	8,560	8,560
Total Income	10,443	10,443	10,443
Business Expense	-133	-133	-133
Discretionary	-328	-328	-328
Non-Discretionary	-4,836	-4,836	-4,836
Unassigned	-52	-52	-52
Total Expenses	-5,349	-5,349	-5,349
Total Income	10,443	10,443	10,443
Total Expenses	-5,349	-5,349	-5,349
Difference	5,094	5,094	5,094

You can also create three different kinds of budget reports/graphs from the Report menu in the Budget window:

- *Budget Report.* Displays a Budget Report for the entire period selected based on your current budget information. Choose Reports, Planning, Budget to access this report.

- *Monthly Budget Report.* Displays a Budget Report that lists each month's actual, budget, and difference amounts separately. Choose Reports, Planning, Monthly Budget to access this report.

- *Budget Variance Graph.* Displays an Actual versus Budgeted Net Income bar chart as well as an Actual versus Budgeted Category Groups bar chart. Choose Reports, Graphics, Budget Variance to access this graph.

12

Viewing the Progress Bar

Using the Quicken Progress Bar, you can visually track the progress on your two most important budget areas or goals. The Progress Bar shows your progress toward meeting a certain savings or budget goals as a percentage. For example, if you set a savings goal of $6,000 and you've saved $3,000 so far, the Progress Bar would indicate 50 percent.

To display the Progress Bar, select Features, Planning, Progress Bar. Figure 12.10 shows the Progress Bar, which appears at the bottom of the screen.

FIGURE 12.10

The Progress Bar lets you track two important goals.

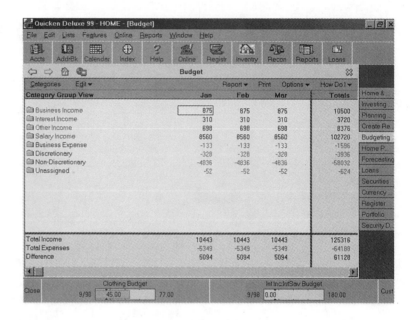

To Do: Customize the Progress Bar

1. Click the Cust button on the right side of the Progress Bar. The Customize Progress Bar dialog box appears, as shown in Figure 12.11.

FIGURE 12.11

Customize how you want to view the progress bar.

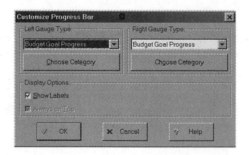

You can select both a Left Gauge Type and a Right Gauge Type.

2. From the drop-down lists, select one of the following:

   • *Savings Goal Progress*. Activates the Choose Goal button. Click the button to open the Choose Savings Goal dialog box (see Figure 12.12) from which you can select a savings goal you created.

   • *Budget Goal Progress*. Activates the Choose Category button. Click the button to open the Choose Category dialog box, shown in Figure 12.13. Select a date range and category you want to track.

FIGURE 12.12

You can track a savings goal with the progress bar.

▼

FIGURE 12.13

You can also track a budget goal.

- *Category Group Budget.* Activates the Choose Category Group button. Click the button to open the Choose Category Group dialog box, illustrated in Figure 12.14.

FIGURE 12.14

View your progress by category group in the progress bar.

12

3. From the Choose Category Group dialog box, select a date range and category group. Then click OK to return to the Customize Progress Bar dialog box.

4. The Display Options group box provides two options:

▼

- *Show Labels.* Displays a descriptive label over the Progress Bar.

▼   • *Always on Top*. Always displays the Progress Bar on top.

    5. Click OK to finish customizing the Progress Bar.

▲   To close the Progress Bar, click the Close button on its left side.

Forecasting Income and Expenses

Quicken also includes the ability to forecast, a useful tool for predicting your potential future income and expenses.

To Do: Set Up a Forecast

1. Select Features, Planning, Forecast. If this is the first time you're creating a forecast, the Automatically Create Forecast dialog box appears, as shown in Figure 12.15.

FIGURE 12.15

You can automatically create your first forecast.

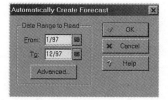

2. In the From and To fields, enter a date range to read. This should be a date range in the past that you want Quicken to use to determine your future income and expenses.

3. Click the Advanced button to open the Advanced AutoCreate dialog box, illustrated in Figure 12.16.

FIGURE 12.16

Determine which sources you want to use for your forecast.

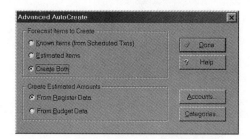

4. Select from the following options included in this dialog box:

    • *Known Items* (from Scheduled Txns). Uses scheduled amounts from the register, Financial Calendar, and Scheduled Transaction List.

▼

- *Estimated Items.* Creates average estimates based on register transactions and budget entries.
- *Create Both.* Uses both known and estimated items.
- *From Register Data.* Includes estimated items, retrieving those estimates from your register data.
- *From Budget Data.* Includes estimated items, retrieving those estimates from your budget data.

5. Click the Accounts button to open the Select Accounts to Include dialog box (see Figure 12.17).

FIGURE 12.17

You can include or exclude certain accounts.

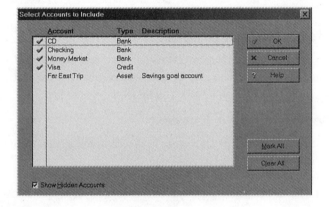

 You can also access this dialog box by selecting Options, Select Accounts.

12

6. Select the accounts you want to include, and then click OK.
7. Click the Categories button to open the Select Categories to Include dialog box, shown in Figure 12.18.
8. Select the categories you want to include, and then click OK.
9. Click Done to return to the Automatically Create Forecast dialog box.
10. Click OK to create your forecast.

 Choose Options, Update Forecast to open the Automatically Create Forecast dialog box again and update your forecast options.

FIGURE 12.18

Specify the categories you want to include in your forecast.

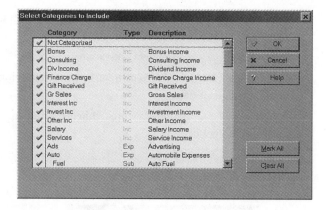

Customizing a Forecast

You can customize your forecast items—income and expense—if you want. For example, you may want to add a new income item to forecast freelance income you hope to receive from graphic design work you do on the weekends.

To Do: Customize a Forecast

1. Select the Income Items button to display the Forecast Income Items dialog box, shown in Figure 12.19.

FIGURE 12.19

You can add, edit, and delete forecast income items.

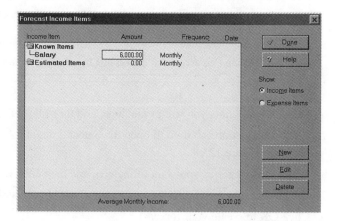

2. To add a new income item, click New to open the Create New Income Item dialog box, shown in Figure 12.20.

3. Click the Income option button to verify that this is an income item.

4. Enter a description and an amount of the item.

FIGURE 12.20

You can create new items to forecast.

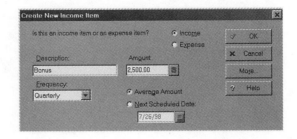

Click the Expense option button to change to an expense item; the dialog box name changes to Create New Expense Item.

5. Select one of the 10 Frequency options—from Only Once to Yearly.

6. Specify how the forecast should treat this item:

   • *Average Amount*. Treats the item as an estimated amount and averages the amount you enter over the specified frequency.

   • *Next Scheduled Date*. Treats the item as a known item—that is, a scheduled transaction. Activates the date field where you can enter the next scheduled transaction date.

7. Click the More button to open the Edit Advanced Info dialog box, shown in Figure 12.21.

FIGURE 12.21

Category and payment tracking are advanced options.

12

8. In this dialog box, you can specify a category for tracking and the number of payments if desired. Click OK to return to the previous dialog box.

9. Click OK to finish and return to the Forecast Income Items dialog box.

10. You can edit the exact amount of an item by selecting the Amount column and typing in a new amount. If you want to modify an amount further, select it and click the Edit button. The Edit Income Item dialog box displays (see Figure 12.22).

    This dialog box is almost identical to the Create New Income Item dialog box.

FIGURE 12.22

You can also edit income items.

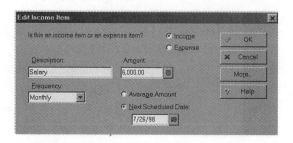

11. Finally, click the Delete button to delete a selected income item.

12. Click Done to close the dialog box and return to the Forecasting window.

> Click the Expense Items button to open the Forecast Expense Items dialog box, which is almost identical to the Forecast Income Items dialog box. Use this dialog box in the same way to add, modify, and delete expense items.

Updating Budgets with Forecast Data

If you want to update your budget with the forecasting information in this window, select Options, Update Budget. Quicken overwrites your existing budget.

To Do: Create Multiple Forecast Scenarios

1. Select Options, Manage Scenarios. Figure 12.23 illustrates the Manage Forecast Scenarios dialog box that opens.

FIGURE 12.23

You can easily manage multiple forecasts.

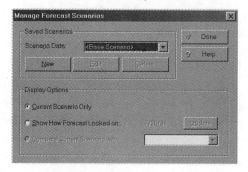

2. Click the New button to open the Create New Scenario dialog box, shown in Figure 12.24.

3. Enter a new name in the Scenario Name field.

▼ 4. Click the Copy Current Scenario check box if you want to save the current fore-casting scenario under this name and click OK to return to the Manage Forecast Scenarios dialog box.

Later, when you want to view one of these scenarios, you can select the forecasting scenario you want to see from the Scenario Data drop-down list.

FIGURE 12.24

You can copy your current scenario when creating a new one.

This dialog box also provides choices on how to display your forecasting scenarios. You can choose to display the current scenario only, show how the forecast looked on a specific date, or compare one scenario to another by creating a third line in the Forecasting window.

5. Click Done to close the dialog box.

▲ You can also edit or delete scenarios by selecting them and clicking the Edit or Delete buttons.

Summary

12

This hour explained the basics of creating and using budgets and forecasts to help you manage and predict your finances. Use a budget to set up and track income and expenses for a specified period of time. Then use the Progress Bar to track visually your progress on your two most important budget goals. Additionally, you can forecast your future income and expenses based on your budget information or the actual data you entered in the register.

Hour 13, "Planning for Specific Goals," introduces you to other Quicken tools that help you plan and manage specific financial goals such as retirement, home purchases, and college.

Q&A

Q My paycheck arrives every two weeks. How do I budget for that?

A Select Edit, 2-Week and enter the amount in the Set Up Two-Week Budget dialog box. Quicken then correctly budgets for this amount every other week.

Q When should I create a forecast rather than a budget?

A Budgets and forecasts are complementary tools. Use a budget to set goals for exactly how much you plan to spend and receive in the near future. Use forecasts to create a big picture prediction of your financial situation further in the future.

HOUR 13

Planning for Specific Goals

This hour introduces Quicken's many interactive calculators and planning tools that help you plan for and analyze common investment goals. With these tools, you can quickly create what-if scenarios that you can use to view your options in planning for loans, refinancing, savings, college, and retirement, among other things.

The highlights of this hour include

- How to plan for loans and investment savings
- When to refinance a loan
- What is the best way to plan for college and retirement expenses
- How to reduce debt
- How to set up a savings goal

Planning for a Loan

The Quicken Loan Calculator helps you analyze loan options for purchasing a home, car, boat, or other item. Using the Loan Calculator, you can quickly create many different what-if scenarios to determine which loan is right for you, how much you can afford, and so on. To do so, select Features, Planning, Financial Calculators, Loan. Figure 13.1 displays the Loan Calculator.

FIGURE 13.1

Quickly determine your loan options with the Loan Calculator.

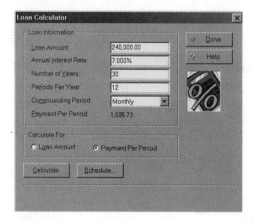

You can either calculate the payment per period or total loan amount based on other variables you enter.

To Do: Determine the Payment Per Period Using the Loan Calculator

1. Select the Payment Per Period option in the Calculate For group box.

2. Enter the total loan amount in the Loan Amount field.

3. In the Annual Interest Rate field, enter the annual interest rate of the loan as a percentage.

4. In the Number of Years field, enter the total number of years it will take to repay the loan.

5. Enter the periods per year. For example, enter 12 for a loan you need to repay monthly or 4 for a loan you repay on a quarterly basis.

6. From the Compounding Period drop-down list, select Daily, Monthly, or Semi-Annually to indicate how often the loan interest will be compounded.

7. Click the Calculate button to display the payment per period.

For example, suppose that you want to purchase a $300,000 home with 20 percent down, but need to determine whether you can afford the monthly payments. A mortgage lender offers you a rate of 7 percent on a $240,000, 30-year fixed loan. The Loan Calculator quickly tells you that your monthly payment would be $1,596.73.

If you already know the loan payment per period and other loan factors, you can use the Loan Calculator to determine the total amount of the loan.

To Do: Determine a Loan Amount

1. Select the Loan Amount option button in the Calculate For group box.

2. In the Annual Interest Rate field, enter the annual interest rate of the loan as a percentage.

3. In the Number of Years field, enter the total number of years it will take to repay the loan.

4. In the Periods Per Year field, enter the periods per year. For example, enter 12 for a loan you need to repay monthly or 4 for a loan you repay on a quarterly basis.

5. From the Compounding Period drop-down list, select Daily, Monthly, or Semi-Annually to indicate how often the loan interest will be compounded.

6. Enter the payment per period.

7. Click the Calculate button to display the total loan amount.

As another example, suppose that you learn from a car dealer that the monthly payment on the car you want to buy is $348.78 for a five-year loan at 8.5 percent. The Loan Calculator tells you that you will pay approximately $17,000, as illustrated in Figure 13.2.

FIGURE 13.2

Starting with a monthly payment, you can determine the amount of a loan.

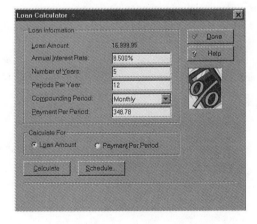

13

Creating a Payment Schedule

After you calculate a loan, you can display or print a schedule that details the principal, interest, and balance at each loan payment. Click the Schedule button to display the Approximate Future Payment Schedule dialog box, shown in Figure 13.3.

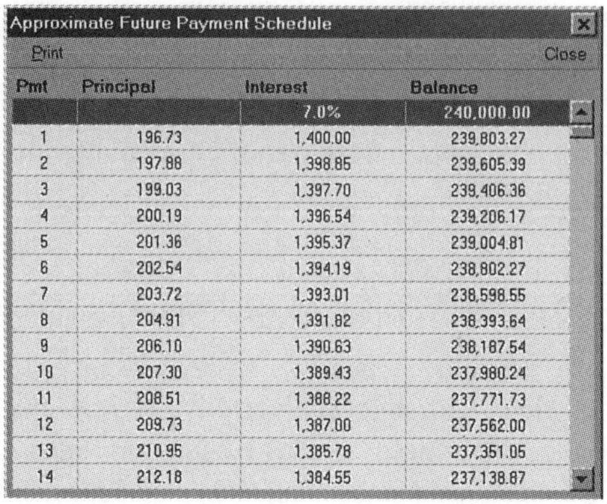

FIGURE 13.3

After you find loan options you like, you can print a detailed schedule of payments.

Approximate Future Payment Schedule			
Print			Close
Pmt	Principal	Interest	Balance
		7.0%	240,000.00
1	196.73	1,400.00	239,803.27
2	197.88	1,398.85	239,605.39
3	199.03	1,397.70	239,406.36
4	200.19	1,396.54	239,206.17
5	201.36	1,395.37	239,004.81
6	202.54	1,394.19	238,802.27
7	203.72	1,393.01	238,598.55
8	204.91	1,391.82	238,393.64
9	206.10	1,390.63	238,187.54
10	207.30	1,389.43	237,980.24
11	208.51	1,388.22	237,771.73
12	209.73	1,387.00	237,562.00
13	210.95	1,385.78	237,351.05
14	212.18	1,384.55	237,138.87

To print the schedule, click the Print button, which opens the Print dialog box. Make any necessary adjustments and click OK. When you're done looking at the schedule, click Close. To close the Loan Calculator, click Done.

Planning to Refinance a Loan

If you already have a loan and want to find out whether it makes sense to refinance it, you can use the Refinance Calculator. If loan rates have decreased, you may save money by refinancing, but you also need to consider new loan expenses such as closing costs and points. The Quicken Refinance Calculator asks you for information about your existing mortgage, the proposed new loan, and its associated costs. The calculator then calculates five key figures to help you determine whether it is worthwhile to refinance using this proposed new loan.

To open the Refinance Calculator, select Features, Planning, Financial Calculators, Refinance. Figure 13.4 illustrates this planner.

FIGURE 13.4

*The Refinance
Calculator helps you
decide whether it's
time to refinance.*

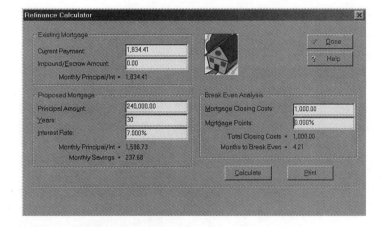

To Do: Analyze a Refinance Opportunity

1. In the Current Payment field, enter the current monthly payment for your existing mortgage.

2. In the Monthly Impound/Escrow Amount field, enter the amount that you pay for these services. These might include property tax, insurance, and so on.

3. Enter the principal amount, years, and interest rate of the new proposed mortgage.

4. Enter any mortgage closing costs or mortgage points associated with the new loan.

5. Click Calculate. Quicken tells you what your new payment would be, how much you would save, and how many months it would take to break even.

6. If you want to print this information, click the Print button, which opens the Print dialog box. Make any necessary adjustments and click OK.

7. When you're done with the Refinance Calculator, click Done to close it.

As an example, suppose that you have an existing 30-year fixed $250,000 mortgage at 8 percent interest with monthly payments of $1,834.41. A mortgage lender offers you a lower rate of 7 percent on your remaining $240,000 loan with closing costs of $1,000 and no points. Your new payment would be $1,596.73, a savings of $237.68 with a break-even time frame of 4.21 months.

13

Planning for Savings

Quicken's Investment Savings Calculator helps you plan, analyze, and strategize your savings goals. Using the Investment Savings Calculator, you can calculate:

- The regular contributions required to achieve a savings goal
- The ending savings balance you'll achieve based on specified contributions

- The opening savings balance required to achieve an ending savings goal with fixed contributions

To open the Investment Savings Calculator, select Features, Planning, Financial Calculators, Savings. Figure 13.5 illustrates this calculator.

FIGURE 13.5

Analyze investment savings options in a variety of ways using the Investment Savings Calculator.

To Do: Calculate Regular Contributions

1. Select Regular Contribution in the Calculate For group box.

2. In the Opening Savings Balance field, enter the savings balance that currently exists in this savings account, if any.

3. In the Annual Yield field, enter the interest percentage rate you estimate you will earn in this account.

4. Enter the number of weeks, months, quarters, or years you will take to achieve your savings goal.

5. Enter the ending savings balance you want to achieve.

6. If you want to include the effect of inflation into your calculations, enter the predicted inflation rate. Quicken's default for this rate is 4 percent.

7. If you want to inflate your calculations based on this percentage, select the Inflate Contributions check box.

8. Select the Ending Balance in Today's $ check box to view the final calculation using today's dollar value.

9. Click Calculate to display your required annual contribution.

For example, suppose that you want to take a trip to the Far East in two years and know that it will cost $6,000 to do so. You currently have $1,000 in an account paying 6 percent interest and want to know how much you'll have to save each month to be able to afford this trip. The calculator tells you the monthly amount to save is $211.22.

You can determine how much you'll save over a period of time by investing a particular amount of money.

To Do: Calculate an Ending Savings Balance

1. Select Ending Savings Balance in the Calculate For group box.
2. In the Opening Savings Balance field, enter the balance that currently exists in this savings account, if any.
3. In the Annual Yield field, enter the interest percentage rate you estimate you will earn in this account.
4. Enter the number of weeks, months, quarters, or years you will take to achieve your savings goal.
5. In the Contribution Each field, enter the contribution you want to make for the period of time you specified in step 4.
6. If you want to include the effect of inflation into your calculations, enter the predicted rate in the Predicted Inflation field. Quicken's default for this rate is 4 percent.
7. If you want to inflate your calculations based on this percentage, select the Inflate Contributions check box.
8. Select the Ending Balance in Today's $ check box to view the final calculation using today's dollar value.
9. Click Calculate to display your ending savings balance.

As an example, suppose that you decide to start putting $100 a month (or $1,200 a year) into a stock mutual fund. You can't be sure of how much you'll earn, but are hoping for about 12 percent. You want to know how much you'll have after five years. Figure 13.6 illustrates this example.

You can determine how much money you need to start with to save a specific amount of money with fixed contributions.

To Do

13

Figure 13.6

*You can determine
the potential future
outcome of a savings
plan.*

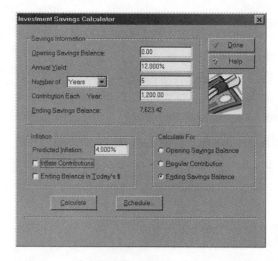

To Do: Calculate an Opening Savings Balance

1. Select Opening Savings Balance in the Calculate For group box.

2. In the Annual Yield field, enter the interest percentage rate you estimate you will earn in this account.

3. Enter the number of weeks, months, quarters, or years you will take to achieve your savings goal.

4. In the Contribution Each field, enter the contribution you want to make for the period of time you specified in step 3.

5. Enter the ending savings balance you want to achieve.

6. If you want to include the effect of inflation into your calculations, enter the predicted rate in the Predicted Inflation field. Quicken's default for this rate is 4 percent.

7. If you want to inflate your calculations based on this percentage, select the Inflate Contributions check box.

8. Select the Ending Balance in Today's $ check box to view the final calculation using today's dollar value.

9. Click Calculate to display the opening savings balance required to achieve your savings goal.

For example, suppose that your daughter wants to buy a car for her birthday six months from now. You estimate that she will need $4,000 to buy a used car. She is going to put her money in a savings account paying 6 percent interest and can contribute $500 a month from her part-time job to help pay for the car. You've offered to help her by giving money to get started with this savings account. Using the Investment Savings Calculator, you can easily see that you will need to provide $933.88 to achieve her dream of buying a car. Figure 13.7 illustrates this example.

FIGURE 13.7

Knowing how much money you'll need to start with can help you achieve an investment goal.

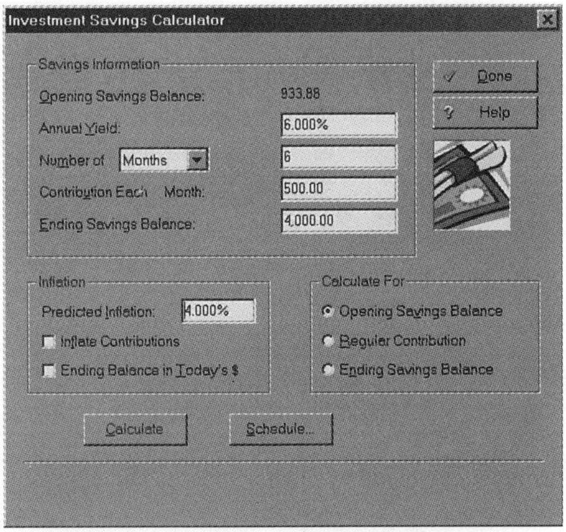

Creating a Savings Deposit Schedule

After you calculate your savings plan, you can display or print a schedule that details the deposit and total amount at each contribution. Click the Schedule button to display the Deposit Schedule dialog box, shown in Figure 13.8.

FIGURE 13.8

Viewing a deposit schedule can help track your progress.

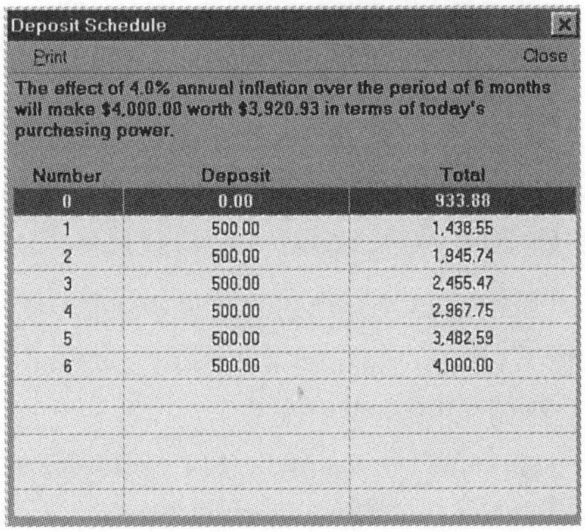

13

To print the schedule, click the Print button, which opens the Print dialog box. Make any necessary adjustments and click OK. When you're done looking at the schedule, click Close. When you're done with the Investment Savings Calculator, click Done to close it.

Planning for College

Paying for your child's college education is a major expense for most parents, and the Quicken College Calculator can help you plan for this.

To access the College Calculator, select Features, Planning, Financial Calculators, College. Figure 13.9 displays this calculator.

FIGURE 13.9

You can determine the annual contributions you need to make for your child's education starting at an early age.

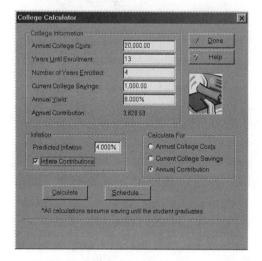

You can also use Quicken's What-If Scenarios to help you plan for expenses such as college and retirement. Select Features, Planning, What-If Scenarios to open the What-If Scenarios window. You can download additional scenarios from the Quicken Web site.

To Do: Determine an Annual Contribution

1. Select Annual Contribution in the Calculate For group box.

2. In the Annual College Costs field, enter the current annual cost for the type of college you estimate your child will attend.

3. Enter the number of years until enrollment. For example, estimate that a 10-year-old child will enroll in college in eight years.

4. Enter the number of years enrolled. For example, enter 4 for a typical bachelor's degree program.

5. Enter the current college savings you've already accumulated, if any.

6. In the Annual Yield field, enter the annual yield you hope to achieve with your college savings.

7. If you want to include the effect of inflation into your calculations, enter the predicted inflation rate. Quicken's default for this rate is 4 percent.

8. If you want to inflate your calculations based on this percentage, select the Inflate Contributions check box.

9. Click Calculate to display the annual contribution required to achieve this savings goal.

For example, suppose that your five-year-old son is already showing signs of rare musical talent and you want to be sure he has the opportunity for the best education possible to cultivate this talent. You estimate that in today's dollars, this type of college education costs about $20,000 per year. Currently you've saved only $1,000 toward this goal, but with a careful mix of stocks and bonds, you hope to achieve an 8 percent return on future investments. Using the College Calculator, you learn that you need to start saving $3,828.59 per year to achieve this goal.

You can also use the College Calculator to calculate annual college costs based on your current savings program or determine how much savings you'll need to start with based on different scenarios. Select these options in the Calculate For group box.

Creating a College Deposit Schedule

After you calculate your college savings plan, you can display or print a schedule that details the deposits, tuition spent, and balance of this account per year. Click the Schedule button to display the Deposit Schedule dialog box, shown in Figure 13.10.

FIGURE 13.10

Create a schedule to verify that your college contributions are on track.

Deposit Schedule

Print   Close

This deposit schedule assumes that your ability to make yearly contributions keeps pace with a 4.0% annual inflation rate.

Year	Deposit	Tuition	Balance
2003	4,658.07	0.00	32,364.46
2004	4,844.39	0.00	39,798.00
2005	5,038.16	0.00	48,020.01
2006	5,239.69	0.00	57,101.30
2007	5,449.28	0.00	67,118.68
2008	5,667.25	0.00	78,155.42
2009	5,893.94	0.00	90,301.79
2010	6,129.70	0.00	103,655.63
2011	6,374.88	33,301.47	82,357.38
2012	6,629.88	34,633.53	58,171.64
2013	6,895.07	36,018.87	30,820.07
2014	6,639.56	37,459.62	0.00

13

To print the schedule, click the Print button, which opens the Print dialog box. Make any necessary adjustments and click OK. When you're done looking at the schedule, click Close. When you're done with the College Calculator, click Done to close it.

Planning for Retirement

Quicken's Retirement Calculator can perform sophisticated what-if scenarios to help you determine how much to save for retirement and to forecast your annual retirement income.

> To create more detailed retirement planning calculations, you can use the Quicken Financial Planner program included in the Quicken Financial Suite. Quicken Deluxe 99 includes a limited version of Quicken Financial Planner. Select the QFP icon on the Iconbar to open the program.

To open the Retirement Calculator, select Features, Planning, Financial Calculators, Retirement. Figure 13.11 illustrates this calculator.

FIGURE 13.11

Analyze numerous options to create a secure retirement.

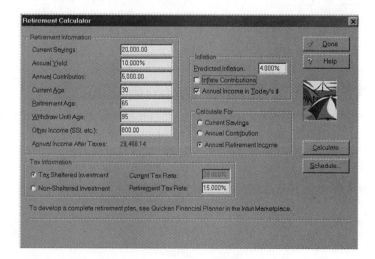

You can use this calculator to determine your annual retirement income based on your current savings and investment plan.

To Do: Determine Your Annual Retirement Income

1. Select Annual Retirement Income in the Calculate For Group box.

2. In the Current Savings field, enter the current amount you've already saved for retirement.

3. In the Annual Yield field, enter the annual yield you hope to achieve on your investments.

4. In the Annual Contribution field, enter, in today's dollars, the annual contribution you plan to make, including any matching contribution on behalf of your company.

5. Enter your current age.

6. In the Retirement Age field, enter the age at which you plan to retire.

7. In the Withdraw Until Age field, enter your anticipated life expectancy.

> It's best to overestimate your life expectancy to avoid running out of money.

8. In the Other Income field, enter the amount of other income, such as social security or pension, you estimate you'll receive.

> To help estimate your future social security benefits, you can request a Personal Earnings and Benefits Estimate Statement (PEBES) from Social Security. Call 1-800-772-1213 or visit the agency's Web site at http://s3abaca.ssa.gov/pro/batch-pebes/bp-7004home.shtml.

9. If you want to include the effect of inflation into your calculations, enter the predicted rate in the Predicted Inflation field. Quicken's default for this rate is 4 percent.

10. If you want to inflate your calculations based on this percentage, select the Inflate Contributions check box.

11. Select the Annual Income in Today's $ check box to view the final calculation using today's dollar value.

12. If your retirement savings are held in a tax-sheltered investment such as an IRA or 401(K) plan, select the Tax Sheltered Investment option button.

▼

13

▼ 13. If your retirement savings are held in a regular investment account, select the Non-Sheltered Account option button.

14. Adjust the Current Tax Rate or Retirement Tax Rate information if desired.

▲ 15. Click the Calculate button to calculate your annual income after taxes.

For example, suppose that you're 30 years old, planning to retire at age 65, and hope to live to 95. You've already saved $20,000 in your company 401(K) plan and currently are investing $5,000 per year in this plan. You're investing with a long-term perspective because you're young and hope these stock investments will return at least 10 percent per year. You guess that you would receive about $800 a month in Social Security benefits in today's dollars. Based on these assumptions, you see that you would have $28,468.14 per year during retirement.

If your retirement income amount isn't enough, you can modify your entries and recalculate or start with the amount you want to have available upon retirement and calculate how much you need to save. To do this, select Annual Contribution in the Calculate For group box.

> You can also determine how much retirement savings you would need to start with based on specific parameters by selecting the Current Savings option in the Calculate For group box.

Creating a Retirement Deposit Schedule

After you calculate your retirement savings plan, you can display or print a schedule that details the deposits, income, and balance of this account based on your age. Click the Schedule button to display the Deposit Schedule dialog box, shown in Figure 13.12.

FIGURE 13.12

Use the Deposit Schedule to track the money coming into and going out of your retirement account.

Deposit Schedule

Print · Close

This deposit schedule assumes that your retirement income keeps pace with a 4.0% annual inflation rate. Note that income is in future, pre-tax dollars.

Age	Deposit	Income	Balance
62	5,000.00	0.00	1,575,760.81
63	5,000.00	0.00	1,738,336.89
64	5,000.00	0.00	1,917,170.58
65	0.00	128,448.17	1,967,594.65
66	0.00	133,586.09	2,017,409.41
67	0.00	138,929.54	2,066,327.86
68	0.00	144,486.72	2,114,025.26
69	0.00	150,266.19	2,160,134.98
70	0.00	156,276.84	2,204,243.95
71	0.00	162,527.91	2,245,887.65
72	0.00	169,029.03	2,284,544.48
73	0.00	175,790.19	2,319,629.73

To print the schedule, click the Print button, which opens the Print dialog box. Make any necessary adjustments and click OK. When you're done looking at the schedule, click Close. When you're done with the Retirement Calculator, click Done to close it.

Planning to Reduce Debt

The Debt Reduction Planner is a Quicken Deluxe feature that analyzes your debts, provides interactive advice, and creates a plan to help you get out of debt sooner while paying less interest. Select Features, Planning, Debt Reduction Planner to open the Debt Reduction window, shown in Figure 13.13.

FIGURE 13.13

Save money on interest expense using the Debt Reduction Planner.

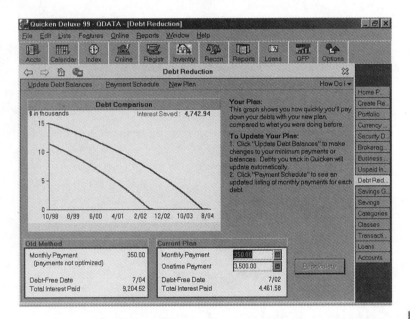

This window provides step-by-step advice on how to reduce your debt by:

- Importing a list of all your debts from your Quicken file.
- Calculating your total debt and monthly payments, and indicating when you will be debt-free based on your current repayment schedule and how much interest you'll pay under this schedule.

13

- Providing advice on paying off loans in the order of the highest interest rate. For example, you would want to pay off a high-interest credit card debt before a lower interest car loan.

- Showing you how much you would save by paying off these higher interest debts.

- Analyzing your savings and suggesting how much to apply toward your debts.

- Giving suggestions on where you could cut back on monthly expenses by focusing on over-budget categories.

- Creating a special action plan for getting out of debt.

Figure 13.14 illustrates this action plan.

FIGURE 13.14

An action plan helps you get started reducing debts.

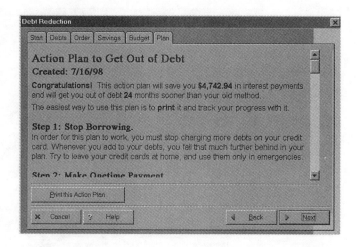

To get started with a debt reduction plan, click the Plan button.

Setting Savings Goals

Another feature that helps you plan and analyze your savings is the Savings Goals window. Select Features, Planning, Savings Goals to open it (see Figure 13.15).

FIGURE 13.15

The Savings Goals window helps you plan for and track major expenditures.

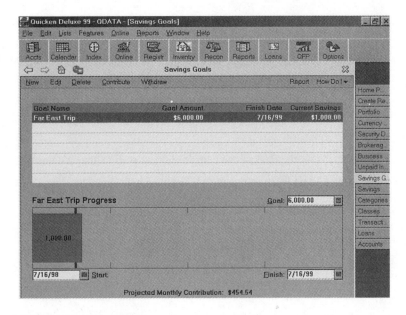

To Do: Set Up a Savings Goal

1. Click the New button to open the Create New Savings Goal dialog box, shown in Figure 13.16.

FIGURE 13.16

You can specify a new goal in the Create New Savings Goal dialog box.

2. In the Goal Name field, enter a name that identifies your goal.

> For additional assistance, click the calculator button next to the Goal Amount field or the calendar button next to the Finish Date field.

3. In the Goal Amount field, enter the final amount you want to save.

4. Enter a finish date in the Finish Date field.

13

5. Select a currency from the Currency drop-down list if you've activated multicurrency support.

6. Click OK. Quicken lists the goal in the Savings Goals window.

7. If you've already made a contribution or want to assign money to this goal, select Contribute from the menu. The Contribute to Goal dialog box appears.

8. In the From Account field, select the account from which you want to contribute funds for this goal.

9. Enter the date of the contribution as well as the amount.

10. Click OK to return to the Savings Goals window. The Progress Bar shows how much you have contributed so far.

> Select Edit from the menu to edit the amount and finish date. Click the Delete menu option to delete the goal.

You can track several goals in the Savings Goals window. Select the goal you want to view from the Goal Name column.

As you continue making contributions, you can track your savings progress on an ongoing basis. Or, if you withdraw money from the account, you can track this progress as well. To do so, select Withdraw from the menu. Figure 13.17 displays the Withdraw from Goal dialog box.

FIGURE 13.17

You can also withdraw money from a savings goal if necessary.

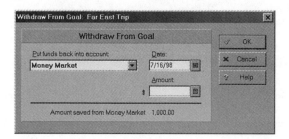

You can specify the date and the amount of funds you put back into another account.

> Select Report from the menu to see a report of your savings goal progress.

In an earlier example, you were saving for a vacation to the Far East in two years. By setting up a savings account, you can track how much you've saved and your contributions. For instance, you could allocate $1,000 for this trip from a money market account containing $5,000. The other $4,000 you want to keep for other uses.

Summary

This hour taught you how to use Quicken's interactive planning tools to plan for your financial future. If you want to analyze loan and refinance possibilities, the Loan Calculator and Refinance Calculator can help make calculations quickly. You can create sophisticated investment projections with the Investment Savings Calculator. And the College Calculator and Retirement Calculator can help you prepare for these future major expenses. Finally, you can reduce debt and better plan for future savings using the Debt Reduction Planner and the Savings Goals window.

Hour 14, "Planning for Taxes," shows you how to use Quicken's interactive tax-planning features to organize and save money on your income taxes.

Q&A

Q I'm not sure how to predict my potential yield in calculations. What are some good guidelines?

A Use these historical returns to help predict potential yield based on your investment mix: international stocks at 13.2 percent, U.S. small company stocks at 12.3 percent, U.S. large company stocks at 10.2 percent, domestic bonds at 5.1 percent, and money market accounts at 3.7 percent.

Q What happens to funds that I allocate for a savings goal? Why doesn't this money still show up in my actual savings account?

A By setting up a savings goal, Quicken reminds you that this money is tagged for the specified goal to help keep you from spending it, but doesn't really remove it from your account. On your net worth report, however, a savings goal is referred to as an "other asset" rather than as a "cash and bank account asset," even though the money still remains in your bank account.

13

HOUR **14**

Planning for Taxes

This hour shows you how to take advantage of Quicken's powerful tax planning and analysis tools. By linking tax forms to categories, you can create a variety of scenarios that help you make tax decisions. Tools such as the Tax Link Assistant, Deduction Finder, Tax Planner, and Capital Gains Estimator can save you time and effort in dealing with taxes. In addition, Quicken directly interfaces with Intuit's tax preparation software and online service, TurboTax.

The highlights of this hour include

- Why you should link categories to tax forms
- How to use the Tax Link Assistant and Deduction Finder
- What's the best way to use the Tax Planner
- How to use the Capital Gains Estimator
- How to interface to TurboTax

Understanding Quicken's Tax Features

The ability to assign tax forms and schedules to categories is a key factor in being able to use Quicken's many tax features successfully. By default, Quicken assigns a tax form or schedule to the categories it includes with the program, but to use this capability most effectively, you should carefully verify the form to which each existing category is linked as well as link new categories you create.

To do so, select Lists, Category/Transfer to display the Category & Transfer List. Select New to create a new category or Edit to edit the selected category. In the dialog box that displays (see Figure 14.1), the Tax group box offers a Form drop-down list from which you can choose the appropriate tax form or schedule.

FIGURE 14.1

Linking categories to tax forms and schedules is essential to good tax planning in Quicken.

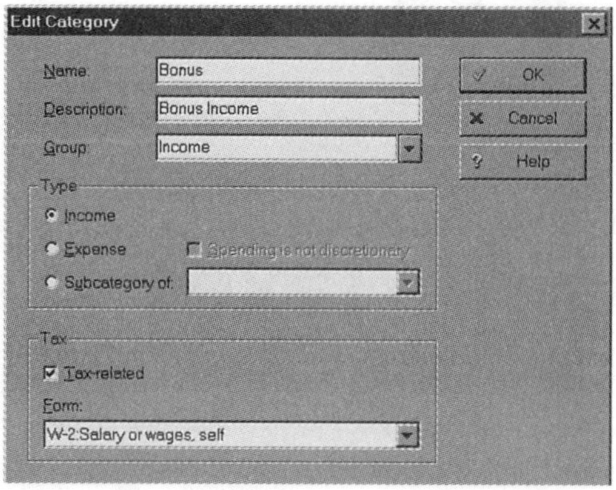

Also be sure to select the Tax-Related check box. If this field doesn't display, you need to set the option to use tax schedules with categories. Select Edit, Options, Quicken Program to display the General Options dialog box (see Figure 14.2).

FIGURE 14.2

You can link tax schedules with categories by selecting this check box.

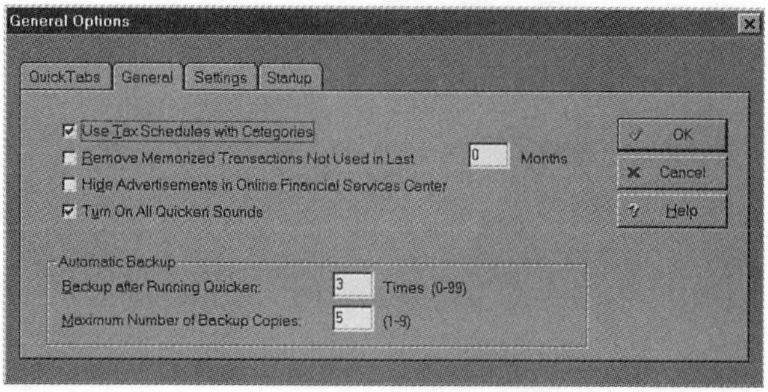

The General tab offers the option to use tax schedules with categories. Select this check box if it's not already selected.

> Although Quicken's many tax planning features can help save you time and hopefully money, they do require that you have some basic knowledge of tax forms and schedules and your own tax situation. In addition, they cannot replace the advice of a tax professional. But if you usually handle your own tax preparation, Quicken's powerful and time-saving tax planning tools can be very beneficial.

Using the Tax Link Assistant

Quicken's Tax Link Assistant helps you to assign categories to tax line items, making it easier to estimate future taxes and analyze your tax situation. With the Tax Link Assistant, Quicken has already done a lot of the work for you. All the default categories already have tax line items assigned to them. So all you need to do is to verify that these assignments are accurate for your own needs and assign tax line items to categories you create yourself.

To Do: Explore the Tax Link Assistant

1. Select Features, Taxes, Set Up for Taxes to open the Tax Link Assistant, illustrated in Figure 14.3.

FIGURE 14.3

Use the Tax Link Assistant to view, add, and change tax line item assignments by category.

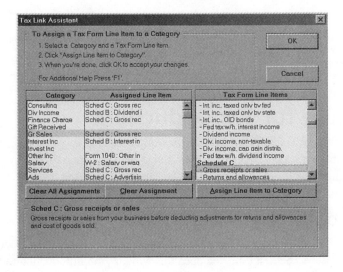

▼

14

▼   2. Select the category to which you want to assign a tax line item from the Category
        column. If an item is already assigned, it displays in the Assigned Line Item
        column.

     3. From the Tax Form Line Items column on the right side of the dialog box, choose
        the appropriate line item to assign the category.

> All tax line items are sorted by tax form (1040, Schedule A, Form 8829, and
> so on). If you're unsure about what each line item is, Quicken offers a
> detailed explanation at the bottom of the dialog box for each selected line
> item. You can also refer to your actual tax forms to verify where to assign
> each category.

     4. Click the Assign Line Item to Category button. Quicken assigns the designated line
        item, overwriting any existing assignment.

     5. When you are finished assigning line items to categories, click OK to close the
▲   Tax Link Assistant.

> If you want to remove a specific assigned line item, click the Clear
> Assignment button. If you want to remove all assigned line items, click the
> Clear All Assignments button.

> Selecting the Clear All Assignments button removes *all* line item assign-
> ments, even those that Quicken provides by default.

Looking for Tax Deductions

Quicken includes several interactive worksheets that help you determine whether you are
eligible for specific tax deductions. Using the Deduction Finder, you can answer a series
of questions about your individual tax situation; Quicken then creates a summary and
detailed action plan based on this information.

To Do: Use the Deduction Finder

     1. Select Features, Taxes, Tax Deduction Finder to open the Deduction Finder win-
        dow. The first time you open this window, the Introduction to Deduction Finder
        dialog box greets you (see Figure 14.4).

FIGURE 14.4

This dialog box explains the five steps for finding potential tax deductions.

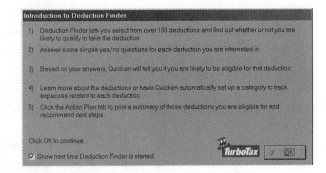

2. Click OK to continue. The first tab, Deductions (see Figure 14.5), provides the interactive worksheets that tell you whether you may be eligible for specific deductions.

FIGURE 14.5

The Deductions tab includes interactive worksheets that help determine the deductions for which you may be eligible.

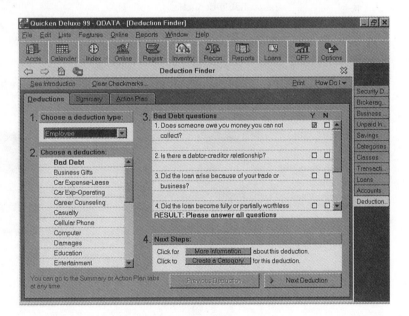

3. In step 1 of the Deductions tab, choose a deduction type. Choices include Employee, Homeowner, Individual, Investor, Medical, or Self-Employed.

4. In step 2 of the Deductions tab, select the deduction for which you want to determine your eligibility.

5. In step 3 of the Deductions tab, answer all the listed questions by clicking the Y check box for yes or the N check box for no.

14

> If you want to start over again, select the Clear Checkmarks button. Quicken removes *all* your responses, and you can enter new information in the Deduction Finder.

After you answer all questions, the RESULT line indicates whether you may qualify for the deduction.

6. In step 4 of the Deductions tab, you can click the More Information button to view a more detailed explanation of the specific deduction or click the Create a Category to create a Quicken category to track expenses for the deduction.

> Click the Previous Deduction and Next Deduction buttons to scroll through the available deductions.

Viewing a Deduction Summary

To see a summary of all available deductions and the number for which you may qualify, click the Summary tab, shown in Figure 14.6.

FIGURE 14.6

The Summary tab tells you how many possible deductions you have and also reminds you of the number of deductions you haven't considered yet.

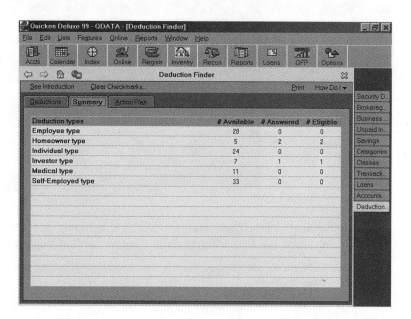

Deduction types	# Available	# Answered	# Eligible
Employee type	28	0	0
Homeowner type	5	2	2
Individual type	24	0	0
Investor type	7	1	1
Medical type	11	0	0
Self-Employed type	33	0	0

Viewing an Action Plan

To view a tax deduction action plan based on your answers to the questions in step 3 of the Deductions tab, click the Action Plan tab, shown in Figure 14.7.

FIGURE 14.7

An action plan provides detailed advice on potential tax deductions.

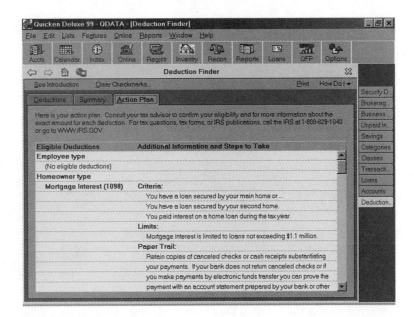

This plan details each deduction for which you may be eligible, including information on criteria, limits, paperwork requirements, and tax forms.

To print your action plan, click the Print button. The Print dialog box displays; select your designated printer and other parameters and click OK.

Using the Quicken Tax Planner

The Quicken Tax Planner is a sophisticated tax planning tool that helps you determine your potential tax payment or refund.

> Be sure to check Quicken's Web site before tax time so that you can download the latest updates for the current tax year.

14

To Do: Plan a Tax Return

1. Select Features, Taxes, Tax Planner. Figure 14.8 illustrates this planner.

2. Select your filing status and the tax year from the drop-down lists.

FIGURE 14.8

The Tax Planner analyzes different tax consequence scenarios.

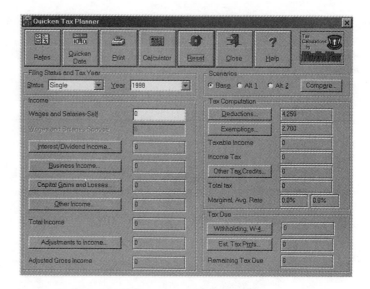

3. Click the Quicken Data button to import your tax data for the year automatically into the Tax Planner. Figure 14.9 illustrates the Preview Quicken Tax Data dialog box that opens.

FIGURE 14.9

You can choose whether to annualize tax items.

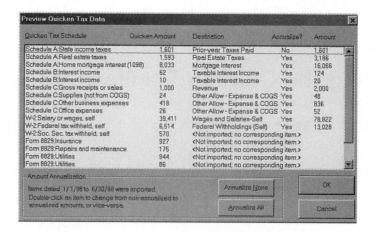

▼   For each tax schedule, Quicken indicates the amount, its destination, whether it is
annualized, and the amount if annualized. Double-clicking an item serves as a toggle to select or deselect annualization.

You'll probably want to annualize items such as salary and mortgage payments that
you know you will continue to pay or receive throughout the year. Payments or
expenses for one-time items, however, don't need to be annualized. If you are calculating taxes for the previous year, you don't need to worry about the problem of
annualization because all 12 months are already included.

NEW TERM   *Annualization* is the process of recalculating a year-to-date amount based on
a full year. For example, $6,000 for a year-to-date total as of June 30th
(six months) annualizes to $12,000.

> You can choose the Annualize All or Annualize None buttons to set annual-
> ization options quickly.

4. Click OK to return to the Tax Planner.

Based on the information you've provided, Quicken estimates your tax or refund
due for the year (see Figure 14.10).

FIGURE 14.10

*You can get an esti-
mate of your tax pay-
ment or refund with
the Tax Planner.*

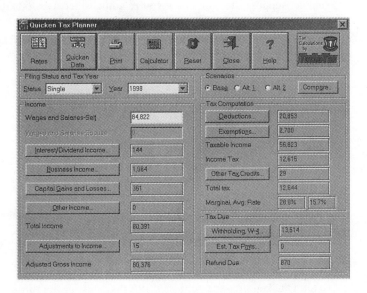

14

To reset the tax planning scenario you just created, select the Reset button. To print the scenario, select the Print button. Enter any specific parameters in the Print dialog box and click OK.

Customizing the Tax Planner

You can adjust many tax areas by clicking the designated buttons to open a customization dialog box. You can adjust

- Interest/Dividend Income
- Business Income
- Capital Gains and Losses
- Other Income
- Adjustments to Income
- Deductions
- Exemptions
- Other Tax Credits
- Withholding W4
- Estimated Tax Payments

For example, suppose that you know you're going to receive some interest or dividend income later this year and want the planner to reflect this income. Click the Interest/Dividend Income button to open the Interest/Dividend Income - Schedule B dialog box, shown in Figure 14.11.

FIGURE 14.11

You can modify income, payments, deductions, and credits to create an accurate tax plan.

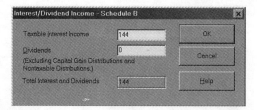

Enter the adjusted amounts and click OK. Quicken then recalculates your tax based on this new information.

Modifying Tax Rates

By default, Quicken uses the published IRS tax rates for the filing status you select. To modify these rates, select the Rates button. Figure 14.12 illustrates the Tax Rates for Filing Status dialog box.

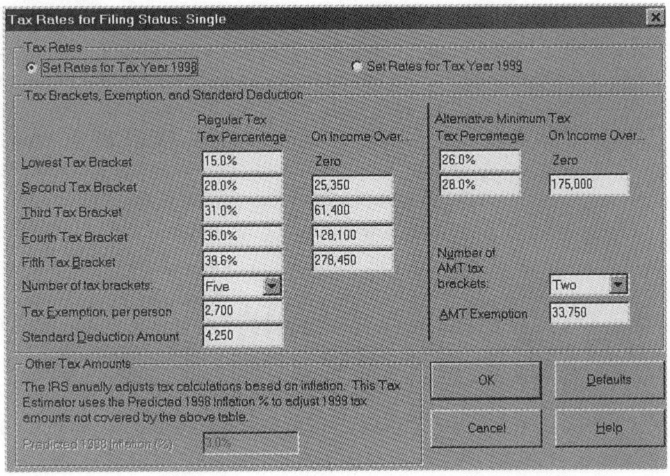

FIGURE 14.12

If the default rates Quicken automatically assigns aren't accurate, you can modify them.

Make any necessary changes and click OK to return to the Tax Planner. Quicken now recalculates information based on the adjusted tax rates. To return to the default tax rates, select the Defaults button in the Tax Rates for Filing Status dialog box.

Creating Alternate Tax Plan Scenarios

You can create two alternate tax plan scenarios to compare and contrast your tax obligations based on different assumptions. To create another assumption, click either the Alt 1 or Alt 2 option button in the Tax Planner's Scenarios group box. Quicken asks whether you want to copy the existing data to this scenario.

Enter the new information to create the scenario. To compare the scenarios you've created, click the Compare button to display the Tax Scenario Comparisons dialog box, shown in Figure 14.13.

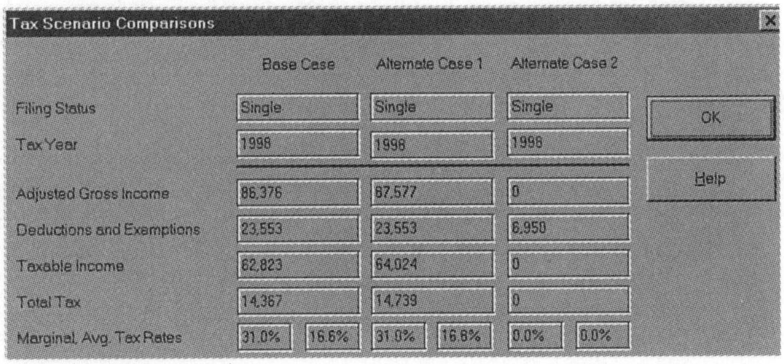

FIGURE 14.13

Comparing multiple scenarios lets you determine which one is most beneficial.

14

Keep in mind that in spite of the power and sophistication of the Tax Planner, its results are only as good as the data you provide it. If you haven't entered all your financial transactions in Quicken, haven't thoroughly linked categories to tax line items with the Tax Link Assistant, or haven't carefully analyzed and adjusted its assumptions, the Tax Planner may not provide an accurate estimate of your taxes.

Estimating Capital Gains

The Capital Gains Estimator is a new Quicken Deluxe 99 feature. You can use it to see quickly the tax implications of selling specific securities.

You must have an existing investment account and at least one investment to open the Capital Gains Estimator.

The Capital Gains Estimator helps you to determine the tax consequences of selling investments such as stocks or mutual funds. Select Features, Taxes, Estimate Capital Gains to open the Capital Gains Estimator, illustrated in Figure 14.14.

In the lower half of the window, under Current Holdings Excluding Tax-Deferred Accounts, Quicken lists all the investments you currently own in regular accounts, by lot.

NEW TERM   A *lot* is the amount of a particular security you bought or sold on a particular date. Lots are important in estimating capital gains, particularly if you purchased the same security several times, because they identify how long you've held each number of shares.

This portion of the window displays each security by name and lists the market price, shares owned, gain/loss, and holding period (either short-term or long-term) for each lot.

Select the lot or lots you want to sell, then click the Add button. Quicken displays these securities in the upper portion of the window, under the Proposed Sales section. To remove lots, select them and click the Remove button.

You can also double-click a lot to add it to the Proposed Sales section.

You can adjust the shares and sales prices to see what the outcome would be. If you change the sales price and want to return to the actual price of the security, click the Current Prices button.

FIGURE 14.14

Estimate the tax implications of a potential investment sale.

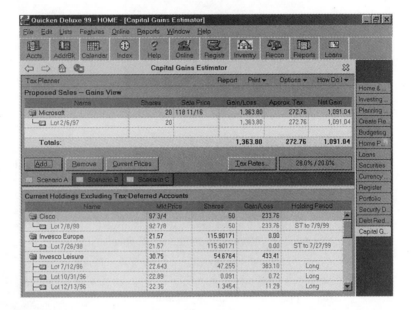

Changing Your Tax Rate

The tax rates that Quicken uses to estimate capital gains are based on the tax rate the Tax Planner calculates for you. The box to the right of the Tax Rates button displays this information.

For example, 31.0% / 20.0 % means that you would pay 31 percent for short-term capital gains and 20 percent for long-term gains. The rate for short-term gains is equivalent to your regular tax rate. If you haven't used the Tax Planner (which automatically calculates your tax rate) or want to adjust the tax rate for capital gains estimates, click the Tax Rates button to display the Select Tax Rates dialog box (see Figure 14.15).

Choose the capital gains rates you want to use, then click OK. The Capital Gains Estimator now uses the new rates to estimate your gains.

Creating Capital Gains Scenarios

14

If you want, you can create multiple scenarios to perform a what-if analysis on your capital gains estimates. To create a second or third scenario, click the Scenario B or Scenario C buttons. Quicken moves to a clear window where you can add new proposed sales information.

FIGURE **14.15**

*You can change your
tax rates if necessary.*

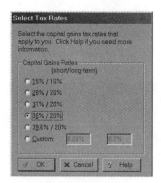

Printing Reports

You can print three different reports based on data you analyze with the Capital Gains
Estimator:

- *Capital Gains Report.* Click the Report button to move to the Create Report window where the Capital Gains report is already selected. Click Create to display the
  Capital Gains Report, illustrated in Figure 14.16.

- *Capital Gains Scenario.* Select Print, Print This Scenario to display an analysis of
  proposed sales (see Figure 14.17), matching what appears in the upper portion of
  the Capital Gains Estimator window.

FIGURE **14.16**

*This report illustrates
the tax effects of your
investment sale.*

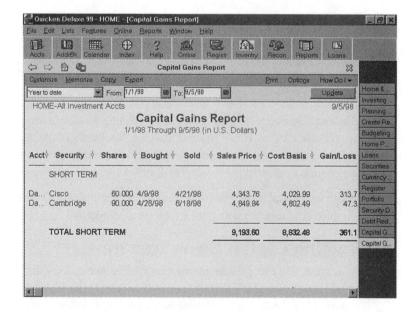

• *Capital Gains Holdings.* Select Print, Print Holdings to display a list of your holdings by lot number (see Figure 14.18), matching what appears in the lower portion of the Capital Gains Estimator window.

FIGURE 14.17

Print the proposed sale scenario you're viewing on screen.

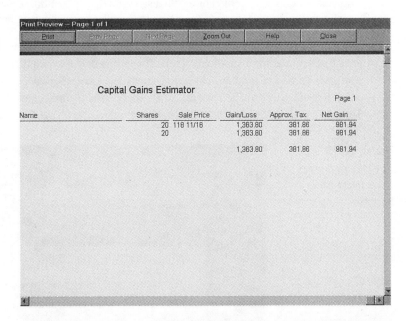

FIGURE 14.18

You can also print a list of your holdings by lot.

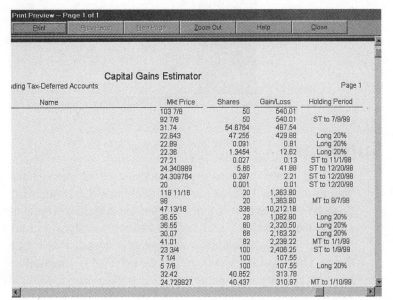

14

Interfacing with TurboTax

If you own Intuit's TurboTax product, you can interface directly to it from within Quicken. To do so, select Features, Taxes, TurboTax. If you don't have TurboTax on your system, Quicken displays a dialog box telling you so.

You can also use Intuit's TurboTax Online feature, which enables you to prepare and file your taxes online for a small fee. TurboTax online doesn't include all the features of the complete TurboTax product, but it does provide a convenient way for people with less complicated returns to file their taxes. To access this feature, select Features, Taxes, TurboTax Online. Figure 14.19 illustrates the initial TurboTax Online screen.

FIGURE 14.19

TurboTax Online lets you prepare taxes on the Web.

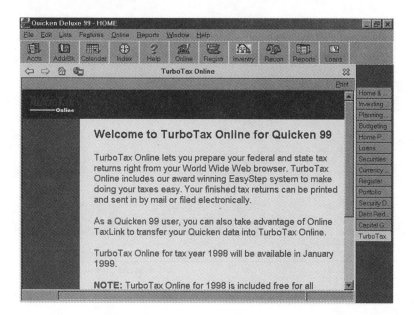

Summary

This hour showed you how to use Quicken's tax features to organize, plan, and analyze your tax situation. Linking categories to tax schedules is the first step in connecting your financial data with the tax forms and schedules it affects. From there you can use tools such as the Deduction Finder and Tax Planner to analyze your tax situation further. And if you're planning to sell investments such as stocks and mutual funds, you can use the Capital Gains Estimator to determine the potential tax implications of such sales. Finally, when tax time arrives, you can use your Quicken data in the regular TurboTax product as well as its online counterpart.

Hour 15, "Setting Up Investment Accounts," start a new section that focuses on how to set up and track your investments and assets.

Q&A

Q What's the best way to get an overall look at my tax situation?

A For an overview of taxes, look at the Tax Center. Select Features, Centers, Tax Center to display this view, which provides information on projected taxes, a tax calendar, and year-to-date income and deductions.

Q Where can I see exactly how my Quicken transactions are linked to tax forms and schedules?

A Quicken includes two tax reports that provide detailed information on the way your financial data is categorized for tax purposes. They are two of Quicken's Home reports: the Tax Summary Report and Tax Schedule Report.

14

PART IV

Setting Up and Tracking Investments

Hour

Hour **15**

Setting Up Investment Accounts

This hour introduces you to Quicken investment accounts. You can quickly set up an investment account to track stocks, bonds, and mutual funds as well as establish a special account to track your 401(k). Quicken investment accounts offer the flexibility of adding extensive detail for future tracking and analysis or the capability to track only basic information.

The highlights of this hour include

- What kind of accounts you should use to track your investments
- Why you might want to track detailed information about your investments
- How to set up an investment account
- How to set up a 401(k) account

Understanding Investment Accounts

Quicken investment accounts track investments you own, such as stocks, bonds, and mutual funds. Using investment accounts, you can track investment purchases and sales, dividends, performance, value, and other useful information. Quicken offers several ways to track your investments, depending on the type of account and what you're tracking. Options include

- *Investment Account*. This account tracks investments you hold with brokerage and mutual fund firms. You can indicate whether the account contains a single mutual fund or numerous stocks, bonds, and funds.

> You should set up only one Quicken investment account for an account you have with a brokerage or mutual fund firm, even if it contains more than one security.

- *401(k) Account*. This type of account is specifically designed to track securities, usually mutual funds, which you hold in a 401(k). Even if your statement doesn't tell you how many shares you hold, a 401(k) account can track this investment.

NEW TERM   A *401(k)* plan is a company-sponsored, tax-deferred retirement plan that lets you make set contributions from your salary on a regular basis. In many cases, the company provides a matching contribution with the contribution percentage often based on your years of employment.

- *Asset Account*. An asset account is most useful for tracking investments such as real estate, but you can also use it to track investments that don't provide detailed information on the number of shares or purchase price. In this case, you could use an asset account simply to track overall price changes of the investment.

Before you set up any investment account, you should have your last statement available. You also need to consider how much detail you want to track in the account. In general, the more detail you provide, the more useful Quicken's investment tracking and analysis tools will be, but it does take more time to set up this kind of detailed information.

For example, you need to decide the time frame for tracking your investments in Quicken before you set up an account. You can track your investments as of

- *Today*. This is the easiest way to start tracking an investment, but this method doesn't enable you to analyze performance or track tax implications for the current year.

15

- *The end of last year.* This method lets you track year-to-date information for tax purposes, but doesn't provide detailed historical data for investment analysis.
- *The date you purchased the security.* This method provides the most detailed information for historical performance analysis and tax planning, but takes the most time to set up.

You can also set investment goals for each security to analyze how your investments are performing by goal. Sample investment goals include

- Aggressive growth
- College fund
- Growth
- High risk
- Income
- International
- Low risk
- Sector
- Small company
- Technology

> Hour 21, "Viewing and Analyzing your Portfolio," shows you how to modify investment goals.

And finally, you can track your investments by asset class. This is optional, but helps you analyze your investment asset allocation. Quicken provides several asset classes from which you can choose:

- Bonds
- Domestic bonds
- Global bonds
- Stocks
- Large cap stocks
- Mid cap stocks
- Small cap stocks
- International stocks

- Money market
- Cash
- Other

You can enter this information yourself or, if you're not sure of the asset mixture (which is common with mutual funds), you can download the asset mix from the Internet.

If you want to enter additional detail when you first set up your investment account, be sure to have the required information and paperwork available. If you don't, however, you can set up a basic account, then add additional information at a later date.

Setting Up an Investment Account

In the Enter a New Investment dialog box, you can set up a new investment with step-by-step EasyStep guidance or use the Summary tab to expedite the setup.

To Do: Set Up an Investment Account

1. Select Features, Investing, Create New Investment to open the Enter a New Investment dialog box, illustrated in Figure 15.1.

FIGURE 15.1

You can get step-by-step guidance on creating an investment account.

2. Select the I Want to Set Up a New Account option button.

You can also set up a new security in an existing account, which is different from creating a new account itself. After you already have an investment account, you can set up many new securities (such as a stock or mutual fund) as you buy them. Hour 16, "Tracking Investments," describes how to set up a new security.

▼   3. Click OK to continue. The Investment Account Setup dialog box displays, as
       shown in Figure 15.2.

FIGURE 15.2

You can move immediately to the Summary tab to simplify data entry.

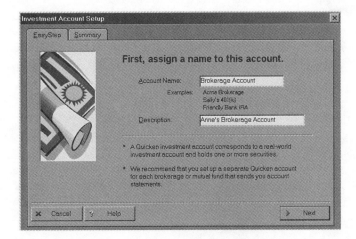

   4. On the EasyStep tab, enter an account name and description for this account.

   5. Click the Summary tab to continue. Figure 15.3 illustrates this tab.

FIGURE 15.3

You can set specific account options if your accounts contains only one mutual fund.

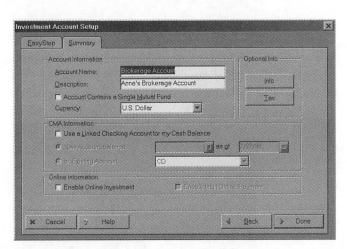

   6. Select the Account Contains a Single Mutual Fund check box if such is the case for
▼   your investment account.

15

> If you select this option, you can track only one fund in this account, and the account can't track cash balances.

7. Select the currency you want to use for this account. The default is the U.S. dollar.

8. Optionally, click the Info button to display the Additional Account Information dialog box, shown in Figure 15.4.

FIGURE 15.4

Enter address and other information about this financial institution if you want.

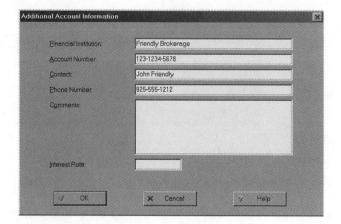

9. You can enter more detailed information about the financial institution in this dialog box. Click OK to return to the previous dialog box.

10. Optionally, click the Tax button to display the Tax Schedule Information dialog box, shown in Figure 15.5.

FIGURE 15.5

Specify tax information in this dialog box.

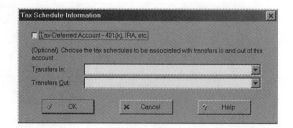

11. Specify whether this is a tax-deferred account, select optional Transfers In and Transfers Out accounts, and click OK to return to the Summary tab.

12. Select the Use a Linked Checking Account for My Cash Balance check box if you can write checks or use a debit card based on this account.

15

If you want to set up a 401(k), you can also use the 401(k) Setup dialog box to set up an account specifically designed to handle 401(k) investment tracking.

Selecting this option activates the lower portion of the CMA Information group box.

13. Click New Account Balance and enter a balance and effective date if you want to create a new account to link to this investment account.

14. Click Existing Account if you want to link to an existing Quicken checking or savings account; select the account from the drop-down list that appears.

15. Select Enable Online Investment if you want to be able to retrieve online statements for this account.

16. Select Enable Intuit Online Payment if you want to be able to pay bills online from this account. You must link this account to a checking account to choose this option.

Enabling online financial services is described later this hour.

17. If you don't choose to enable online services, the Done button appears. Click this button to continue to the next EasyStep setup series.

Setting Up Securities in Your Account

Clicking the Done button in the previous series of steps opens another dialog box, Security Setup (see Figure 15.6).

FIGURE 15.6

You can set up multiple securities in the Security Setup dialog box.

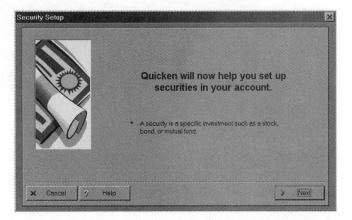

To Do: Set Up Securities

1. Click Next to move from this informational dialog box to the next step (see Figure 15.7).

FIGURE 15.7

Provide basic information about this security.

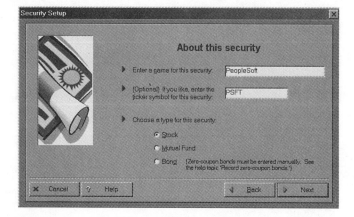

2. Enter a name and ticker symbol for this security.

3. Specify whether this security is a stock, mutual fund, or bond and click Next. You then move to the next step, shown in Figure 15.8.

FIGURE 15.8

An investment goal helps you track your investment's performance.

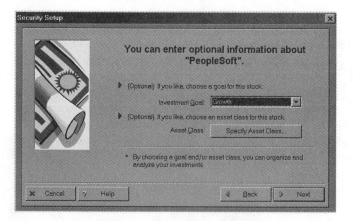

4. Select an optional investment goal from the drop-down list. This isn't required, but is useful in tracking and analyzing your goals.

5. If you want to choose an optional asset class to assign to this security, click the Specify Asset Class button to display the Asset Class Information dialog box, shown in Figure 15.9.

▼

FIGURE 15.9

If you don't know the asset class of a mutual fund, you can download this information from the Internet.

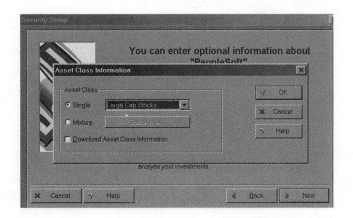

6. If this investment belongs to a single asset class, select it from the Single drop-down list. Stocks usually belong to a single asset class.

7. If this investment contains a mixture of asset classes (which is common with mutual funds), you can click the Download Asset Class Information check box and have Quicken download the exact mix details from the Internet.

If you already know the exact asset class mix, you can click the Mixture option button and then the Specify Mixture button to display the Asset Class Mixture dialog box, where you can enter the precise information. It's highly unlikely, however, that you'll already know the exact asset mix of your mutual funds. You'll probably get more accurate results by downloading them from the Internet.

To download from the Internet, you first need to set up Quicken to access the Internet. Hour 23, "Using Online Financial Services," tells you how to do this if you haven't already done so.

8. Click OK to return to the Security Setup dialog box and click Next to move to the next step, shown in Figure 15.10.

15

FIGURE 15.10

Set a time frame for tracking your investments.

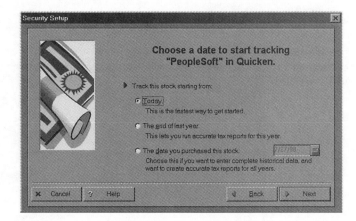

9. Determine whether you want to track this investment as of today, the end of last year, or the date you purchased it and click Next. You then see the next step, shown in Figure 15.11.

FIGURE 15.11

Provide more detailed information on this security.

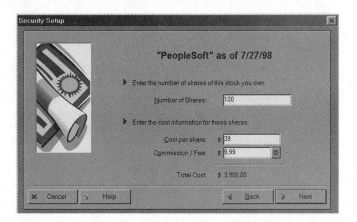

10. As of the date you specified in the previous step, enter the number of shares you purchased, the cost per share, and the commission or fee. Then click Next. Figure 15.12 illustrates the next step.

11. Specify whether you want to track your cost basis by lot identification or average cost. Then click Next to display the next step, shown in Figure 15.13.

> **NEW TERM**   A *lot* is the amount of a security that you bought or sold at a particular time. Purchasing the same security at two different times results in two separate lots.

Tracking by lot identification (each purchase of shares tracked separately)
provides you more detailed information for determining and analyzing the
capital gains consequences of your investment sales. Tracking by average
cost spreads the cost of each share purchase for a particular security over
the time you own it.

15

FIGURE 15.12

You can track stocks by lot identification.

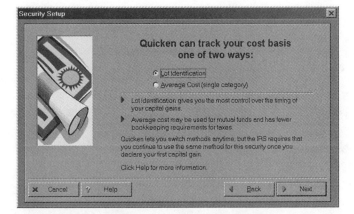

FIGURE 15.13

You can add multiple securities in this dialog box.

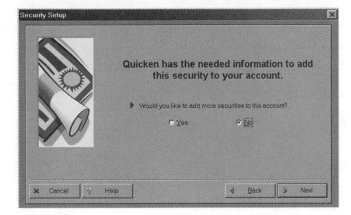

12. If you want to add more securities, click Yes; Quicken then repeats the last few
    steps. Otherwise, click No and then select the Next button to continue to the final
    step, shown in Figure 15.14.

13. This step summarizes the security setup information you entered. Click Done to
    open the register for this investment, shown in Figure 15.15.

FIGURE 15.14

You can see a summary of the securities you set up.

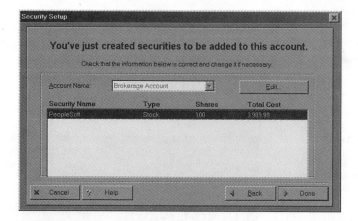

FIGURE 15.15

Quicken displays the register for the investment account you just created.

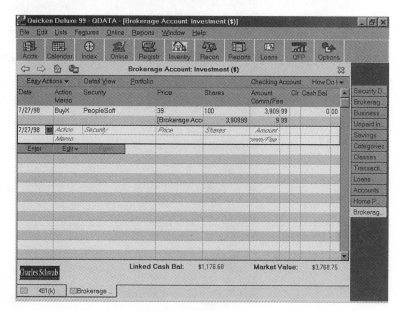

> Click Edit to display the Stock Information dialog box, where you can make any last-minute changes.

Setting Up an Account with Online Services Enabled

You can choose to enable online services in the Investment Account Setup dialog box by clicking the Enable Online Investment check box as shown in Figure 15.16. Just click Next, and Quicken provides the steps described in the following "To Do" section (see Figure 15.17).

FIGURE 15.16

Select online services and you can continue in the setup process.

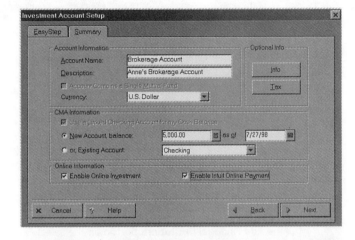

FIGURE 15.17

If you already set up your financial institution, you can select it from the drop-down list.

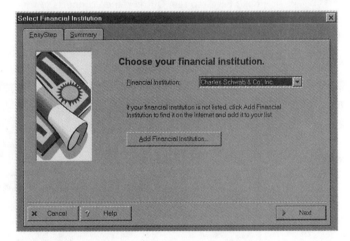

To Do: Set Up an Account with Online Services Enabled

1. Select the appropriate Financial Institution from the drop-down list and click Next. Figure 15.18 illustrates this next step.

2. Specify whether you want to use online investment tracking and/or Intuit online payment. Then click Next. The next step displays (see Figure 15.19).

FIGURE 15.18

Indicate which online financial services you want to set up.

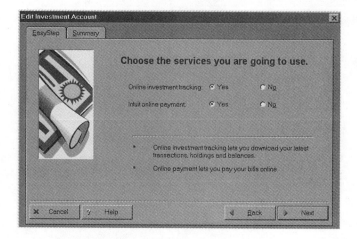

If you haven't set up a financial institution to use online services yet, click the Add Financial Institutions button on the Select Financial Institution dialog box's EasyStep tab. Quicken then connects to the Internet to set up this institution. Hour 23, "Using Online Financial Services," provides more detail about setting up Quicken's online services.

FIGURE 15.19

Enter the appropriate account and customer numbers.

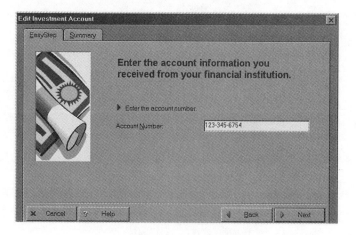

You can't jump to the Summary tab in this dialog box; you must use the EasyStep process.

▼   3. Enter your account number and customer ID (provided by your financial institution) in the next two steps and click Next to proceed to the standard Summary tab.

4. Click Next to move to the final summary step, which summarizes your online banking selections, shown in Figure 15.20.

FIGURE 15.20

Finalize your online setup in the Summary tab.

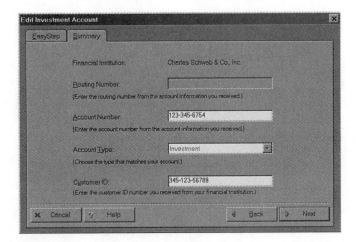

▲   5. Click Done to complete setting up your account.

Setting Up a 401(k) Account

A 401(k) account is similar to a regular investment account, but your employer's 401(k) statements may or may not contain the same detail as a regular investment. Because of this, Quicken offers special setup guidance for 401(k)s so that you can track this investment whether or not your statement provides detailed shares and purchase price information.

To Do: Set Up a 401(K)

1. Select Features, Investing, Track 401(k) to open the 401(k) Setup dialog box, illustrated in Figure 15.21.

2. The initial dialog box provides basic information about setting up a 401(k) in Quicken. Click Next to continue to the next step (see Figure 15.22).

3. Enter an account name and description for this 401(k) and click Next. Figure 15.23 illustrates the next step.

▼

▼
    4. Enter the ending date of your most recent 401(k) statement.

    5. Enter the number of securities (usually mutual funds) that your 401(k) contains and click Next to continue (see Figure 15.24).

Unlike the investment account setup, a 401(k) setup requires you to use the EasyStep process.

FIGURE 15.21

Quicken's 401(k) setup takes into consideration the specifics of tracking a 401(k).

FIGURE 15.22

Enter basic information about your 401(k) in the dialog box.

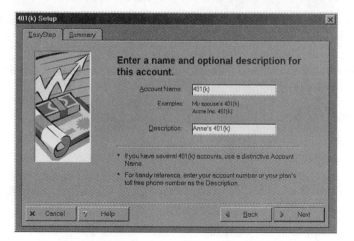

▼

FIGURE 15.23

Enter information from your last 401(k) statement.

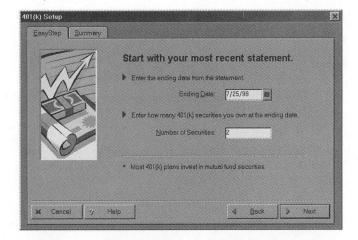

FIGURE 15.24

You can set up a way to track your company's matching contributions.

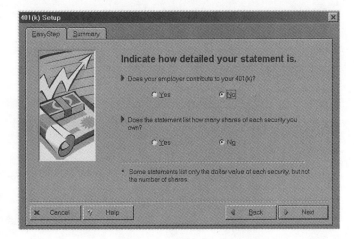

6. Specify whether or not your company provides a matching contribution to your 401(k).

7. Specify whether or not your 401(k) statement indicates how many shares of each security you own. Then click Next. Figure 15.25 illustrates the following step.

8. Enter the security name, the total shares you own, and the ending balance based on your most recent statement. Then click Next to continue.

> The Total Shares field is available only if you indicated in the previous step that your statement lists the total shares you own.

FIGURE 15.25

*Provide information
from your most recent
401(k) statement.*

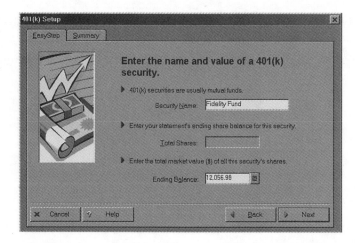

Quicken displays this same dialog box again for as many securities as you indicated
that the 401(k) contains.

9. After you finish entering the last security, click Next. The Summary tab displays,
   as shown in Figure 15.26.

FIGURE 15.26

*You can revise any
incorrect information
on the Summary tab.*

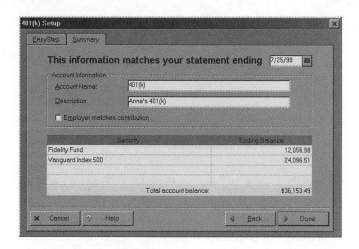

10. If any of this information is incorrect, correct it on the Summary tab.

11. When you're satisfied with the information, click Done.

Quicken creates an account for this 401(k) as well as a 401(k) View from which you can
analyze and update your account. Figure 15.27 illustrates the 401(k) View.

FIGURE 15.27

The 401(k) View provides an overview of your 401(k) investments and performance.

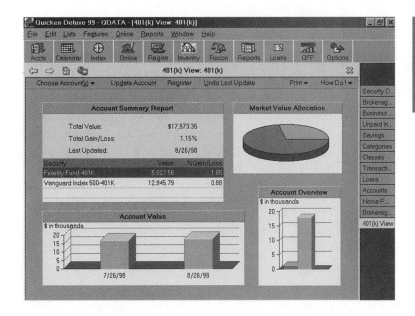

15

Hour 16, "Tracking Investments," covers how to update and enter information in your 401(k) account.

Summary

This hour explained how to set up both regular investment accounts and special accounts to track a 401(k). You can set up investment accounts with as much or as little detail as you want, depending on the type of investment analysis you want Quicken to perform.

Hour 16, "Tracking Investments," continues with information on how to enter and track investment transactions in the accounts you just set up.

Q&A

Q I own many different stocks and mutual funds, but I'm not sure how many accounts to set up.

A You should set up one investment account for each brokerage account you have, regardless of how many securities that account contains. For example, suppose that you have an account with a brokerage firm. That account contains two individual stocks and four mutual funds. You also have an account with a mutual fund company. That account contains just one mutual fund. Even though you own seven securities, you need to create only two Quicken investment accounts.

Q Can I set up a 401(k) in a regular investment account?

A If your 401(k) statement tells you how many shares you own and the price you paid to purchase these shares, then you can also track a 401(k) in a regular investment account. But Quicken's 401(k) account structure provides added flexibility by enabling you track your 401(k)'s performance even without this detailed information. In addition, you can take advantage of the special 401(k) View when you set up your account as a 401(k) rather than a regular investment account.

HOUR 16

Tracking Investments

This hour illustrates how to enter transactions in your investment and 401(k) accounts. Quicken makes it easy to record purchases, sales, and distributions of the stocks, bonds, and mutual funds in your investment account register. If you make more sophisticated investment transactions, such as margin trading, you can track these expenses as well. For 401(k) accounts, Quicken offers a special update tool that takes into consideration differences in 401(k) statements.

The highlights of this hour include

- What types of investment transactions Quicken can track
- How to enter investment transactions in the register
- Where to record advanced transactions
- How to update your 401(k)

Understanding Investment Transactions

Quicken enables you to enter investment transactions in an investment account register. This register is similar in appearance to a register tracking a bank account, but includes fields for entering price, shares, and commissions rather than payments and deposits. Figure 16.1 illustrates a sample investment account register.

FIGURE 16.1

You can record many different kinds of investment transactions in the register.

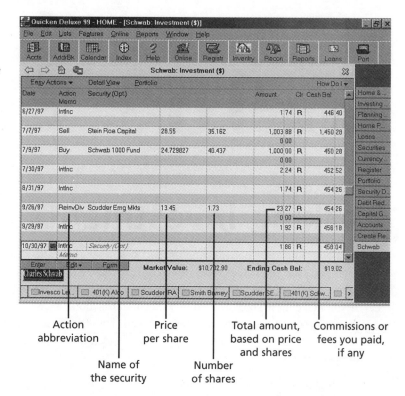

Action abbreviation

Name of the security

Price per share

Number of shares

Total amount, based on price and shares

Commissions or fees you paid, if any

You open an existing investment account just as you would any other account—click the Accts icon on the Iconbar and then double-click the account whose register you want to view.

To enter a transaction in the register, you need to specify an action (buy, sell, reinvest, and so on) and security, and then provide the details of that transaction such as price, shares, and so on.

You can enter a transaction manually or you can use the Easy Actions menu to open a form that provides guidance on entering specific transaction types. Until you become very familiar with the investment register, you probably want to use the Easy Actions menu to help you enter data.

No matter which method you use, it's still a good idea to be familiar with Quicken's investment actions and their abbreviations so that you are able to understand the way the investment register records your transactions. Table 16.1 lists some of the most common investment actions you use, showing both their abbreviation and description. These display in the Action field in the register.

16

TABLE 16.1. QUICKEN INVESTMENT ACTIONS.

Action	Description
Buy	Buy a security with the cash available in your investment account.
BuyX	Buy a security with cash you transfer from another account.
CGLong	Record a long-term capital gain distribution in your investment account.
CGLongX	Record a long-term capital gain distribution and transfer the funds to another account.
CGMid	Record a medium-term capital gain distribution in your investment account.
CGMidX	Record a medium-term capital gain distribution and transfer the funds to another account.
CGShort	Record a short-term capital gain distribution in your investment account.
CGShortX	Record a short-term capital gain distribution and transfer the funds to another account.
Div	Record a dividend distribution in your investment account.
DivX	Record a dividend distribution and transfer the funds to another account.
IntInc	Record interest income in your investment account.
IntIncX	Record interest income and transfer the funds to another account.
ReinvDiv	Record the reinvestment of additional security shares from a dividend distribution.
ReinvInt	Record the reinvestment of additional security shares from an interest distribution.
ReinvLg	Record the reinvestment of additional security shares from a long-term capital gains distribution.
ReinvMd	Record the reinvestment of additional security shares from a medium-term capital gains distribution.
ReinvSh	Record the reinvestment of additional security shares from a short-term capital gains distribution.
Sell	Sell a security and place the proceeds in your investment account.
SellX	Sell a security and transfer the proceeds to another account.
StkSplit	Record a stock split.

Buying and Selling Shares

You can enter the purchase of shares directly in the register or an investment account.

To Do: Buy Shares

1. Select Easy Actions, Buy/Add Shares to open the Buy/Add Shares dialog box,
   shown in Figure 16.2.

FIGURE 16.2

Enter a buy transaction in the Buy/Add Shares dialog box.

2. Click the Summary tab. Figure 16.3 illustrates this tab.

FIGURE 16.3

Use the Summary tab to record your purchase faster.

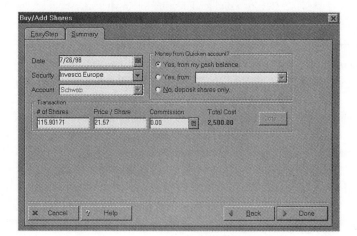

3. Enter the Date of the purchase.

4. Select the Security from the drop-down list or enter the name of a new security.

▼ If you enter a new security, Quicken opens the Set Up Security dialog box when
   you tab out of this field. This dialog box is illustrated in Figure 16.4.

FIGURE 16.4

Set up a new security
in this dialog box.

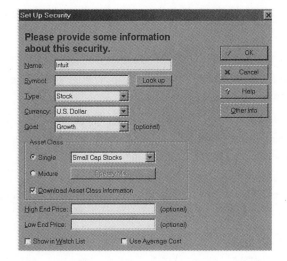

16

5. The Name defaults from your previous entry.

6. Enter the Symbol for this security or click the Look Up button and Quicken
   connects to the Internet to look up the symbol for you.

> You must set up Quicken to connect to the Internet before you can use this
> feature.

7. Select the Type of security from the drop-down list. This list includes all default
   security types plus those you add to Quicken.

8. Select a Currency for this purchase. The U.S. dollar is the default.

9. Choose an optional investment Goal. Quicken prompts you with the goals included
   in the Investment Goal List.

10. You can enter optional asset class information in the Asset Class group box. If this
    security has a single asset class, select it from the Single drop-down list options
    such as Large Cap Stocks, Global Bonds, and so on. Individual stocks and bonds
    usually belong to a single asset class.

11. If this security includes a mixture of asset classes, such as a mutual fund, select
    the Download Asset Class Information check box and Quicken downloads this
▼   information the next time you log on to the Internet.

> You can enter your own asset class mix by selecting the Specify Mix button, but unless you are very sure about the exact mixture, you get more accurate results by downloading this information from the Internet.

12. Enter an optional High End Price and Low End Price for price tracking.

13. Select the Show in Watch List and/or Use Average Cost check boxes to activate these options.

14. Click OK to return to the Buy/Add Shares dialog box.

15. In the Money from Quicken Account group box, specify the source of funds to purchase these shares. Options include the cash balance in your investment account, another account, or the ability to deposit shares only.

16. Next, indicate the number of Shares you bought, the Price per Share, and any Commission you paid. Quicken totals this amount in the Total Cost field.

17. Click Done. Quicken records the transaction in the register.

To Do: Sell Shares

1. Select Easy Actions, Sell/Remove Shares to open the Sell/Remove Shares dialog box, illustrated in Figure 16.5.

FIGURE 16.5

Choose the security you want to sell.

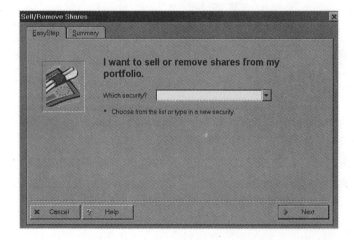

2. Click the Summary tab to continue to the next step, shown in Figure 16.6.

3. Select a Date, Security, and Account.

4. In the Record Proceeds group box, indicate where you want to record the proceeds of the sale. Options include the cash balance of your investment account, another account, or the ability to record share withdrawal only.

FIGURE 16.6

The Summary tab makes recording a security sale even easier.

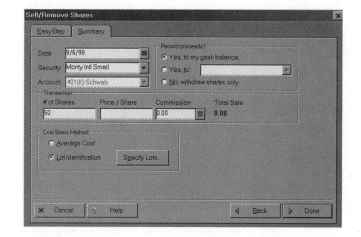

16

5. Next, enter the number of Shares you sold, the Price per Share, and any Commission you paid. Quicken totals up this information in the Total Sale field.

6. Specify the Cost Basis Method you want to use by choosing Average Cost or Lot Identification.

7. If you are only selling some of the shares you own of this security and not all shares, click the Specify Lots button to open the Specify Lots dialog box, shown in Figure 16.7.

8. Use this dialog box to estimate which specific shares to sell. By clicking the First Shares In, Last Shares In, Minimum Gain, and Maximum Gain buttons you can create different scenarios in the upper portion of the dialog box.

FIGURE 16.7

To minimize the tax implications, you can specify the lots you sell.

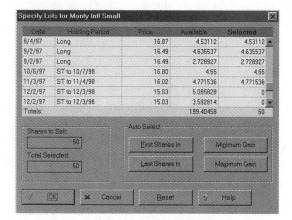

> You can also use the Capital Gains Estimator to analyze the tax implications of selling your securities. Hour 14, "Planning for Taxes," covers this tool in more detail.

9. Click OK to return to the Sell/Remove Shares dialog box.

10. Click Done to record the transaction.

> To start over again, click the Reset button.

> Be aware that selling investments can create numerous tax implications. You can use Quicken tax analysis tools to help you determine these consequences if you are already familiar with your own tax situation. Otherwise, contact your tax professional for more guidance on dealing with investment sale taxes.

Entering Capital Gains, Dividends, and Income

You can enter distributions such as capital gains (short-, medium-, and long-term), dividends, and interest income in one dialog box.

New Term   *Capital gains* refers to the profit (or loss) achieved by selling a security. A dividend is a distribution a company makes to its shareholders based on quarterly earnings.

> If you are reinvesting your proceeds, be sure to use the Reinvest Income dialog box rather than the Record Income dialog box.

To Do: Record Income

1. Select Easy Actions, Record an Income Event to open the Record Income dialog box, illustrated in Figure 16.8.

2. Verify the Date and Account information.

FIGURE 16.8

Record income you receive from capital gains, dividend, and interest distributions.

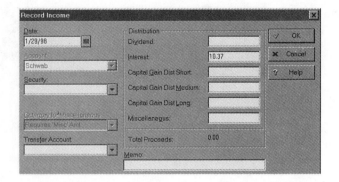

▼

Your brokerage firm statement should indicate the type of income you received so that you can properly record it.

3. Select the Security for which you received income from the drop-down list. Leave this field blank if the income you received was from the account's cash balance.

4. In the Distribution group box, enter the exact amount you received for each type of income.

Entering a Miscellaneous distribution activates the Category for Miscellaneous drop-down list. Select the appropriate category for this miscellaneous distribution so that Quicken knows how to record it.

▲

5. Enter an optional Transfer Account and/or Memo and click OK to record the transaction.

Entering Reinvestments

You can also record distributions that you reinvest in additional shares of a stock or mutual fund by using the Reinvest Income dialog box. Select Easy Actions, Reinvest Income to open this dialog box, displayed in Figure 16.9.

Reinvest Income is almost identical to Record Income, but it includes an extra column for recording the Number of Shares you received (and reinvested) for each distribution.

FIGURE **16.9**

If you reinvest your distributions, record them in this dialog box.

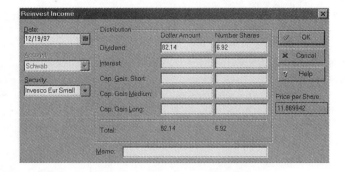

Recording Stock Splits

If a stock splits, you can record this activity and adjust the shares you own and their price accordingly. It's important to record stock splits if you want to maintain accurate records of your investments.

To Do: Record a Stock Split

1. Select Easy Actions, Stock Split to open the Stock Split dialog box (see Figure 16.10).

FIGURE **16.10**

It's important to properly track stock splits.

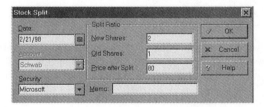

2. Verify the Date and Account information.

3. Select the stock that split from the Security drop-down list.

4. Enter the Split Ratio in terms of New Shares and Old Shares. For example, a 2 for 1 stock split is a common ratio.

5. Enter the new Price After Split.

▲   6. Add a Memo if you want and click OK to record the split in the register.

Recording Account Fees

At times, a brokerage or mutual fund firm charges you an account fee, separate from commission fees that you pay to buy or sell securities. This is most common with retirement accounts, particularly those with low balances.

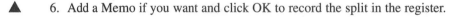

To Do: Record Miscellaneous Account Fees

1. Select Easy Actions, Miscellaneous Expense to open the Miscellaneous Expense dialog box, shown in Figure 16.11.

FIGURE 16.11

Record fees that your brokerage or mutual fund firm charge.

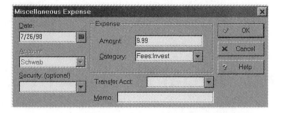

16

2. Verify the Date and Account information and select a Security if the charge pertains to it rather than to the account as a whole.

3. Enter the Expense Amount and select a Category to track it from the drop-down list.

4. Enter an optional Transfer Acct or Memo if needed.

▲   5. Click OK to record the transaction.

Transferring Cash

Quicken also enables you to easily record the transfer of cash into and out of your investment accounts. For example, you might want to buy some new mutual funds and add $10,000 to a mutual fund account to do so. Or you might want to sell some stock in a brokerage account and transfer it to your checking account to pay for a trip or another purchase.

To Do: Transfer Cash into an Investment Account

1. Select Easy Actions, Transfer Cash Into Account. Figure 16.12 displays the Transfer Cash In dialog box.

FIGURE 16.12

You can transfer cash from another account into your investment account.

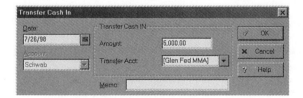

2. Verify the Date and Account information.

▼   3. Enter the Amount of cash you want to transfer.

▼   4. Select the account from which you want to transfer funds in the Transfer Acct drop-down list.

▲   5. Add a Memo if desired and click OK to record this activity.

To transfer cash out of an investment account, select Easy Actions, Transfer Cash From Account to open the Transfer Cash From dialog box, which is almost identical to Transfer Cash In.

Dealing with Special Investment Situations

In addition to basic investment transactions, Quicken has the power and sophistication to deal with more complicated investment dealings as well. Select Easy Actions, Advanced to view a list of advanced investment transaction options. From this menu you can do the following:

- Record margin interest expenses
- Transfer shares between accounts
- Record a corporate name change
- Record corporate securities spin-offs and acquisitions
- Create reminder transactions

Figure 16.13 illustrates an example of an advanced investment transaction, recording margin interest expense.

FIGURE 16.13

If you incur margin interest expense you can record it in the register.

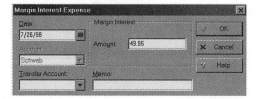

Tracking 401(k) Accounts

If you set up a special 401(k) account to track your 401(k), you update it differently from a regular investment account.

Be sure to have your current statement on hand before updating your 401(k) in Quicken.

To Do: Update a 401(k)

1. Select Features, Investing, Track 401(k) to open the Track My 401(k) dialog box, shown in Figure 16.14.

FIGURE 16.14

Indicate that you want to update your 401(k).

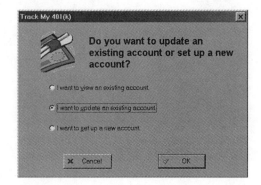

16

2. Choose the I Want to Update an Existing Account option and click OK. Figure 16.15 displays the next step.

FIGURE 16.15

If you have more than one 401(k), you can select the one you want to update.

3. Select the Account Name of the 401(k) you want to update and click OK to continue to the Update 401(k) Account dialog box (see Figure 16.16).

4. Enter the date of the current statement and click Next. Figure 16.17 illustrates the next step.

5. Select the securities you still have in your account.

6. If you added a new security since your last statement, click the Add New Security button. The Add New Security dialog box displays (see Figure 16.18).

FIGURE **16.16**

Enter information from your current statement.

You must use the EasyStep process to update your 401(k). You cannot immediately move to the Summary tab.

FIGURE **16.17**

Specify which securities are in your 401(k).

7. Enter the new Security Name and click OK to return. Click Next to continue to the next step (see Figure 16.19).

8. For each selected security, Quicken displays a step that asks you to enter your total contribution, your employer's contribution, dividends/interest earned, and the ending balance. Click Next to continue to the next step, shown in Figure 16.20.

9. Select Yes if you transferred money from one security to another, otherwise enter No.

FIGURE 16.18

Enter a new security purchase in the Add New Security dialog box.

▼

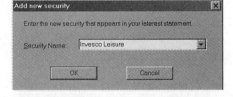

FIGURE 16.19

Enter details about your latest 401(k) activity.

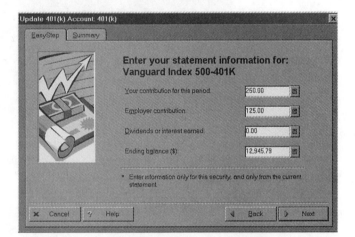

16

FIGURE 16.20

Specify whether you made any transfers.

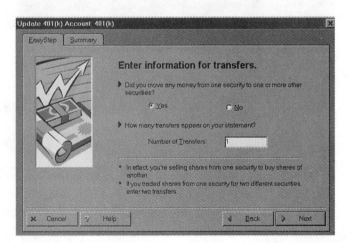

10. If you did transfer funds, indicate how many transfers you made in the Number of Transfers field and click Next. Figure 16.21 displays the next step that appears

▼   only if you responded Yes to this question.

FIGURE 16.21

Then enter the details of this transfer.

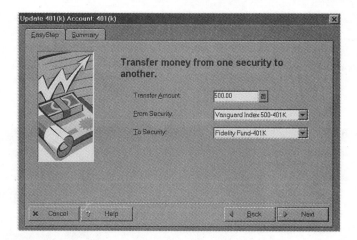

▼

11. Enter the amount of money you transferred, the security you transferred from, and the security you transferred to and click Next. Figure 16.22 illustrates this final step, the Summary tab.

FIGURE 16.22

The Summary tab provides an overview of your current 401(k) status.

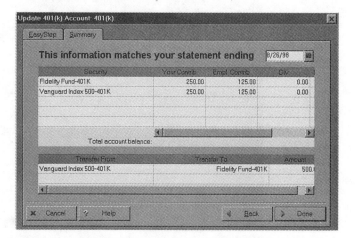

12. Verify the information on this tab, make any necessary changes, and click Done.

13. Quicken displays the 401(k) View that provides an updated look at your most recent 401(k) activity. Figure 16.23 illustrates this view.

▲

If the information in the view looks inaccurate, you can undo the transactions you just entered by selecting Undo Last Update.

Figure 16.23

*The 401(k) View pro-
vides a visual glimpse
of how your 401(k) is
performing.*

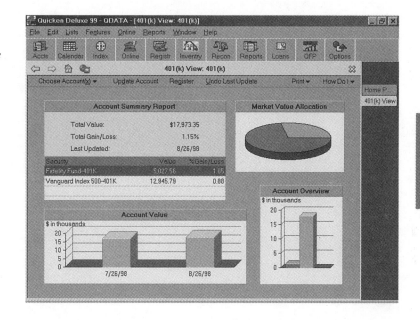

16

Summary

This hour showed you how to enter and track securities in your investment and 401(k)
accounts. Use the investment register to record many common transactions, such as
buying and selling securities. You can also record many complex securities transactions
in the register as well. Use the special 401(k) update feature to help you track your
401(k) regardless of how detailed your statements are.

Hour 17, "Tracking Real Estate," shows you how you to track another important
investment—your home.

Q&A

Q What if I'm not sure what kind of transaction I need to record?

A Some types of transactions such as dividends and capital gains distributions can
be confusing, but usually your account statement should specify the exact type
of transaction that occurred. If you are still confused, call your brokerage or
mutual fund firm to find out the exact nature of the transaction and then record
it accordingly.

Q How can I get a list of my investment transactions?

A Run the Investment Transaction Report that you can access from the Investment
tab in the Create Report window.

HOUR 17

Tracking Real Estate

You can use Quicken 99 to track your real estate investments. When you do, Quicken helps you keep accurate records of your real estate investments, payments, expenses, and current values.

Simply described, the equity in your home is the difference between what the home is worth today (resale value) and how much you owe on it. Of course, in the "real world" this does not necessarily equate the true dollar amount that you would obtain if you sold your home. Many other factors would be considered in this equation, including home improvements needed to be done to sell the house, real estate fees, advertising fees, inspection fees, closing costs (often negotiated between the buyer and the seller), and possible home vacancies during the time the property is on the market.

If you are like many of us in today's fluctuating real estate market, it is sometimes difficult to know whether you currently have positive equity in your home. By periodically assessing your real estate investments, you can easily obtain the "big picture" regarding your real estate holdings.

To track your real estate equity you need two accounts:

- A liability account that shows how much you currently owe on your mortgage. Quicken creates this account automatically when you set up a loan.

- An asset account to track the market value of your real estate. The asset account is an account that you set up yourself.

A loan has a balance that goes down as you make regular payments. A loan in which the amount of principal and interest changes with each payment is called an *amortized* loan. With real estate loans, Quicken keeps track of both the amount of interest you've paid and the loan's outstanding principal balance. As you make payments each month from a checking or savings account to your mortgage company, Quicken transfers the principal portion of the payment to your liability account to decrease its balance. Your decreasing debt and increasing equity is then reflected in your net worth report.

The highlights of this hour include

- How Quicken 99 can calculate the value of your real estate

- How you can use Quicken to pay your home loan

- Updating your home value when it changes

- Managing rental property with Quicken

Tracking Your Home as an Asset

When you begin to track your home as an asset, you must set up a loan account. Quicken asks for basic information about your loan, such as the amount owed, length of the loan, interest rate, and payment method. Quicken creates a liability account to track the principal remaining on the loan. It is a good idea to have your latest mortgage statement handy before you begin.

> You probably receive monthly mortgage statements for your home that reflect the current payment due, the loan balance, and the amounts of the last payment that were credited to interest and principal. These hard copy statements are a good backup and an additional way to double-check the accuracy of your Quicken accounts.

To Do: Set up a Liability Account

To Do

Scenario: You have just received your latest mortgage statement and want to set up a liability account for your home.

1. With the Quicken program open, select File, New. Click the New Quicken Account radio button, and then click the OK button.

2. Click on the Liability radio button, and then click the Next button. Follow the prompts to enter an account name, statement date, and balance due.

3. After desired information is entered, as shown in Figure 17.1, click the Done button.

FIGURE 17.1

The first step in printing a check is to enter a transaction in your checking account.

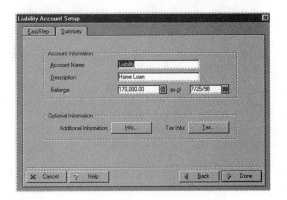

17

Now that you have used the Liability Account Setup wizard, you can set up an amortized loan as well as an asset account for your home. Because you are still in the setup mode, you are prompted to set up an amortized loan and an asset account. You could also set up an asset account by selecting File, New.

A friendly set of dialog boxes prompts you for all the information Quicken needs to break down your loan into payments.

To Do: Set up an Amortized Loan

1. Click the Yes button to set up an amortized loan to be associated with the account.

2. Follow the steps in the Loan Setup Wizard to complete your loan setup. Use the existing liability account you just defined as your associated account, as shown in Figure 17.2.

3. After the amortized loan setup is complete, you are prompted to set up a loan payment. In the Setup Loan Payment dialog box, verify (and change if necessary) your Interest rate and Principal and Interest payment. Select a payment method from the Type drop-down menu in the transaction area of the dialog box. Enter a payee in the Payee field. If you selected a printed check as your payment method, you can click the Address button and enter an address for the payee. Click the Payment Method button to select a memorized, scheduled, or online payment.

FIGURE 17.2

Your loan payments are linked to your associated liability account.

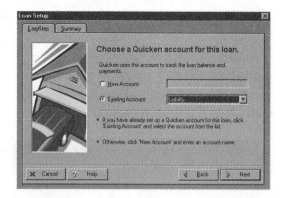

▼

4. When you've completed the dialog box, click the OK button.

5. Next, you are prompted to set up an asset account to go along with this loan. Enter today's date and the value of your home. Remember that the current value is probably not the same amount as the current loan balance due.

▲   After you enter a current value for your home, Quicken automatically opens the liability account you just defined. You can make payments to your loan account from your checking account, as shown in Figure 17.3.

FIGURE 17.3

Defined loan payments can be made from your checking account.

You can also view the status of your home loan, as well as the value of your home from the Quicken 99 Home Page. In Figure 17.4, this information is displayed in the lower-left quarter of the Home Page.

Updating the Market Value of Your Home

As real estate values fluctuate, you want to update the value of your home, thus adjusting your net worth.

To Do: Update Your Home Value

Scenario: You have recently spoken to a real estate agent and have requested "comps" for your property. Surprisingly, your home is valued at a higher amount than you had originally

▼ thought it was worth. You want to update your asset account and view the changes to your asset account.

FIGURE 17.4

Quicken gives you a quick picture of your home assets and liabilities.

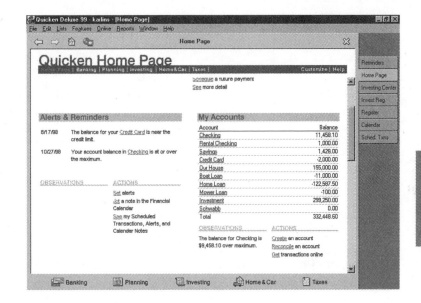

1. Click the link to your Home Loan in the Quicken Home Page.

2. Click the Update Balance button. Remember that this is an asset account, not a loan. The current asset balance is considered to be the value of the asset, not the amount due on your home loan.

▲ 3. Enter a new balance and adjustment date, and then click the OK button.

A net worth report reflects your current assets, liabilities, and total net worth as of a given date.

Now that you have updated you asset account, you can print a net worth report.

To Do: Print a Net Worth Report

1. Click the Home & Car icon on the Activity bar, and then click "Report on my net worth."

2. Scroll through the report to view your total assets, total liabilities, and overall total.

3. Select File, Print Report. Click OK to print the report. The report includes the assets and liabilities associated with your home, as shown in Figure 17.5.

FIGURE 17.5

Quicken includes home value in your net work.

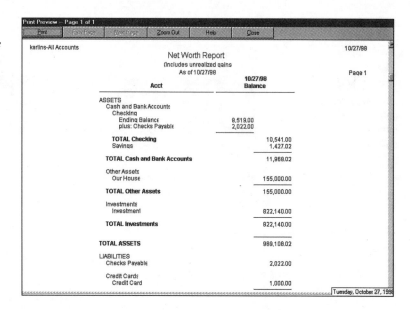

Hour 19, "Creating and Customizing Reports," provides more detailed information on customizing a report.

> Because the real estate market is constantly changing, it is a good idea to set a time frame, such as every six months, to obtain information on the current value of your home. By tracking home values on a regular basis, you are able to gain a good picture of your homes' potential value in the future.

Tracking Home Improvements

Home improvements can add to the value of your home. Home improvements can either be paid for as you go, or they can be financed by either taking out an additional loan on your home or completely refinancing your home.

If you are to pay for home improvements with an additional loan, be sure to set up another liability account for this loan. If you are to refinance your home and pay off your original loan, you must close out the original loan in Quicken as well as set up a new loan.

After home improvements have been made, the added value of the home improvement should be added to your home's asset account. Keep in mind that the cost of the improvement may not be the same as the increased value.

For instance, if you were to remodel your bathroom yourself, you may be able to purchase all the necessary plumbing fixtures, materials, and wall coverings for around $1,500, yet the increase to your homes' value may be $3000.

Conversely, some home improvements are done to suit the homeowners' taste, but may add little or no resale value to the home.

To Do: Track Home Improvements

1. In the Quicken Home page, click the link to the asset account associated with your home loan.

2. Click the Update Balance button, and then enter a new balance based upon the value the home improvement adds to your property. Enter an adjustment date.

3. Select Home Repair as the Category for Adjustment and click the OK button.

> For tax purposes, when a house is sold, you may be able to add the cost of improvements to the original purchase price. To do this, you must keep accurate records. Your receipts, contracts, and canceled checks all serve as hard copy documentation. It is a good idea to keep ongoing home expense records as well. Quicken is an excellent vehicle for this record keeping.

Tracking Rental Property

Rental property can be tracked in Quicken similarly to a home. However, with rental property an income and expense account must be set up as well as a liability account to track real estate loans and an asset account to keep track of the current value.

The market value of rental property can be recorded in an asset account. Keep in mind that the current value of rental property is what you can sell the property for, but that the intrinsic value the property has to you includes both income you can derive from the property as well as tax benefits or liabilities you may incur from rental property.

To gain a "true picture" of the possibilities rental properties have for you, it is advisable to consult with real estate and/or tax experts.

The income and expense account should keep track of the initial deposits received from tenants, monthly payments made by tenants, payments you make for repairs, property taxes, mortgage payments, and refunds made to tenants.

Setting Up Accounts

If you keep a separate checking account for your rental properties, your income and expense account can be recorded in this account. Deposits and payments received from tenants should be assigned an income category. All payments made in conjunction with the rental property should be assigned an expense category.

If your liability account is associated with the loan for this property, you can designate which account the payment is transferred from. As you make payments from the checking account, the memorized mortgage transaction is automatically recorded in the liability account. The correct principal amount is deducted from the loan balance.

To Do: Create a Separate Checking Account to Track Property Transactions

Scenario: You have purchased a duplex apartment building as rental property. You want to set up a checking account to track transactions associated with this property.

1. With the Quicken program open, select File, New. Click the New Quicken Account radio button, and then click the OK button.

2. Click the Checking radio button. Enter a name for this new checking account and a description (such as "Rental Property Checking Account"). Click the Next button.

▲ 3. Follow the prompts to complete the Checking account setup.

> If you have several rental properties and you have multiple accounts for each property, you may want to store each property as a separate Quicken file rather than just another account within the same file.

Tracking Income and Expenses

After your income and expense account is set up, you should enter all transactions associated with your rental property. You may want to develop a daily, weekly, and/or monthly routine for entering this information. If you neglect to enter payments or credits, you do not have a clear picture of the value of your rental investment. Organizing a routine helps you to maintain accurate records.

Let's say that you have received the first month's rent and security deposits from the tenants in both of your duplex apartments. You also have to pay the current mortgage payment on your property. Quicken can help you manage this.

To Do

To Do: Track Rental Income and Expenses

1. Set up liability and asset accounts for your mortgage loan.

2. Enter your rental receipts in your rental checking account, and then enter a check to your mortgage company for the current mortgage payment.

▲ 3. Switch to your liability account and view the recorded mortgage payment.

> For the correct decrease to be recorded in your liability account, your liability and amortized loan must be set up correctly. It is a good idea to have a few months of mortgage statements handy and compare the principal and interest amounts on these statements. If they differ from those recorded in Quicken, you need to go back and readjust the original figures in your account setups.

17

Summary

Mortgage loans are recorded in a liability account. As mortgage payments are made, the principal amount of the payment is deducted from the loan balance. The current value of real estate is recorded in an asset account. This value fluctuates with time and does not necessarily correspond to the loan balance or original loan amount. Home improvements (or conversely, damage to real estate) should be recorded in an asset account to reflect the current home value.

Rental property is also recorded in liability and asset accounts. Additionally, an income and expense account, such as a checking account, should be set up to record all transactions associated with the rental property.

Q&A

Q If I have a liability account set up that shows the current balance due on my loan, why do I also need an asset account?

A Although you owe a given amount on your home, this is not necessarily the worth of the home. An asset account reflects what the home is worth, not just how much is owed.

Q How do I know whether the correct principal is being deducted from my liability account when I record a transaction for a mortgage payment from my savings or checking account?

A View the liability account to find out what decrease is being recorded. Compare this amount against your mortgage statement.

HOUR **18**

Tracking Household Inventory and Personal Financial Records

This hour introduces you to two Quicken Deluxe features—Quicken Home Inventory and the Emergency Records Organizer. Quicken Home Inventory lets you track the contents of your entire house, including the value of all items. The Emergency Records Organizer is a repository of essential information regarding your finances, home, and family. Both of these features provide you with an organized written record of your life for both day-to-day reference and in case of an emergency.

The highlights of this hour include

- What information to track in Quicken Home Inventory
- How to add, edit, delete, and print inventory information
- Which emergency records are important to keep
- How to track and print emergency records

Using Quicken Home Inventory

To open Quicken Home Inventory, select the Inventory icon on the Iconbar. The first time you open Quicken Home Inventory, a welcome dialog box greets you. After that, you'll move directly into the main application, illustrated in Figure 18.1.

FIGURE 18.1

Use Quicken Home Inventory to track the value of your possessions.

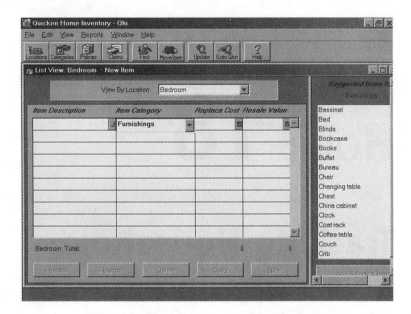

Quicken Home Inventory lists all your valuable household items (furniture, appliances, and so on) by room and lets you track their replacement cost, resale value, and other pertinent information about their purchase. This hour doesn't go into the details of every feature of Quicken Home Inventory, but rather shows you how to perform the most common and essential tasks.

Before you can start an inventory of your home, you first need to set up locations, categories, and other important information.

To Do: Update Locations

1. Click the Locations icon in the Iconbar to display the Locations dialog box, illustrated in Figure 18.2.

   This dialog box lists common household locations. Because it provides only one bedroom and one bathroom listing, however, you'll probably need to add some additional locations.

▼

FIGURE 18.2

You can customize the available locations based on your own home.

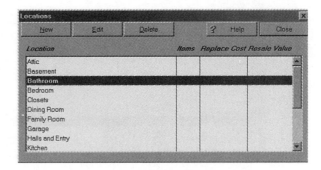

▼

2. To add a new location, click the New button, which displays the New Location dialog box shown in Figure 18.3.

FIGURE 18.3

Add extra bedrooms and baths in the New Location dialog box.

18

3. Enter a new location name, such as Bedroom 2, and click OK. Quicken adds the new location name to the list.

 To rename an existing location—for example, Bathroom to Bathroom 1— click the Edit button and enter the new name in the dialog box.

4. To delete a location that you don't need, select it and click the Delete button. Quicken verifies that you want to delete the location and proceeds with the deletion.

▲ 5. When you've finished modifying locations, click Close.

To Do: Update Categories

1. Click the Categories icon in the Iconbar to display the Categories dialog box, illustrated in Figure 18.4.

   This dialog box lists common household inventory categories, but you'll probably want to update this information to match your household more precisely.

2. To add a new category, click the New button, which displays the New Category dialog box shown in Figure 18.5.

▼

FIGURE 18.4

The Categories dialog box displays a list of default categories.

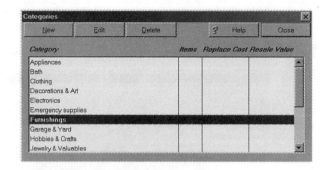

FIGURE 18.5

Use the default categories or create your own category.

3. Enter a new category name, such as Computer Equipment, and click OK. Quicken adds the new category to the list and returns you to the Categories dialog box.

> To rename an existing category, click the Edit button in the Categories dialog box and enter the new name in the dialog box.

4. To delete a category that you don't need, select it and click the Delete button. Quicken verifies that you want to delete the category and proceeds with the deletion.

5. When you've finished modifying categories, click Close.

Updating Insurance Policies

You'll want to indicate which insurance policy covers each household item. Quicken already includes four default policy types:

- Automobile
- Homeowner/Renter
- Special Rider
- Unassigned

If you want to edit these or add additional policies, you can do so in the Policies dialog box. Click the Policies icon on the Iconbar to display this dialog box, illustrated in Figure 18.6.

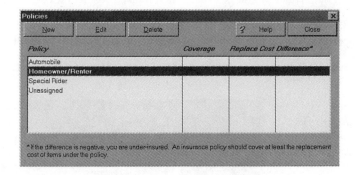

The Policies dialog box is similar to the Locations dialog box and the Categories dialog box. The way in which you can add, edit, and delete policies is almost identical.

> You can also track insurance claims in Quicken Home Inventory. Select the Claims icon on the Iconbar to open the Insurance Claims dialog box.

Entering Home Inventory Items

After you've updated the locations, categories, and policies to match your needs, you can start your home inventory.

> Before entering this information in Quicken, it's a good idea to go through your house writing down an inventory list on paper. To give you an idea of what to inventory, take a look at the lists of suggested items per category.

Select the first location you want to inventory from the View by Location drop-down list. There are two ways to enter your inventory information:

- You can enter the item description and then choose an appropriate item category if you have an exact list of what you want to inventory and know how you want to categorize it. You then enter your own replace cost and resale value.

- You can select an item category first and then use the list of suggested items on the right side of the screen to help you choose appropriate items to inventory. When you find an item, select it to move it to the Item Description list. Quicken also automatically enters an estimated replace cost and resale value that you can edit.

In general, it's probably easier to use the second method, checking off items from your paper list; use the first method only for items that Quicken doesn't automatically list.

Figure 18.7 shows an example of what you might enter for a typical living room.

FIGURE 18.7

A typical living room probably includes several valuable items.

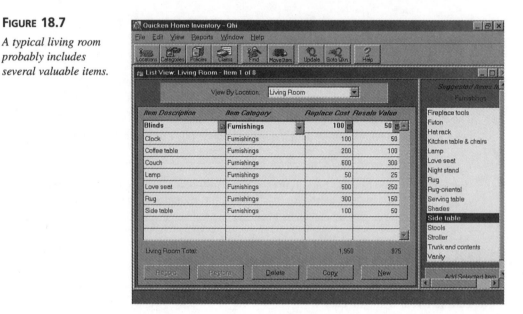

After you finish your home inventory, click the Update icon on the Iconbar. A dialog box asks whether you want to send the information to Quicken. Click Yes if you do. Your open Quicken account is then updated with the information in your home inventory. The next time you run a net worth report, for example, Quicken will include the assets you listed in Quicken Home Inventory.

Deleting, Copying, and Moving Data

After you create a basic home inventory, you can always go back and add new items as you purchase them as well as delete, copy, and move other items.

To delete an item you no longer own, select it in the List View and click the Delete button. After verification, Quicken deletes the item.

You may want to copy an existing inventory item, for example, to save on data-entry time or to enter multiple items. To do so, select the item in the List View and click the Copy button to copy the item to the next line.

If you want to move items, select the MoveItem icon on the Iconbar to open the Move Item dialog box, shown in Figure 18.8.

FIGURE 18.8

You can move items to new locations if you redecorate or move to a new home.

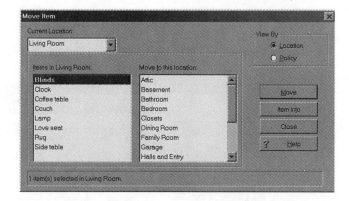

Select the location from the Current Location list and then choose the item you want to move. Finally, select the new location from the Move to This Location list and click the Move button. When you're finished moving items, click Close.

Printing a Home Inventory Report

When you finish entering data, you can print several different reports analyzing this information. Report options include

- Inventory Value Summary
- Inventory Detail
- Insurance Coverage Summary
- Insurance Coverage Detail
- Insurance Claim Summary
- Insurance Claim Detail

To access these reports, select Reports from the menu and choose the report you want to run. Figure 18.9 displays the Inventory Value Summary Report.

You can view this report by category, location, or policy. To preview the report, select the Preview button. The report displays as it will on paper (see Figure 18.10).

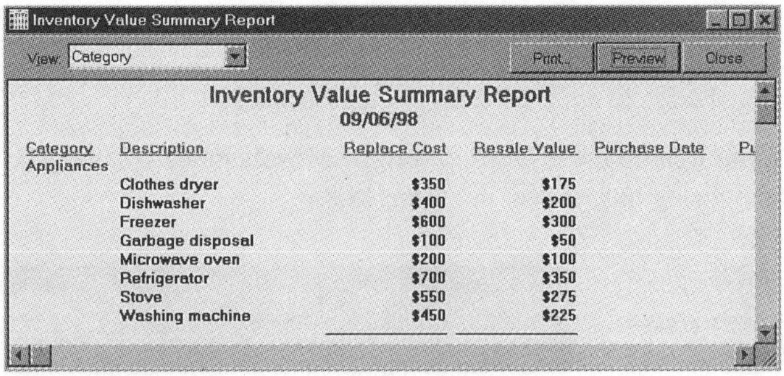

FIGURE 18.9

*An inventory summary
is one of many reports
you can create.*

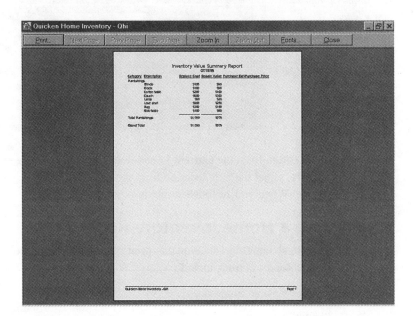

FIGURE 18.10

*Preview your report to
see what it will look
like when printed.*

You can zoom in and out from this view as well as change report fonts. When you're
done previewing, click Close.

To print the report, click the Print button to open the Print dialog box.

Select the destination printer as well as other options and then click OK.

Exiting Quicken Home Inventory

To exit Quicken Home Inventory, choose File, Exit. A dialog box prompts you to back
up your data. To return to Quicken, leaving Quicken Home Inventory open, select the
GoTo Qkn (Go to Quicken) icon on the Iconbar.

Using the Emergency Records Organizer

The Emergency Records Organizer helps you organize your family's medical, legal, and financial records. To use it, select Features, Planning, Emergency Records Organizer. Figure 18.11 displays the Emergency Records Organizer.

FIGURE 18.11

Track important medical, legal, and financial records in the Emergency Records Organizer.

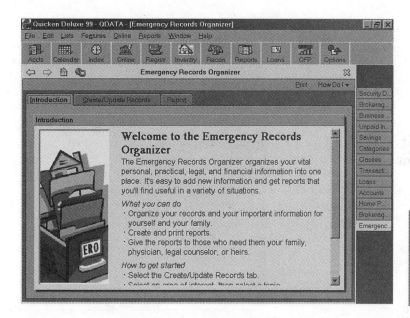

 Before you start, you should assemble all the medical, legal, and financial information you want to record, or have easy access to it.

To Do: Enter Records

1. Click the Create/Update Records tab, shown in Figure 18.12.

   You can enter information on the following areas:

   - Adults' Emergency Info
   - Children's Emergency Info
   - Adults' Important Info
   - Children's Important Info
   - Personal and Legal Docs
   - Accounts

18

- Income
- Invest and Retirement
- Home/Auto/Property
- Insurance
- Mortgage/Loans

FIGURE 18.12

You can create records in three steps.

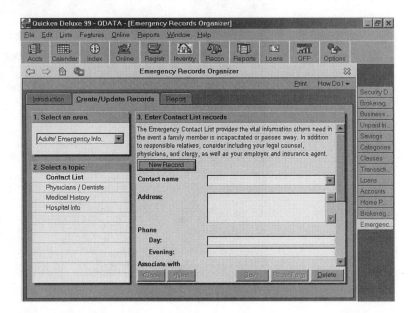

2. Choose one of these areas in the drop-down list in Step 1 of the Create/Update Records tab.

3. Step 2 of the Create/Update Records tab provides a list of related topics. Select a specific topic. The right side of the window then displays a form for you to fill out.

4. In Step 3 of the Create/Update Records tab, fill out the form with as much detail as you want.

5. When you finish entering information in the form, click Save.

6. You can add another record for this topic by selecting the New Record button, or continue to another topic.

7. Continue through Steps 1, 2, and 3 until you've entered all the records you want to track.

You can delete a record by selecting the Delete button.

You can scroll through the records you've entered by clicking the Back and Next buttons.

Printing an Emergency Records Report

After you've finished entering all your emergency records, you can create a variety of reports, each targeted for a specific situation or person. These include:

- Emergency Report
- Caretaker Report
- Survivor's Report
- Summary of Records Entered Report
- Detail Report

To run one of these reports, select the Report tab, shown in Figure 18.13.

FIGURE 18.13

You can print a variety of emergency record reports.

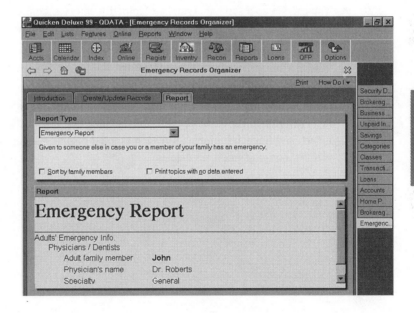

You can sort the report by family member or choose to include or exclude topics that have no data. The lower part of the window previews the selected report's contents.

To print the report, click the Print button. Quicken prints the report using default settings.

Summary

This hour showed you how to use the Quicken Home Inventory and Emergency Records Organizer to track the important details of your life. Use Quicken Home Inventory to

Organizer to track the important details of your life. Use Quicken Home Inventory to inventory and value all the contents of your home, for informational and emergency use. Use the Emergency Records Organizer to help you track your medical, legal, and financial records in as much—or as little—detail as you want.

Hour 19, "Creating and Customizing Reports," starts a new section devoted to viewing and analyzing your Quicken data.

Q&A

Q I have a vacation home. How do I track the inventory for this home separately?

A You can set up a separate Quicken Home Inventory account for it. Select Edit, Options to display the Options dialog box. In the General tab, you can specify a different Quicken Account Name for this home.

Q Which emergency records are the most important for me to keep?

A If you're going to use the Emergency Records Organizer, be sure to track essential medical information such as doctors' names and important medical history facts, legal information such as your attorney's name and the location of legal documents, and financial information such as a list of major accounts and numbers as well as mortgage and loan details.

PART V
Analyzing Your Financial Data

Hour

HOUR 19

Creating and Customizing Reports

This hour introduces you to Quicken's reporting features. After you've entered substantial data, you will probably want to create reports analyzing this information. Quicken includes many ready-made reports—dealing with your personal, investment, and business finances—that you can run instantly. You can also customize these reports and memorize them for future use. Finally, if you would rather just ask a question in plain English than determine what kind of report you need, Quicken offers EasyAnswer reports to make things even simpler.

The highlights of this hour include

- What kinds of Quicken reports you can create
- Why you might want to create an EasyAnswer report
- Where in the register you can create a QuickReport
- How to create a report
- How to customize and memorize a report
- How to print a report

Determining the Kinds of Reports You Can Run

Quicken includes many ready-made reports for banking, planning, investment, taxes, and business use. Before you create any reports at all, you should familiarize yourself with the available reports and report types.

Looking at Banking Reports

Quicken includes five reports that specifically detail your banking activity. These include

- *Account Balances*. Displays a summary of account balances.
- *Transaction*. Displays transactions from selected accounts.
- *Missing Checks*. Displays checking account transactions, highlighting missing and duplicate checks.
- *Summary*. Displays transactions summarized by category.
- *Comparison*. Displays income and expense comparisons by category.

Figure 19.1 illustrates an example of an Account Balances Report.

FIGURE 19.1

The Account Balances Report is one of five Quicken banking reports.

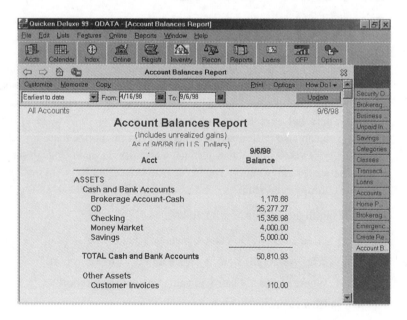

Looking at Planning Reports

Quicken also offers several reports that help you plan and analyze your finances, including

- *Net Worth*. Displays assets and liabilities by account value.
- *Monthly Budget*. Displays a comparison of your budget estimates versus your actual income and expenses.
- *Budget*. Displays a comparison of income and expenses against a preset budget.
- *Itemized Categories*. Displays an itemization of all transactions subtotaled by category.
- *Cash Flow*. Displays summarized income and expenses by category.
- *Comparison*. Displays a comparison of income and expenses by category over specified periods.

Figure 19.2 shows an example of a Cash Flow Report.

FIGURE 19.2

A Cash Flow Report is just one of many reports for home users.

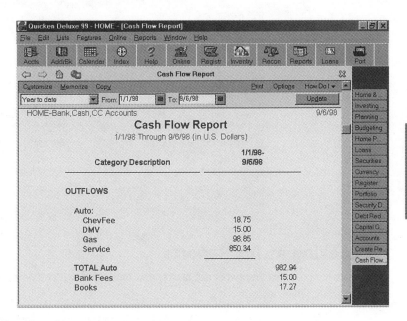

Looking at Investment Reports

Quicken also offers five reports for investors. Investment reports detail and analyze the stocks, bonds, and mutual funds you hold in your investment accounts. These include

- *Portfolio Value*. Displays the total value of investment accounts.
- *Investment Performance*. Displays the average annual total return of your investments.
- *Investment Income*. Displays a summarized list of investment income and expenses.
- *Capital Gains*. Displays capital gains on investments you sold.
- *Investment Transactions*. Displays a list of investment transactions you entered in the register.

Figure 19.3 offers an example of a Portfolio Value Report.

FIGURE 19.3

This investment report shows you the total value of your investment portfolio.

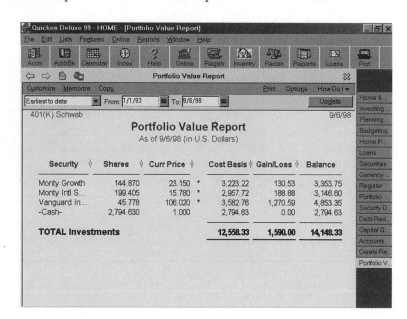

Looking at Tax Reports

Quicken provides three specific tax reports that offer necessary financial information at tax time. These include

- *Tax Summary*. Displays a list of tax-related transactions by category.
- *Capital Gains*. Displays capital gains on investments you sold.
- *Tax Schedule*. Displays a list of tax-related transactions subtotaled by line item.

Figure 19.4 offers an example of a Tax Summary Report.

FIGURE 19.4

A Tax Summary Report can help you do your income taxes.

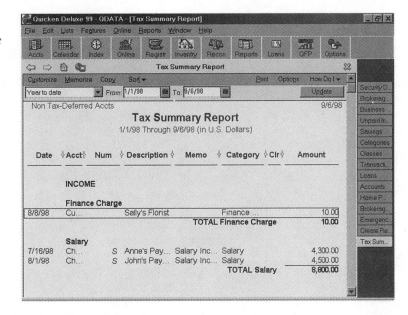

Looking at Business Reports

If you use Quicken to track business income and expenses, you can create a variety of reports to analyze these transactions and their results. The business reports include

- *Profit & Loss Statement*. Displays a summarized profit and loss statement by category.
- *Profit & Loss Comparison*. Displays a profit and loss statement comparing two selected periods.
- *Cash Flow*. Displays summarized income and expenses by category.
- *A/P by Vendor*. Displays a summarized list by vendor of bills to pay.
- *A/R by Customer*. Displays a summarized list by customer of payments to be received.
- *Job/Project*. Displays a summarized list of income and expenses by class.
- *Payroll*. Displays a summarized list of income and expenses by employee.
- *Balance Sheet*. Displays a business balance sheet, calculating equity, assets, and liabilities.
- *Missing Checks*. Displays checking account transactions, highlighting missing and duplicate checks.
- *Comparison*. Compares income and expenses by category over specified periods.

Figure 19.5 previews an example of a Profit & Loss Statement Report.

FIGURE 19.5

*You can also create
reports for your small
business, such as this
Profit & Loss
Statement Report.*

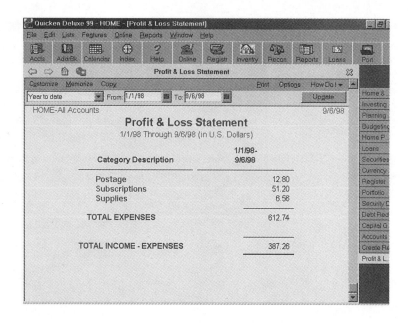

Creating an EasyAnswer Report

If you aren't sure which report you need or you want to ask a question in plain English,
an EasyAnswer report can simplify your reporting needs.

To create an EasyAnswer report, select Reports, EasyAnswer Reports. Figure 19.6 shows
the EasyAnswer Reports & Graphs dialog box.

FIGURE 19.6

*Ask a question in plain
English, and get a
report as your answer.*

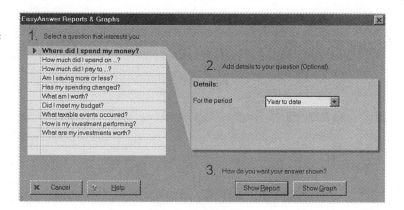

In Step 1 of the EasyAnswer Reports & Graphs dialog box, you select the question you want to ask. Questions include

- *Where did I spend my money?* Asks you to enter a period of time. Displays a Cash Flow Report.

- *How much did I spend on...?* Asks you to select an optional category and period of time. Displays an Itemized Categories Report.

- *How much did I pay to...?* Asks you to specify a payee and period of time. Displays an Itemized Categories Report.

- *Am I saving more or less?* Asks you to compare data between two periods. Displays a Comparison Report.

- *Has my spending changed?* Asks you to select a category and two periods. Displays a Comparison Report.

- *What am I worth?* Asks you enter a period of time. Displays a Net Worth Report.

- *Did I meet my budget?* Asks you for a period of time. Displays a Budget Report.

- *What taxable events occurred?* Asks you to enter a period of time. Displays a Tax Summary Report.

- *How is my investment performing?* Asks you to select an investment (or investments) as well as a period of time. Displays an Investment Performance Report.

- *What are my investments worth?* Asks you to select a period of time. Displays a Portfolio Value Report.

In Step 2, you specify additional information related to this question, such as the period on which you want to report.

Finally, click the Show Report button to display the requested report.

> The EasyAnswer Reports & Graphs dialog box also enables you to create graphs based on this same information. Hour 20, "Creating and Customizing Graphs," covers this in more detail.

19

Running a QuickReport

A QuickReport is a report that analyzes the transactions in a register. You can quickly summarize all of the open register's transactions or report on a specific payee or entry you've selected. For example, suppose that you have a bank CD and want to know how much interest you've received this year. With the register open for this account, select one of the interest transactions and click the Reports button. A menu of available options displays, as shown in Figure 19.7.

FIGURE 19.7

Select from several QuickReport options.

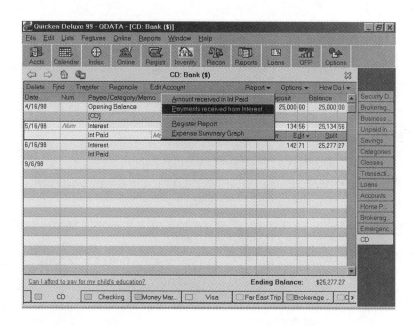

One of the options is to show the payments received from interest. Select this option; a report displays showing you this total amount for the year (see Figure 19.8).

FIGURE 19.8

A QuickReport reports on data in the register.

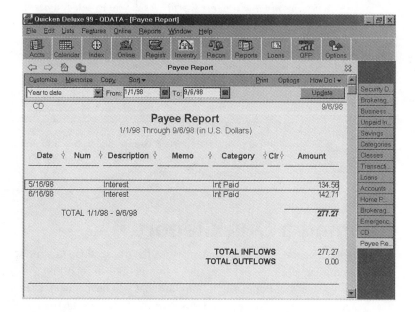

To Do: Create Quicken Reports

1. Click the Reports icon on the Iconbar to open the Create Report window, shown in Figure 19.9.

FIGURE 19.9

You can run one of many ready-made reports from the Create Report window.

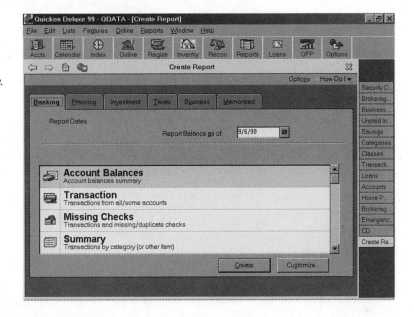

You can also open the Create Report window by selecting Reports, and then either Banking, Planning, Investment, Taxes, or Business to display a menu of available reports.

19

2. Click the tab of the report category you want to view, such as Banking or Investment.

3. Select the specific report you want to display from the list of reports. The upper portion of the window changes to display selection criteria for this report.

4. Select the report criteria, such as report dates and time frames.

5. Click the Create button to display the requested report.

You can scroll up and down to see the entire report. Figure 19.10 displays a sample of
▼ the Net Worth Report.

FIGURE 19.10

Scroll through your report to see it in its entirety.

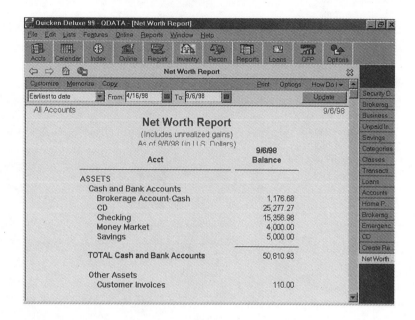

▲

QuickZooming to More Detail

To view the detail behind a summarized item, you can request a QuickZoom report. To do so, select the line to which you want to zoom. Double-click the QuickZoom button that displays (a magnifying glass with a *z*) to open the report. Figure 19.11 displays a QuickZoom report.

Click the Close window icon (the X) to return to the original report.

Updating Reports with New Information

If you want to change report parameters, select new options in the drop-down lists in the customize bar and then click the Update button (see Figure 19.12). The report is updated based on the new parameters.

If the customize bar doesn't appear, select the Options button in the report window and verify that the Show the Customize Bar check box is selected in the Report Options dialog box that displays.

FIGURE 19.11

QuickZoom provides a way to zero in on more report details.

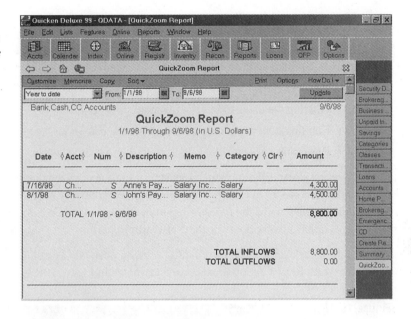

FIGURE 19.12

Change your basic report parameters and see the updated information displayed immediately.

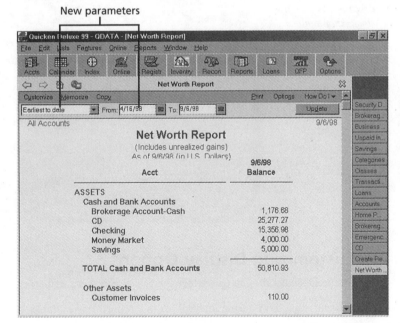

19

Customizing Reports

If none of the existing reports suits your needs, you can customize a report. Quicken offers a multitude of customization options, many of which you may never use. The most common report customizations include:

- Altering the dates to include different time periods
- Limiting a report to only certain accounts, categories, or classes
- Renaming a report title

There are slight differences in the customization options available, depending on what kind of report you're customizing. But in general, customizing Quicken reports is very similar regardless of the types of reports you are customizing. As an example, examine the customization options for the Net Worth Report.

To do so, select the Customize button from an open Net Worth Report. The Customize Net Worth Report dialog box appears, as shown in Figure 19.13.

FIGURE 19.13

Quicken includes many customization options.

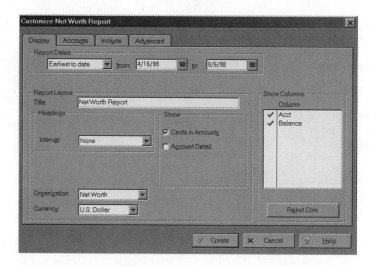

Customizing Display Options

On the Display tab, you can select specific report dates and enter a report title.

You can also select a time interval for this report. For example, if you want to compare your net worth by year and have three years' worth of data in your Quicken file, you can select the Year interval to view the report this way. If you want to summarize your net worth as of today, select None as your interval option.

In the Organization field, you can choose to display this report either as a Net Worth Report (for an individual or family) or as a Balance Sheet Report (for a business).

The Currency field defaults to the U.S. dollar. If you want to display your report in another currency, select it from the list.

Select the Cents in Amounts check box to display amounts with two decimal places such as $193.87. If you leave this check box blank, the amount would display as $194, rounded to the nearest dollar.

Select the Account Detail check box to provide more detailed information about each account, such as a list of investments in each investment account.

Finally, you can choose which columns to display by selecting or deselecting the available columns in the Show Columns group box.

Customizing Account Options

On the Accounts tab, shown in Figure 19.14, you can specify the exact accounts to include in your report.

FIGURE 19.14

Specify the accounts or account types on which to report.

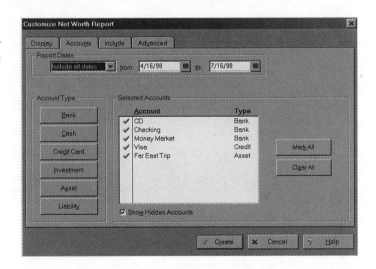

19

To include all accounts of a certain account type, such as Bank, Credit Card, or Investment, click the corresponding button in the Account Type group box. To select or deselect accounts individually, click the accounts in the Selected Accounts list. A green check mark appears before selected accounts.

Click the Mark All button to include all accounts. Click the Clear All button to exclude all accounts and start again.

If you want to include hidden accounts, click the Show Hidden Accounts check box.

Customizing Categories and Classes

On the Include tab, you can select specific categories and classes to include. Figure 19.15 illustrates this tab.

Select either the Categories or Classes button to display the appropriate list and then select the categories or classes you want to include. The report will include those categories and classes with a green check mark.

FIGURE 19.15

Selecting specific categories and classes can even further narrow down your report.

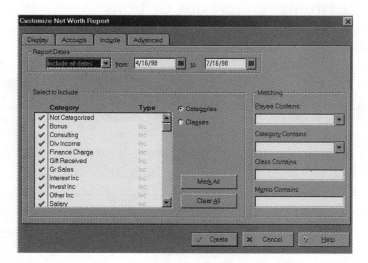

To save time, you can mark all or clear all the options in the list.

You can also create an exact match by payee, category, class, or memo by selecting the desired item from the drop-down lists in the Matching group box.

Setting Advanced Report Options

On the Advanced tab (see Figure 19.16), you can set a variety of other options.

FIGURE 19.16

The Advanced tab includes several more sophisticated options for your report.

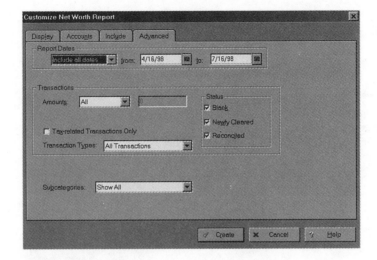

You can include all amounts, or only those less than, equal to, or greater than a specified amount.

Select the Include Unrealized Gains check box to include these gains in your net worth. Select the Tax-Related Transactions Only check box to include only transactions whose category you designated as relating to taxes.

You can specify the exact transaction types you want to include: all transactions, payments, deposits, or unprinted checks. And you can determine how to handle transfers: include all, exclude all, or exclude internal transfers.

In addition, you can show all, hide all, or show reversed subcategories. Reversed subcategories reverse the order in which categories and subcategories display. For example, if you created Gas and Service subcategories for the Auto category, your report would normally display Gas and Service directly under Auto. Reversing the transactions would display Gas and Service separately.

Finally, the Status group box lets you choose the status of the transactions you include: Blank, Newly Cleared (c), and/or Reconciled (R). The status refers to the entry in the Clr register field.

Completing Report Customizations

When you've made all necessary customizations, click the Create button to redisplay your report. If the results aren't what you expected, you can make further customizations. After you customize a report, you will probably want to refer to it again. Rather than continually making the same customizations, you can memorize the customized report for future use.

19

To Do: Memorize a Customized Report

1. Click the Memorize button in the Create Report window. Figure 19.17 shows the Memorize Report dialog box, which displays.

FIGURE 19.17

Memorize your custom reports so that you can refer to them in the future.

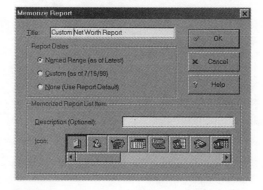

> Click the Edit button to edit the information in this dialog box after you've saved it.

2. In the Title field, enter a new title for this report.

3. Specify the report dates to use. Options include Named Range (which includes transactions as of the day you run the report), Custom (which include transactions as of the day you created the report), or None (which uses the report default).

4. If you want to create an icon for this report, enter the icon description and choose from the list the icon to display. This icon appears next to the report name in the list of memorized reports.

> The icon you associate with a memorized report does not appear on the Iconbar.

Quicken adds all memorized reports to the report list under the Memorized tab in the Create Report window.

> Under the Reports menu, you'll find a list of the last four reports you've memorized for easy access.

▲

Deleting a Memorized Report

To delete a report you customized and memorized, select the Memorized tab in the Create Report window. Choose the report you want to delete and click the Delete button. Quicken verifies you want to delete the selected report before deletion.

Customizing Default Report Options

To customize reporting options, click the Options button. Figure 19.18 displays the Report Options dialog box.

FIGURE 19.18

Customize report defaults in this dialog box.

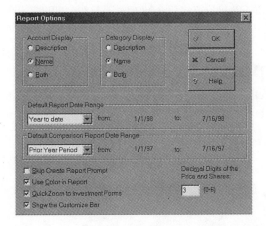

 You can also access this dialog box by clicking the Options icon and selecting the Reports button.

19

You can set the following options:

- *Account Display*. Specifies whether to display the description, the name, or both the name and description of the account in your report.
- *Category Display*. Specifies whether to display the description, the name, or both the name and description of the account in your report.
- *Default Report*. Date Range and Default Comparison Report Date Range. Specifies the default date range for the type of report. The drop-down list offers 12 different options—you can include all dates, or specify a certain month, quarter, year, and so on.

- *Skip Create Report Prompt.* Immediately displays the actual report when you select it from the menu. If you don't select this option, the Create Report window opens when you select a report from the menu, highlighting the designated report.

- *Use Color in Report.* Displays the report in color onscreen.

- *QuickZoom to Investment Options.* Displays the appropriate investment form when you QuickZoom in an investment report. If you don't select this option, QuickZoom displays the register transaction.

- *Show the Customize Bar.* Displays the bar that lets you change date parameters and update the report.

- *Decimal Digits of the Price and Shares.* Sets the number of decimal places that are used in your report's figures. Choices range from 0 to 6 decimal places.

Printing Reports

To print a report, click the Print button in the Create Report window. The Print dialog box displays, as shown in Figure 19.19.

In the Print To group box, select the printer to which you want to print and then click OK.

FIGURE 19.19

After you've seen your report onscreen, you may want to print it.

Summary

This hour explored the many different ways you can create reports in Quicken. If you want to create a report based on a question asked in plain English, try an EasyAnswer report. If you want to analyze or summarize data in a register, a QuickReport can provide an easy answer. For the most flexibility, Quicken provides numerous other ready-made reports for personal, investment, and business finances that you can customize if necessary.

Hour 20, "Creating and Customizing Graphs," introduces you to the related tasks of creating graphs to analyze your Quicken data.

Q&A

Q What is the easiest way to run a report?

A If you're in a hurry or don't know a lot about reports yet, creating an EasyAnswer report or QuickReport is the way to go. But later you'll want to explore the more powerful capabilities of Quicken's other ready-made reports, which are also easy to use and customize.

Q I can't see all the data in my report columns. What can I do?

A You can adjust the width of report columns by selecting them and dragging the mouse to adjust the size.

19

HOUR **20**

Creating and Customizing Graphs

This hour shows you how to create graphs, including bar charts and pie charts, that analyze your financial data. You can display one of five ready-made graph types or customize these to create a specific graph that suits your needs. You can also memorize these custom graphs for future use. Finally, if you want to ask a question in plain English and see a response in a graphical format, Quicken offers EasyAnswer graphs to make things even simpler.

The highlights of this hour include

- What kinds of Quicken graphs you can view
- Why you might want to create an EasyAnswer graph
- How to create a graph
- How to customize and memorize a graph
- How to print a graph

Determining the Kinds of Graphs You Can Run

Quicken includes five ready-made graphs that graphically summarize your spending, net worth, and investments. Before you create a graph, you should first familiarize yourself with what each displays:

- *Income and Expenses Graph.* Displays a monthly income and expenses bar chart as well as a pie chart analyzing net savings versus expenses per category. Figure 20.1 illustrates this graph.

FIGURE 20.1

The Income and Expense Graph is one of five Quicken graphs that you can use to analyze your financial data.

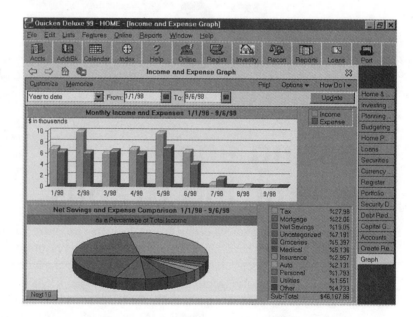

- *Budget Variance Graph* (see Figure 20.2). Displays two bar charts—actual versus budgeted net income, and actual versus budgeted category groups (discretionary, nondiscretionary, and so on).

FIGURE 20.2

You can view your budget information in two ways using the Budget Variance Graph.

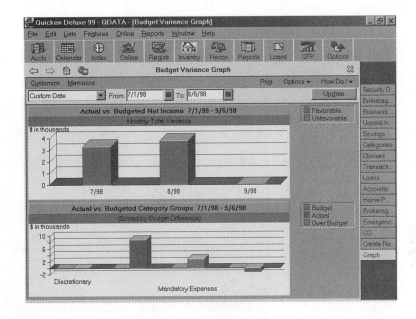

• *Net Worth Graph.* Displays a bar chart illustrating your assets, liabilities, and net worth. Figure 20.3 shows this graph.

FIGURE 20.3

Determine your net worth in relation to assets and liabilities is easy with a Net Worth Graph.

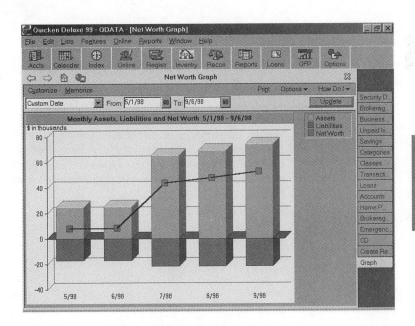

20

- *Investment Performance Graph* (see Figure 20.4). Displays two bar charts, one illustrating your monthly portfolio value and the other your average annual total return. You can display by security type (stock, mutual fund, and so on), investment goal, security name, account, or asset class.

FIGURE 20.4

Knowing the value of your portfolio and its average return is essential to developing a sound investment strategy.

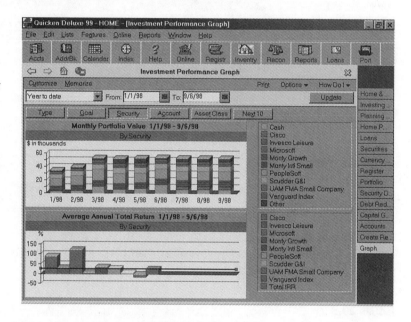

- *Investment Asset Allocation Graph* (see Figure 20.5). Displays a pie chart that details the percentage of your portfolio invested in each asset class, such as large cap stocks, international stocks, and so on.

You can specify the asset class of each investment when you set it up using the Set Up Security dialog box. If you're not sure of the asset class or if you have mutual funds with a mixture of asset classes, you can retrieve this information online by selecting Update Prices, Get Asset Classes from within Portfolio View.

FIGURE 20.5

Use this pie chart to determine how much of your money you have in specific asset classes.

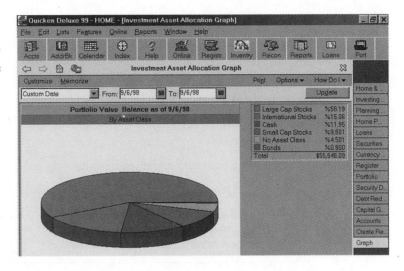

Creating an EasyAnswer Graph

If you want to ask a question in plain English and view a graphical answer to this question, try a Quicken EasyAnswer graph. To create an EasyAnswer graph, select Reports, EasyAnswer Reports. Figure 20.6 shows the EasyAnswer Reports & Graphs dialog box.

FIGURE 20.6

Ask a question in plain English and Quicken will answer your question graphically.

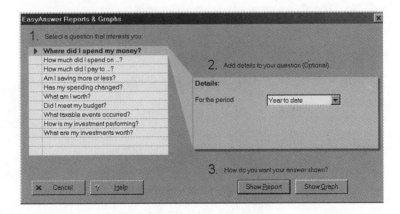

20

Only 4 of the 10 questions listed in Step 1 of the EasyAnswer Reports & Graphs dialog box provide the option to display a graph that answers the question. These include:

- *Where did I spend my money?* Asks you to enter a period of time. Displays an Income and Expense Graph.

- *What am I worth?* Asks you enter a period of time. Displays a Net Worth Graph.

- *Did I meet my budget?* Asks you for a period of time. Displays a Budget Variance Graph.

- *How is my investment performing?* Asks you to select an investment (or investments) as well as a period of time. Displays an Investment Performance Graph.

In Step 2, you specify additional information related to this question, such as the period on which you want to report.

Finally, click the Show Graph button to display the relevant graph.

You can also create a report based on any of the 10 available questions in the EasyAnswer Reports & Graphs dialog box. Hour 19, "Creating and Customizing Reports," covers this in more detail.

Creating Quicken Graphs

To view one of Quicken's ready-made graphs, perform the steps in the following "To Do" section.

To Do: Create a Quicken Graph

1. Click the Graphs icon on the Iconbar to open the Create Graph dialog box, shown in Figure 20.7.

FIGURE 20.7

You can run one of many ready-made graphs from the Create Graph dialog box.

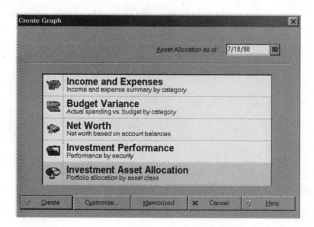

> You can also open the Create Graph dialog box by selecting Reports, Graphs, and then the name of the graph from the menu that displays.

2. Select the specific graph you want to display from the list of graphs. The upper portion of the dialog box changes to display selection criteria for this graph.

3. Select the graph criteria, such as dates and time frames.

▲   4. Click the Create button to display the requested graph.

Updating Graphs with New Information

If you want to change graph parameters, select new options in the drop-down lists in the customize bar and then click the Update button (see Figure 20.8). Quicken updates the graph based on the new parameters.

FIGURE 20.8

Update your graph immediately with new date parameters.

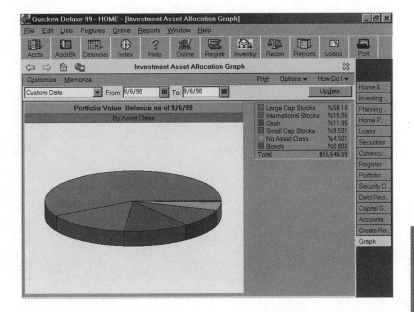

> If the customize bar doesn't appear, click the Options button and choose Show Customize Bar from the menu that displays.

Printing Graphs

To print a graph, click the Print button in the graph window. Quicken automatically prints the graph.

Customizing Graphs

You can customize a graph by altering date parameters and selecting only specific accounts, categories, or classes to include. There are slight differences in the customization options available depending on which graph you're customizing. But in general, customizing is quite similar for each type of Quicken graph. As an example, examine the customization options for the Income and Expenses Graph.

To do so, select the Customize button from an open Income and Expenses Graph. The Customize Graph dialog box appears, shown in Figure 20.9.

FIGURE 20.9

Quicken includes several customization options for your graphs.

You can select specific graph dates just as you can in the customize bar. You can also choose to show subcategories in a graph, which expands on the detail you see in the Net Savings and Expense Comparison pie chart.

The Currency field defaults to the U.S. dollar. If you want to display your graph in another currency, select it from the drop-down list.

The Currency field displays only if you select Multi-currency Support on the Settings tab in the General Options dialog box.

Next, select the accounts, categories, and classes you want to include from the tabs of the same name. A green check mark appears before selected items. To select an item, click it.

To include all listed items, click the Mark All button. Click the Clear All button to exclude all items and start again.

On the Accounts tab, click the Show Hidden Accounts check box if you want to include hidden accounts.

When you're finished customizing your graph, click OK. The revised graph displays. If the results aren't what you expect, you can make further customizations.

Memorizing a Customized Graph

After you customize a graph, you will probably want to refer to it again. Rather than continually making the same customizations, you can memorize the customized graph for future use. To do so, click the Memorize button in the graph window. Figure 20.10 shows the Memorize Graph dialog box that displays.

FIGURE 20.10

Memorize custom graphs so that you can refer to them in the future.

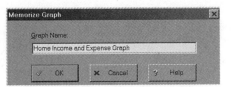

20

Enter a new graph name for this memorized graph. To open a memorized graph at some time in the future, you can:

- Select the Graphs icon on the Iconbar, click the Memorize button in the Create Graph dialog box that displays, and choose a memorized graph from the Memorized Graphs dialog box (see Figure 20.11).

- Select Reports, Graphs, Memorized Graphs from the menu and choose the graph from the Memorized Graphs dialog box that displays.

FIGURE 20.11

After you memorize a graph, you can display it again and again.

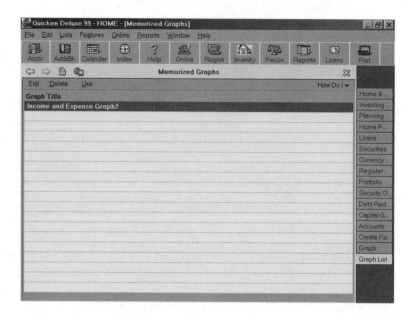

Deleting a Memorized Graph

To delete a graph you customized and memorized, select the graph from the graph list in the Memorized Graphs dialog box and click the Delete button. Quicken confirms you want to delete the graph and then proceeds with the deletion.

Customizing Default Graph Options

You can customize the default graph options if you want. Quicken offers three ways to do this. You can:

- Select Edit, Options, Graphs to display the Graph Options dialog box, shown in Figure 20.12.

FIGURE 20.12

Customize graph defaults in this dialog box.

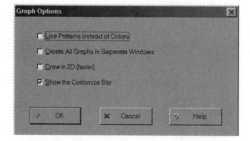

- From an open graph, right-click and select Options from the shortcut menu to open the Graph Options dialog box.

- From an open graph, click the Options button to display a menu of similar options that appear in the Graph Options dialog box (see Figure 20.13).

FIGURE 20.13

You can also set graph options from a menu.

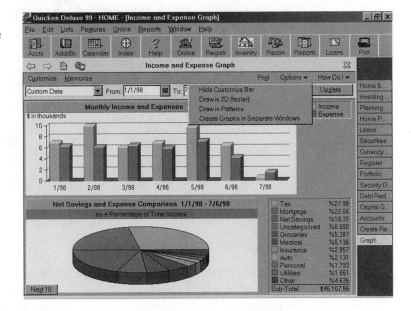

These options include:

- *Use Patterns Instead of Colors*. Displays graphs as patterned textures rather than solid colors. With some printers, this results in faster printing.

- *Create All Graphs in Separate Windows*. Normally, graphs that include two illustrations are combined in one window. If you want to separate these windows, however, you can.

- *Draw in 2D (Faster)*. Displays the graph in two dimensions (2D) rather than three dimensions (3D). Quicken displays 2D faster than 3D, particularly on a slower computer. Figure 20.14 displays a graph in 2D.

- *Show the Customize Bar*. Displays the bar that lets you change date parameters and update the report.

Select the default option or options you want; click OK if you're using the Graph Options dialog box.

20

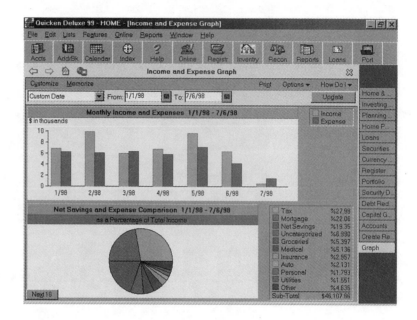

FIGURE 20.14

You can change your graph's format to 2D if desired.

Summary

This hour focused on creating graphs in Quicken. If you want to create a graph based on a question in plain English, try an EasyAnswer graph. You can also view one of five ready-made Quicken graphs through the Create Graph window. And for maximum flexibility, you can customize any of these graphs and memorize them for future use.

Hour 21, "Viewing and Analyzing Your Portfolio," shows you how to use a Quicken portfolio to view, analyze, organize, and update your investments.

Q&A

Q What is the easiest way to create a graph?

A If you're in a hurry or don't know a lot about graphs yet, creating an EasyAnswer graph is the easiest way to go. But be sure also to explore Quicken's other graph options later on so that you can maximize your ability to analyze your data in a graphical format.

Q Should I create a graph or report to analyze my data?

A A lot depends on how you best understand information and the level of detail you need to have. Visual people tend to like graphs because they can *see* their financial performance this way. Graphs are also a good way to view and summarize a great deal of information quickly. Reports, however, can usually provide a lot more detail and content. So, depending, on your needs, you'll probably want to use a combination of reports and graphs to view your Quicken financial data.

20

Hour 21

Viewing and Analyzing Your Portfolio

This hour shows you how to view, analyze, and evaluate the investments you own. Using Portfolio view, you can get an overall picture of your investments, sorted and organized in many different ways. Security Detail view provides even more information on an individual security. You can then use security types and investment goals to further analyze your investments. Finally, Quicken's reporting and graphing tools offer additional ways to look at this information.

The highlights of this hour include

- How to view your investments in Portfolio view
- Where to get detailed information on a particular security
- Why you should use security types and investment goals
- How to create investment reports and graphs
- Where to find a list of all securities you own or track

Viewing Your Portfolio

After you create at least one investment account and enter data in it, you can start using Quicken's tools for viewing and analyzing your portfolio. Select Features, Investing, Portfolio view to display Portfolio view, shown in Figure 21.1.

FIGURE 21.1

Portfolio view gives you an overall picture of your investment performance.

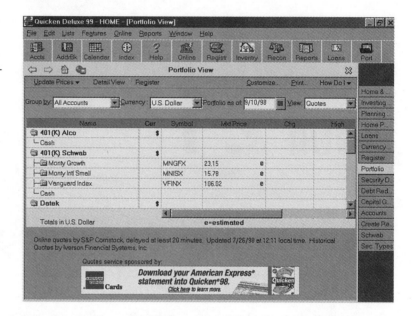

Portfolio view enables you to evaluate your portfolio based on several different grouping and viewing options. You can also specify the exact currency for this Portfolio view (if you have investment accounts in more than one currency) as well as exact date parameters.

Grouping Investments

In Portfolio view you can display the securities you own in a variety of ways by making selections in the Group By drop-down list. Options include the capability to group by:

- *All Accounts*. Displays securities by account for all investment accounts you have.

- *Selected Accounts*. Displays securities in the accounts you select from the dialog box that opens.

- *Security*. Displays all securities you own.

- *Security Type*. Displays securities by security type, such as stock, bond, or mutual fund.

- *Investment Goal.* Displays securities by investment goal, such as growth, income, or low risk.
- *Asset Class.* Displays securities by asset class, such as large cap stocks, small cap stocks, global bonds, and so on.
- *Watch List.* Displays all securities you have in your current watch list.
- *Individual Account.* The drop-down list also includes the actual names of your investment accounts. So, for example, you could choose to view everything in investment accounts such as Anne's 401(k) or Smith Barney Investments.

Figure 21.2 illustrates the Portfolio view with different grouping parameters.

FIGURE 21.2

You can group your securities in many different ways.

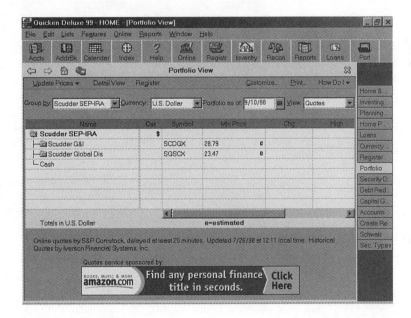

Creating Custom Views

You can also specify the exact information you want to see for each listed security by applying a view. Quicken includes five ready-made views:

- *Holdings.* Lists the market price, shares owned, market value, cost basis, and gain/loss.
- *Performance.* Lists the market price, shares owned, amount invested, amount returned, and ROI (return on investment).
- *Valuation.* Lists the market price, shares owned, amount invested, amount returned, and market value.

21

- *Price Update*. Lists the market price, shares owned, last price, market value, and change in market value.

- *Quotes*. Lists the symbol, market price, market price change, high price, low price, and trading volume.

Figure 21.3 illustrates the Portfolio view using the Performance view.

FIGURE 21.3

Portfolio view offers several views that let you analyze specific information.

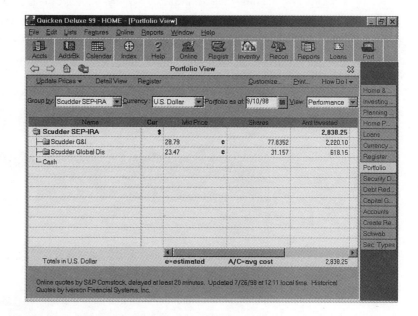

To Do: Modify a Custom View

Quicken also includes two custom views you can modify.

1. Click the Customize button to open the Customize Portfolio dialog box (see Figure 21.4).

2. In the View drop-down list, select the view you want to customize. You can modify one of the five existing views or create your own view by starting with a Custom view.

3. If you want to rename the view, click the Change Name button to open the View Name dialog box, shown in Figure 21.5.

4. Enter the new view name and click OK.

5. To change the date parameters for displaying investment data, click the Date Range button in the Customize Portfolio dialog box, which opens the Portfolio View Date Range dialog box, shown in Figure 21.6.

▼

FIGURE 21.4

You can customize a Portfolio view if you want.

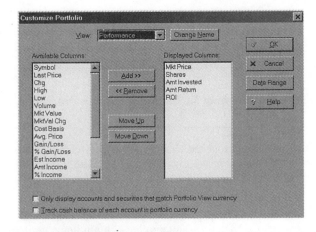

FIGURE 21.5

Create a meaningful name for your new view.

FIGURE 21.6

You can view investment performance for the current year or since you purchased your investments.

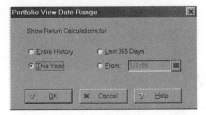

6. Select the date range you want to use for calculating the investment return and click OK. Options include

   - *Entire History*. Since the date you purchased the securities.

   - *This Year*. A year-to-date amount.

   - *Last 365 Days*. The return for a 12-month period.

   - *From*. Lets you enter a specific date from which to calculate return.

7. From the Available Columns list in the Customozie Portfolio dialog box, choose the information item you want to display and click Add to move the item to the Displayed Columns list.

21

To select multiple items at once, drag the mouse over those items or use the Ctrl key to make multiple selections and then click Add.

8. To remove an item from the Displayed Columns list, select it and click Remove.

You can change the location of a displayed column item by selecting it and clicking the Move Up or Move Down button. This changes the order in which you see the column in Portfolio view.

9. Continue adding, deleting, and moving column items until you have the list you want.

10. Select the Only Display Accounts and Securities that Match Portfolio View Currency check box to limit the accounts to those that are in the same currency as the one you selected in Portfolio view. This option is only valid if you have accounts in more than one currency.

11. Select the Track Cash Balances of Each Account in Portfolio Currency if you want to track these balances in the currency you selected in Portfolio view. Again, this is a useful option if you have investment accounts in more than one currency.

12. Click OK to return to Portfolio view.

Viewing Security Details

You can also view more details about each individual security in your portfolio. To do so, select the security and click the Detail View button. Figure 21.7 illustrates the Security Detail view for that security.

The window provides an overview of your position in the selected security in the upper-left corner box. You can also choose another security to evaluate from the drop-down list.

In the upper-right corner box, the window displays a history of your transactions. In the lower portion of the window you can view historical pricing information (see Figure 21.8).

From the left drop-down list, select either Price History or Market Value to view a graph based on the selected parameter. In the second drop-down list you can specify the time-frame you want to see. Finally, choose the Adjust for Split check box if the security was split and you want the graph to reflect this.

FIGURE 21.7

Security Detail view provides more insight into a particular security.

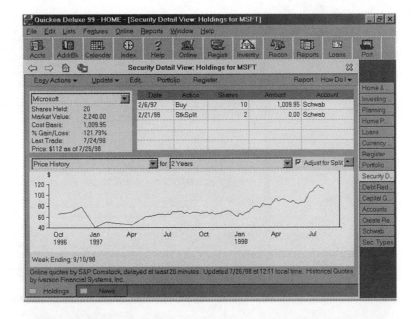

FIGURE 21.8

You can also view a graph based on market value.

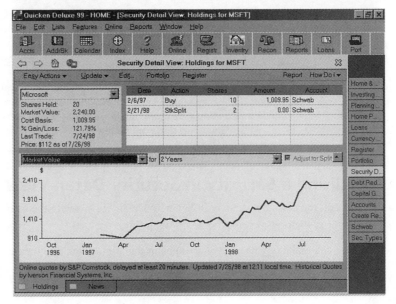

21

Viewing Security News

To view the latest news for this security, click the News tab at the bottom of the dialog box. This brings up the screen shown in Figure 21.9.

FIGURE 21.9

Download the latest security news from the Internet.

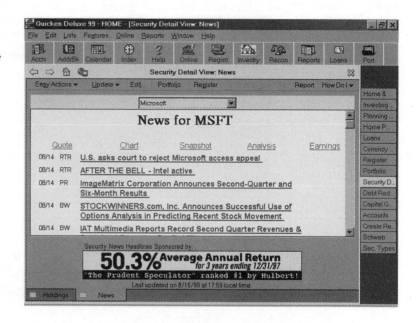

To update this tab with the latest news, select Update, Get Online Quotes and News. Quicken connects to the Internet to update your information.

> You need to set up Quicken to connect to the Internet to use this feature. Hours 23, "Using Online Financial Services" and 24, "Accessing Online Information" provide more details on going online with Quicken if you aren't already using these online features.

Editing a Security in Security Detail View

To edit the selected security in Security Detail view, select the Edit button. The Edit Security dialog box appears, as shown in Figure 21.10.

You can make any necessary changes in this dialog box and then click OK to return to Security Detail view.

From this view you can also

- *Perform Easy Action transactions.* Choose Easy Actions and then the action you want to perform. Options include buying and selling shares, recording interest information, and so on. This is the same as the Easy Action menu that displays in the Register.

FIGURE 21.10

You can modify this security if you want.

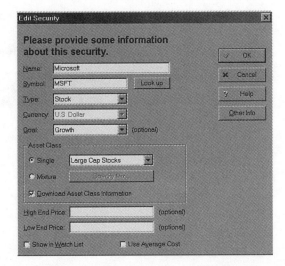

- *Update information from the Internet.* Choose Update and the appropriate online action such as Get Online Quotes or Get Asset Classes.
- *Return to Portfolio view.* Choose Portfolio to return to Portfolio view.
- *Return to the Register.* Choose Register to return to the Account Register that contains this security.

Creating New Security Types

You can view a list of your current security types as well as add new types to better analyze your portfolio. To do so, select Lists, Investment, Security Type. Figure 21.11 displays the Security Type List.

The available security types may be all you need, but if you have other forms of investments you can add new types.

Be careful not to confuse security type with investment goal or asset class when you consider adding a new type.

To add a new security type, click New to open the Set Up Security Type dialog box (see Figure 21.12).

Enter a new Type and specify whether you want to display prices as a Decimal or Fraction. Click OK to return to the list.

21

FIGURE 21.11

View all the available security types in the Security Type List.

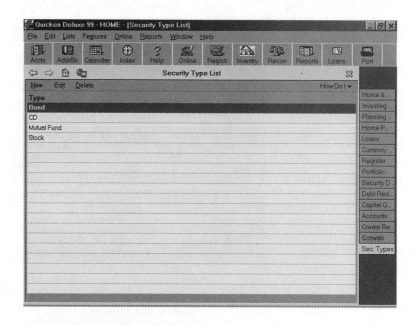

FIGURE 21.12

If the default security types don't suit your needs, you can create a new one.

You can also edit an existing type by selecting it and clicking Edit. In the Edit Security Type dialog box, which is identical to the Set Up Security Type dialog box, you can make modifications.

Finally, to delete this security type, select it and click Delete. Quicken verifies that you want to delete and then proceeds with the deletion.

To print this list, select File, Print List. Choose print parameters from the Print dialog box and click OK.

Creating New Investment Goals

You can view a list of your current investment goals as well as add new goals to better analyze your portfolio. To do so, select Lists, Investment, Investment Goal (see Figure 21.13).

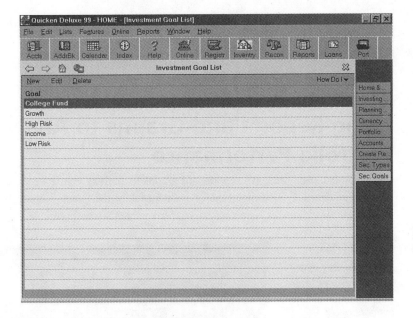

FIGURE 21.13

View your investment goals in this list.

The Investment Goal List details all existing investment goals. The available goals may be all you need, but you can add new goals as well. For example, you may want to specify a goal for your retirement fund or track aggressive growth investments.

Be careful not to confuse investment goal with security type or asset class when you consider adding a new goal.

To add a new investment goal, click New to open the Set Up Investment Goal dialog box (see Figure 21.14).

FIGURE 21.14

You can create new goals in this dialog box.

Enter a new Goal and click OK to return to the list.

You can also edit an existing goal by selecting it and clicking Edit. In the Edit Investment Goal dialog box, which is identical to the Set Up Investment Goal dialog box, you can make modifications.

21

Finally, to delete this goal, select it and click Delete. Quicken verifies that you want to delete and then proceeds with the deletion.

To print this list, select File, Print List. Choose print parameters from the Print dialog box and click OK.

Using Reports and Graphs to Analyze Portfolio Performance

You can use Quicken's reports and graphs to analyze your investment portfolio in even more detail. For example, the Investment tab of the Create Report dialog box includes several options for reporting on your investments (see Figure 21.15).

FIGURE 21.15

The Create Report dialog box includes several investment reporting options.

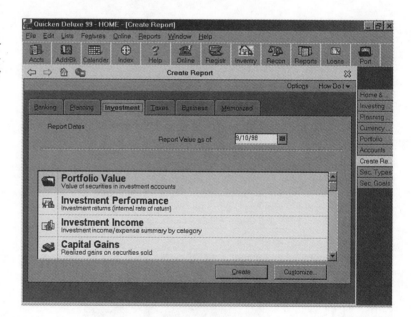

Figure 21.16 illustrates the Portfolio Value Report, one of many investment reports you can create.

From the Create Graph dialog box (see Figure 21.17) you can create the Investment Performance Graph and the Investment Asset Allocation Graph to visually display your investments.

FIGURE 21.16

The Portfolio Value Report quickly tells you how much your investments are worth.

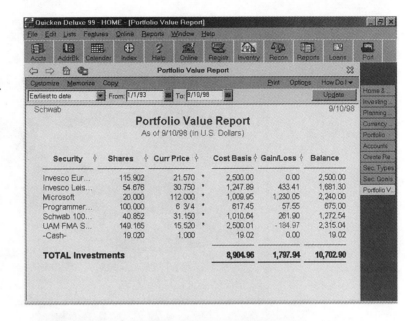

FIGURE 21.17

Quicken provides two graphs that analyze your investments.

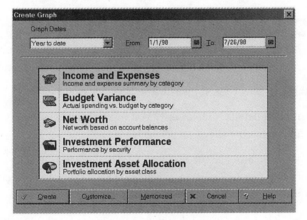

Figure 21.18 illustrates the Investment Asset Allocation Graph.

Hours 19, "Creating and Customizing Reports" and 20, "Creating and Customizing Graphs" cover the use of reports and graphs in more detail.

21

FIGURE 21.18

Determine your asset allocation in this graph.

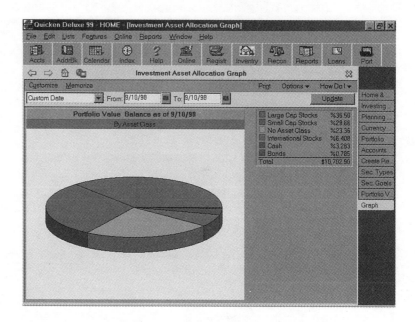

Viewing a List of Securities

After you set up your investment accounts and assign goals and security types to these securities, you can go to the Securities List to see all this information in one place.

To open this list, select Lists, Investment, Security (see Figure 21.19).

The Security List details each security you own with its symbol, type, investment goal, currency, and watch list status.

To edit this information, select a security and then click Edit. The Edit Security dialog box appears (see Figure 21.20) in which you can add or modify details such as the symbol or investment goal.

You can also delete a security for which you never entered transactions. To do so, select the security and click Delete. Quicken verifies that you want to delete and performs the deletion. You can't delete securities for which you've recorded transactions, but you can hide them.

Hiding Securities

If you no longer own a security, you can hide it. That way it doesn't display automatically in your lists and doesn't appear on reports, but the data and transactions related to it still reside in your Quicken file for historical tracking.

FIGURE 21.19

See the details on all your securities in this list.

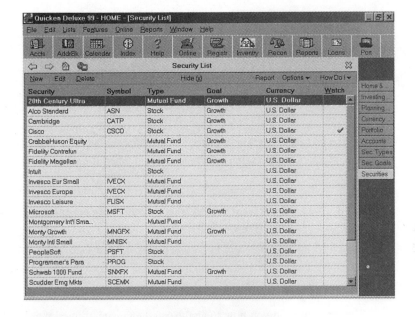

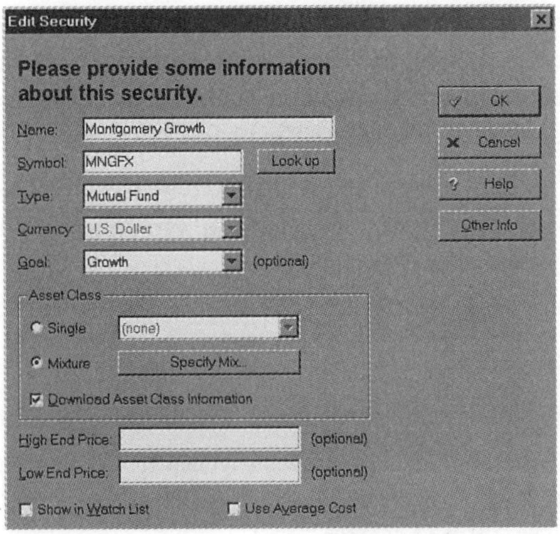

FIGURE 21.20

You can easily edit a security in this dialog box.

To hide a security, select it and click Hide. The security disappears from the Security List, but is not deleted. To view a hidden security, select Options, View Hidden Securities. The security displays on the list again, with a small hand icon next to the security name to identify that it's hidden.

21

When you create Quicken reports and graphs, you can choose whether to include these hidden securities.

Adding a Security to the Watch List

You may want to track a security you don't currently own. To do so, select the security in the list and click the Watch column. This adds the security to the watch list and Quicken downloads current pricing information for it when it updates your existing portfolio.

If you want to track a security that's not on your current Security List, click New to set up a new security.

Summary

This hour showed you how to analyze and evaluate all the investment data that currently exists in your Quicken system. You can use the Portfolio view to get an overview of how your investments are performing. Then use the Security Detail view to look at one particular security. Quicken also includes the capability to associate investments with security types and goals to further analyze specific performance criteria.

Next in Hour 22, "Using Quicken Financial Activity Centers," you'll learn how to use Quicken financial activity centers to tie all your information together into overall snapshots that cover a particular financial area.

Q&A

Q How important is it for me to track investment goals and security types?

A It isn't essential, but it's a good idea if you want the flexibility to analyze your portfolio in several ways and determine whether your investments are achieving what you want them to achieve.

Q What's the best way to quickly see how my investments are doing?

A You can do this in several ways. Portfolio view provides a detailed look, that you can sort and customize, of the securities in your investment portfolio. A Portfolio View Report offers much of this same information in printed format. For the big picture view of your investment activity, go to the Investing Center where you can see your holdings, performance, and asset allocation all on one page.

HOUR 22

Using Quicken Financial Activity Centers

This hour introduces you to Quicken financial activity centers—customized views that help you analyze and organize financial information. Quicken centers combine snapshots of important financial information from your Quicken records as well as useful advice and links to other related areas of the program. Quicken includes six ready-made centers that you can view as is or customize.

The highlights of this hour include

- What advantages Quicken centers offer
- How to use Quicken centers to view and analyze financial information
- Where to customize center views
- How to delete customized center views

Understanding Quicken Centers

Centers are a new feature in Quicken Deluxe 99. They are a vast expansion of the use of snapshots in previous versions.

After you enter a substantial amount of data in Quicken, you can use its centers to

- View and customize snapshots of your financial performance
- Analyze information on a particular financial topic such as investments or banking
- Easily perform common tasks related to the center's topic
- Navigate to related information in Quicken or on the Web

From within a center, you can vary the way you view its contents as well as make changes to the actual data itself. You can also create your own center views with content you specify.

In the left column, Quicken provides summarized snapshots of your financial activity pertinent to the center's topic. The right column includes links to related desktop activities as well as Internet sites. And under the Cool Stuff heading, you'll find other useful information.

Viewing the Quicken Home Page

The Quicken Home Page displays by default when you start Quicken. You can also access it by selecting Features, Centers, Home Page or by clicking the Go to My Quicken Home Page button on the toolbar. This center provides a quick snapshot of your finances, as illustrated in Figure 22.1.

This center offers the following sections:

- *Scheduled Transactions*. Lists scheduled transactions by date and payee. Right-click to display an options menu that lets you create, edit, skip, or enter scheduled transactions.
- *Alerts & Reminders*. Lists alerts and reminders you've entered or downloaded. Right-click to set up and download alerts.
- *My Accounts*. Lists all your accounts and their balances. Right-click to update, edit, delete, or create accounts.

  Select the accounts you want to display (indicated with a green check mark) and click OK. In this dialog box, you can mark all or clear all accounts or choose to display hidden accounts.

FIGURE 22.1

Get an overall view of your finances in this center.

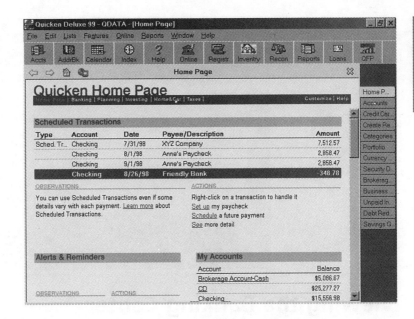

22

- *Watch List.* Lists the latest price of securities you've added to your watch list. Right-click to enter a buy or sell transaction for the selected security, add, edit, or remove securities from the watch list, or display a price graph.

- *Credit Card Analysis.* Lists credit card names, balances, credit limits, and interest rates. Tells you the percentage of total spending allocated to credit cards. Right-click to add, edit, or delete credit card accounts as well as set up alerts for them.

- *Income vs. Expenses.* Displays a graph showing year-to-date expenses by month. Lets you know whether your income exceeds your spending and by how much. You can customize the graph, request a full-screen view, or display a Cash Flow Report.

To customize this snapshot, select Customize This Graph from the menu that displays. Figure 22.2 shows the Customize Snapshot dialog box.

In this dialog box, you can select the accounts, categories, and classes you want to include as well as specify dates. Click OK when you're done customizing; the center reflects these changes.

FIGURE 22.2

Customize the graphs in Quicken centers to see only the information you want.

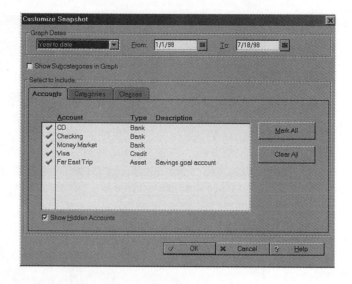

Viewing the Banking Center

The Banking Center provides information and analysis of your bank accounts. You can access this center by selecting Features, Centers, Banking Center. Figure 22.3 displays the Banking Center.

This center includes the following features:

- *Account Overview*. Lists all accounts and associated currency, balance, interest rate, and year-to-date interest received.

- *Credit Card Analysis*. Lists credit card names, balances, credit limits, and interest rates. Tells you the percentage of total spending allocated to credit cards. Right-click to add, edit, or delete credit card accounts as well as set up alerts for them.

- *Income versus Expenses*. Displays a graph showing year-to-date expenses by month. Lets you know if your income exceeds your spending and by how much. You can customize the graph, request a full screen view, or display a Cash Flow Report.

- *Account Activity*. Lists all accounts and associated deposits, ATM withdrawals, checks, transfers, and other transactions.

Right-click any of these sections to update, edit, delete, or create accounts as well as set up account alerts.

FIGURE 22.3

You can quickly see the current status of your banking activities.

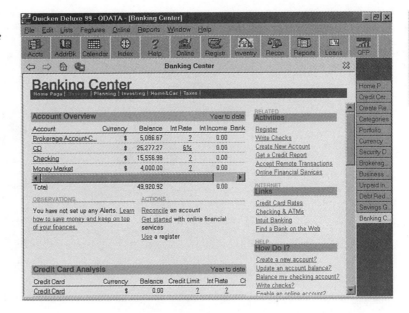

22

Viewing the Planning Center

The Planning Center shows you how well you've been planning your savings, spending, and budgets. Select Features, Centers, Planning Center to view this center, illustrated in Figure 22.4.

Areas of the Planning Center include

- *Savings Analysis*. Displays total savings, the amount specified for an emergency fund, and your rate of savings. Also lets you know whether you are saving enough money.

- *Expenses*. Displays a pie chart that analyzes the percentage of total spending allocated to each category. Right-click to customize the graph or display it full-screen.

- *Budgets*. Lists budgeted, actual, and difference amounts as well as category groups based on the budget information you enter. Also displays the information in a bar chart.

- *Net Worth*. Displays your total assets, liabilities, and net worth. Illustrates this information as a monthly bar chart for the past year. Right-click to customize or enlarge the graph.

- *Financial Plan Summary*. Summarizes a plan you create with the Quicken Financial Planner.

FIGURE 22.4

The Planning Center shows how much you're saving and spending.

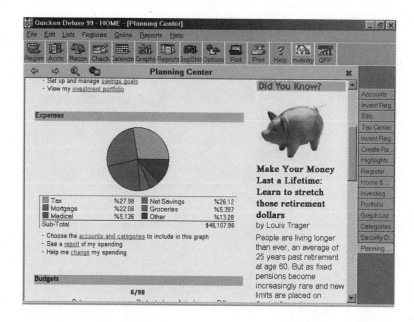

To Do: Specify an Emergency Fund

1. Click the underlined Emergency Fund text to open the Customize Savings dialog box, shown in Figure 22.5.

2. Click the Emergency Fund button to display the Customize Emergency Fund dialog box, shown in Figure 22.6.

3. Select the account or accounts you want to designate as containing emergency funds. Usually these are savings or money market accounts.

4. Click OK to return to the Customize Savings dialog box.

5. In the Minimum Monthly Spending field, enter the minimum amount of money you spend each month on necessities.

FIGURE 22.5

You can customize the way you view your savings.

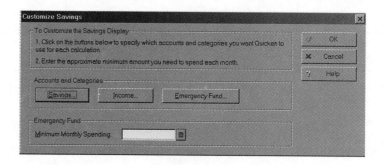

▼ 6. Click OK to return to the center. Based on the account you designate as an emergency fund, Quicken displays the number of months this money will last.

▲

You can also customize which accounts, categories, and classes to consider as savings and income in this dialog box.

FIGURE 22.6

Set up an emergency fund to cover several months' worth of expenses.

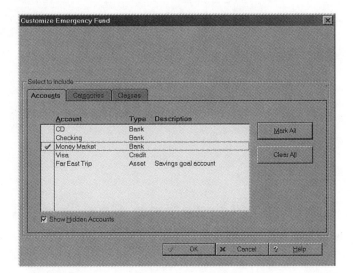

Viewing the Investing Center

The Investing Center helps you track and analyze your investment portfolio. Select Features, Centers, Investing Center to access the center, shown in Figure 22.7.

The Investing Center includes the following sections:

- *Watch List*. Lists the latest price of securities you've added to your watch list. Right-click to enter a buy or sell transaction for the selected security, add, edit, or remove securities from the watch list, or display a price graph.

- *My Portfolio*. Lists account balances for all investment accounts.

- *Asset Allocation*. Displays a pie chart showing the percentage of your investments allocated to each asset class. Right-click to customize or enlarge the chart.

- *Investment Returns*. Illustrates the percentage return of each investment account.

FIGURE 22.7

You'll know very quickly how your investments are performing by looking at the Investing Center.

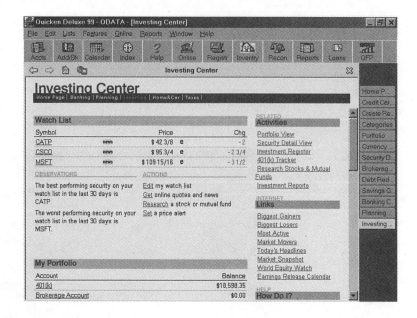

Viewing the Home and Car Center

Select Features, Centers, Home and Car Center to open the Home and Car Center, which tracks your mortgage, car loan, and home and car expenses. Figure 22.8 illustrates this center.

Areas in this center include

- *Asset Accounts.* Displays a list of your assets and their value. You can customize this section by right-clicking it. You can edit the account, update its value, create a new account, or set up alerts.
- *Loan Summary.* Lists the balance, interest, and principal paid for each loan you have. Customization options include editing the loan, payment, or interest rate as well as making an extra payment, deleting a loan, or creating a new loan.
- *Auto Expenses.* Displays year-to-date, month-to-date, and average monthly auto expenses. You can customize the snapshot or view an Itemized Categories report.

Viewing the Tax Center

The Tax Center offers a snapshot of your tax-related financial activity. Select Features, Centers, Tax Center to access the center (see Figure 22.9).

FIGURE 22.8

Track your assets, mortgages, and car loans in this center.

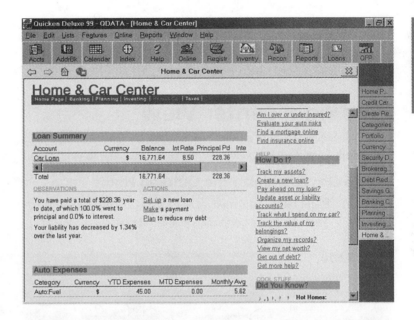

22

FIGURE 22.9

Features such as projected taxes and a tax calendar can help save you money at tax time.

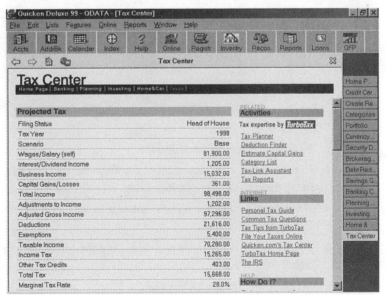

Highlights include

- *Projected Tax.* Provides information relating to your projected tax for the year, including income, deductions, exemptions, credits, and other details.

- *Tax Calendar*. Displays a tax calendar of important tax dates for the year.
- *Income YTD*. Lists year-to-date income by category.
- *Tax-Related Expenses YTD*. Lists year-to-date deductions by category.

Printing a Center View

You can easily print all the information on a Quicken center view. To do so, select File, Print Page. Quicken automatically prints the page to your default printer.

To Do: Customize the Quicken Home Page

1. Right-click and then choose Customize This View from the menu. The Customize View dialog box appears, as illustrated in Figure 22.10.

FIGURE 22.10

You can create a cus-tomized center view to look at information in a different way.

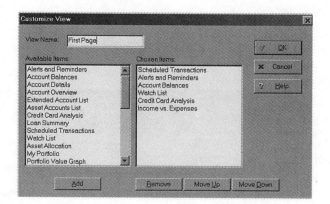

2. Revise the View Name if desired.

3. Choose the sections you want to add from the Available Items list and click Add to move them to the Chosen Items list.

4. If you want to delete a section, select it in the Chosen Items list and then click Remove.

5. To change the order of chosen items, use the Move Up and Move Down buttons to adjust their order.

6. When you're finished, click OK.

7. The contents of the center change based on your customizations. To look at views you've created, click Customize and choose the view from the menu's Show View section.

22

Creating a Center View

If you want to create your own view rather than just customize the Home Page, click Customize and choose Create a New View from the menu. The Customize View dialog box appears, but without any chosen items. Add the items you want to appear in the view and save it.

Deleting a Center View

To delete a center view that you created, click Customize and choose Delete This View from the menu. Quicken verifies you want to delete and then does so.

 You can delete only a view you create, not one of the regular center views Quicken provides, such as the Banking Center or Investment Center.

Summary

This hour introduced you to Quicken centers. These centers provide views and snapshots of particular aspects of your finances such as investments and banking. You can use the center views as they are or create a customized view. You can also use these centers to navigate quickly to other parts of Quicken or perform common tasks related to the center's topic.

Hour 23, "Using Online Financial Services," starts a new section covering Quicken's many Internet and Web capabilities.

Q&A

Q Why can't I customize the center I'm viewing?

A You can customize only the Home Page. None of the other Quicken centers (Banking Center, Planning Center, and so on) is customizable.

Q I tried clicking one of the links to the Web and it doesn't work. What's the matter?

A If you're not already connected to the Internet, Quicken dials your Internet connection to link to the Web. To connect to the Internet, however, you must have already set up a Quicken Internet connection. To do so, select Online, Internet Connection, Setup.

PART VI

Going Online with Quicken

Hour

HOUR 23

Using Online Financial Services

You can connect Quicken with the Internet to perform two types of financial activity. You can do financial research on the Internet, or you can conduct actual financial transactions over the Internet. In Hour 24 you explore the possibilities for financial research on the Internet. In this hour, you learn to conduct online banking using Quicken.

The highlights of this hour include

- Finding out whether your bank supports online banking with Quicken
- Setting up online account access
- Setting up online payments
- Managing your investments with Quicken

Understanding Quicken's Online Financial Services

Basically, you need the following two things to do your banking online with Quicken:

- Access to the Internet
- A bank that supports online banking with Quicken

The first requirement, access to the Internet, is pretty easy to manage. If you already have a modem on your computer, and an Internet Service Provider (ISP), you're all set. Quicken identifies your Internet connection, and you can work online seamlessly.

If you don't have a modem, you have to install one to work online. A full discussion of working on the Internet is beyond the scope of this hour, but there are many accessible books that can provide you with an overview of that, including *Sams Teach Yourself the Internet Starter Kit in 24 Hours*. If you have a modem but not Internet Service Provider (ISP), Quicken helps you contract with one through an easy-to-follow wizard.

Connecting with a bank that provides online support for Quicken may be more of a challenge. If your bank does not support online access from Quicken, you have two options—find another bank that does support Quicken, or use your bank's proprietary online banking software.

Right now, the online banking system is somewhat fragmented. The main reason is that banks are reluctant to surrender online access to third-party interfaces such as Quicken out of fear that after you rely on Quicken as your banking connection, you look to Quicken and not your bank as your financial provider.

If you are committed to utilizing Quicken's powerful online banking features, and your bank doesn't support Quicken, you may have to start with the substantial list of banks that *do* support Quicken, and choose one of them as your bank.

Connecting to the Internet from Quicken

There are two possible options for connecting to the Internet from Quicken:

- You don't have an Internet connection, and you want Quicken to help you get one.
- You already have an Internet connection.

In this section of this hour, we explore both ways of connecting to the Internet through Quicken.

To Do: Sign Up for an Internet Service Provider

1. Select Online, Online Financial Services Setup from the main Quicken menu. The Get Started With Online Financial Services Setup dialog box appears, as shown in Figure 23.1. Click the Setup button in the dialog box.

2. If you do not currently have an Internet Service Provider (such as America Online, Microsoft Network, and so on), click the Tell me how to sign up for an Internet account radio button in the Internet Connection Setup dialog box, as shown in Figure 23.2. Click Next in the dialog box.

FIGURE 23.1

Setting up your Internet connection.

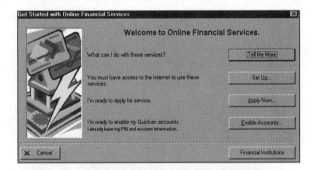

FIGURE 23.2

Quicken can help you find an Internet Service Provider.

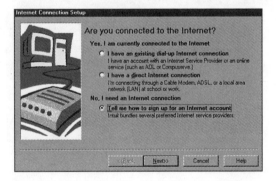

If you already have an Internet Service Provider, skip ahead to the next section of this hour, "Connecting to the Internet Through Your ISP."

3. The How to Sign up for an Internet account dialog box, Quicken advises you on how to sign up with an ISP. The Help button provides some additional advice. Your package of Quicken included some special sign-up offers for Internet connection. You need to find and sign-up with an Internet Service Provider before you can continue with Quicken's online features.

Connecting Quicken to the Internet with your ISP

After you set up an Internet Account, you can have Quicken locate that account and use it to connect you to the Internet when you need to access online features.

To Do: Log On with Quicken

1. Select Online, Online Financial Services Setup from the main Quicken menu. The Get Started With Online Financial Services Setup dialog box appears, as shown earlier in Figure 23.1. Click the Setup button in the dialog box.

2. Select one of the top two radio buttons. Select the I have an existing dial-up Internet account if your computer is connected directly to the Internet. Select the I have a direct Internet Connection radio button if you are constantly logged on to an Internet server. After you select one of the top two radio buttons, click the Next button. Quicken searches your system files and determines which Internet access providers you are signed up with.

3. In the Internet Connection Setup dialog box shown in Figure 23.3, Quicken lists all your Internet providers (if you have only one, that one will be listed). Click one of the Internet providers on the list, and then click the Next button.

FIGURE 23.3

Selecting an Internet connection for Quicken.

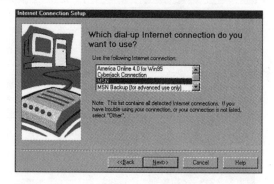

4. In the Browser Preference dialog box, you are prompted to select a browser that works well with your Internet connection. Or, if there is no choice, you read a short description of your selected browser. Click the Next button in this dialog box.

5. The Which Web Browser Would You Like to Use dialog box prompts you to pick from your installed browsers, if you have more than one. Click one of the listed browsers (or just leave your one browser selected) and click the Next button.

6. The Would You Like to Send Diagnostic Data? dialog box gives you the option of sending information about your computer system to the makers of Quicken. There's no need for you to select the Yes radio button, your connection works just

▼ as well if you click No. After making a choice in this dialog box, click the Next
button.

> If you click the Yes radio button in the Would You Like to Send Diagnostic
> Data? dialog box, Quicken periodically sends information about your system
> to the makers of Quicken including the type of modem you have, the name
> of your ISP, the phone number you use to log onto the Internet, and infor-
> mation about software on your computer.

7. The final setup dialog box summarizes your log-on information, as shown in
Figure 23.4. After you review this information, click the Finish button.

FIGURE 23.4

*Quicken summarizes
your Internet connec-
tion information for
you.*

▲ After you define your Internet connection, you return to the Get Started with
Online Financial Services dialog box.

Setting Up Online Account Access

There are, once again, two basic options for setting up an online banking account with
Quicken. Either your bank supports online banking with Quicken, or you can open an
account with a bank that does support Quicken. Of course if you have a lot of pull with
your bank, you might be able to get them to sign up with Quicken, but assuming you're
not that influential, the preceding are your two basic choices.

When you go to the Apply for Online Financial Services view in Quicken, you see a list
of banks and other financial institutions that support online transactions with Quicken. If
you don't see your bank on the list, most of the banks that are listed advertise attractive
sign-up offers. Some list the cost of online transactions. For example, in Figure 23.5,

23

a bank is offering a free trial period and lists the charges for paying bills online with Quicken.

FIGURE 23.5

You can comparison-shop for online banking with Quicken.

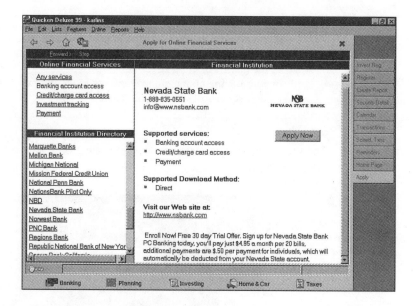

Setting Up an Online Account

The first step in engaging in online banking is to apply for an online account from your bank. (If you don't have a bank that supports online banking, you can shop for one as well, using the following steps).

To Do: Apply for an Online Account

1. Select Online, Financial Institutions from the Quicken main menu. The Apply for Online Financial Services dialog box appears. Click the category of financial institution you are looking for in the list at the top left of the window (Any services, Banking account access, Credit/charge card access, Investment tracking, or Payment). If you're not sure which list includes your institution, click the Any Services link.

2. Peruse the list of financial institutions that support Quicken 99. If you don't see your financial institution, click different ones in the list on the lower left of the window. Listed financial institutions have a page that describes their online services and, in many cases, their fees. They also describe which Quicken online banking services they support. Most of these financial institutions also have toll-free numbers and links to their web pages. If you do not currently have an account

▼ with a bank that supports Quicken, you can select a financial institution from this list to apply for an account with.

3. After you have an account, click your financial institution, and then click the Apply Now button in the Get Started with Online Financial Services dialog box. You are connected to an online application form at your bank.

4. The online application form at your financial institution varies. You are asked to fill out an application similar to the one you see in Figure 23.6. This application is not an application to open a bank account. It's an application to associate online banking with an existing account. If you don't have an account with a bank that supports Quicken, you need to apply for that separately (see step 2).

23

FIGURE 23.6

Signing up for online banking.

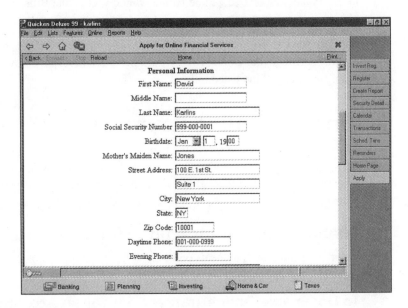

You should read over the application for online banking provided by your financial institution carefully. Find out what fees are charged, and review other rules and terms associated with online transactions.

5. Different banks have different procedures for validating and accepting your application to do online banking with Quicken. You need to study the information provided by your financial institution to see exactly how and when your online banking account becomes active.

After you have established an online account, you can use that account to make financial transactions.

View Your Bills Online

One additional online financial service available through Quicken is the ability to see your bills online.

At this point, only a small number of utilities provide this service, but if your power company does, you can see your utility bill online through Quicken.

To see or receive bills online, select Online, Get Bills Online from the main Quicken menu. In the Welcome to Online Billing window, click the Biller list button. If companies to whom you make payments are listed, you can see your bill online.

Navigate back to the Welcome to Online Billing view by clicking the Back button *below* the Back arrow in the Online Bills view. Then click the Apply Now to apply for online billing with one of the listed billers.

Setting Up Online Payments

After you have signed up for online banking, you can conduct all kinds of financial transactions online. You can make payments without writing checks, and have the amount automatically deducted from your associated account. If your employer supports online paychecks, you can have your pay sent directly to your account.

Enable Online Transactions for an Account

Before you can make payments online, you need to edit the properties of the associated account.

To Do: Enable Online Transactions for an Account

1. Select Lists, Account from the main Quicken menu.

2. Right-click an account that you want to use for online transactions. Select Edit from the context menu. The Edit Bank Account dialog box appears.

3. Select the Enable Online Account Access and Enable Online Payment check boxes, as shown in Figure 23.7.

4. After you enable both types of online transactions, click the Next button, and select your financial institution from the drop-down menu in the Select Financial Institution dialog box. Click the Next button.

FIGURE 23.7

Enabling online transactions.

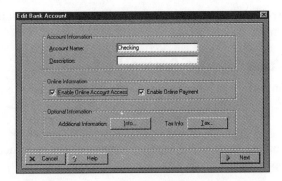

23

5. The next several dialog boxes prompt you for information about your online bank account. Supply information provided by your financial institution in these dialog boxes. When you have completed all the dialog boxes, click the Done button in the final one. You see a dialog box warning you that online transactions are subject to fees and rules set by your bank. Think about that for a minute, and then click the only button in the dialog box—the OK button.

After you've enabled online activity for an account, you can define online transactions.

Assign Online Payment to a Memorized Transaction

You can assign bills to be paid through online transfers.

To Do: Set Up an Account for Online Payment

1. Select Lists, Memorized Transactions to see a list of your memorized transactions. (You can review Hour 8 for a discussion of memorized transactions).

2. Right-click a memorized transaction, and select Edit from the context menu. In the Edit Loan dialog box, select Online Pmt from the Type drop-down menu, as shown in Figure 23.8. Then click OK.

3. Fill in the fields in the Set Up Online Payee dialog box, and then click the OK button.

FIGURE 23.8

Assigning online payment status to a memorized transaction.

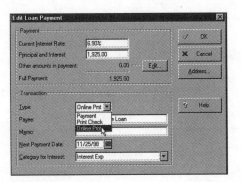

After you enter online status for a transaction, the memorized bill is paid with an online transfer from the associated account.

Editing Your Online Payee List

After you define one or more online transactions in the Memorized Transaction List, you can edit or add online payees in the Online Payee List.

To see the Online Payee List, select Lists, Online Payees from the main Quicken menu. If you have more than one online banking account, select an account from the Financial Institution drop-down list.

You can click the New button to define additional payees to whom you issue online payments. Or, you can right-click a payee in the list and select Edit from the context menu to edit online payment information.

Making Online Payments

You can pay bills online if the payee is set up to accept online payments.

To Do: Make an Online Payment from your Checking Account

1. Select Lists, Account, and double-click your checking account in the list of accounts.
2. In the first available blank transaction line, select Send Online Payment from the drop-down menu in the Num column, as shown in Figure 23.9.

FIGURE 23.9

Assigning online payment status to a memorized transaction.

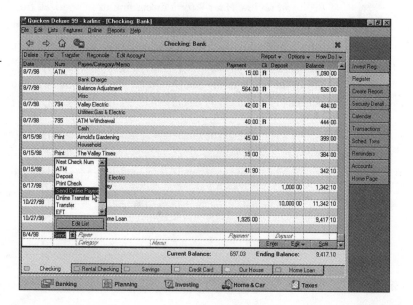

▼ 3. In the Payee column, select one of the payees to whom you have enabled online
      payments.

> If you need to make a payment to a payee who is not defined for online
> payments, go to the Online Payee list and add this payee.

23

   4. Click the Enter button in the register. An online payment is generated.

   5. Select Online, Online Center from the main Quicken menu. Click the Payments tab
      in the Online Financial Services center. Any registered online payments are listed,
      as shown in Figure 23.10.

FIGURE 23.10

*The final step of an
online payment—send-
ing the information to
your bank.*

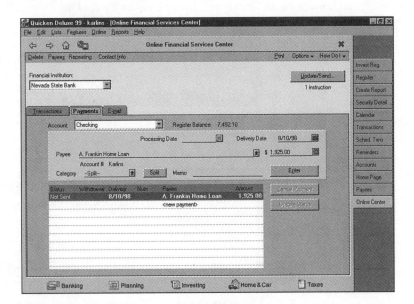

   6. Click the Update/Send button to send your online transaction information to your
      financial institution, and to have your bank issue a payment. Depending on your
      financial institution, you may be prompted for a PIN number or other information
▲   before sending your transaction information online.

Setting Up Online Investment Tracking

You can manage your investment transactions online in basically the same way you
learned to make payments from your checking account earlier in this hour.

First, you need to sign up for an online account with a financial institution. Then, you associate investment transactions with the online account.

Applying for an Online Investment Account

The first step in conducting online investment tracking is to sign up with a provider. Start by selecting Online, Online Financial Services Setup from the main Quicken menu. In the Get Started with Online Financial Services dialog box, click the Apply now button.

Quicken logs you onto the Internet and displays the Apply for Online Financial Services dialog box. Click the Investment Tracking link in the upper-left corner of the window to see a list of online trading and investment tracking institutions that work with Quicken 99.

You can click a financial institution with whom you have an existing account, or you can learn about the different listed companies by clicking their link, as shown in Figure 23.11.

FIGURE 23.11

Signing up for online trading with Quicken.

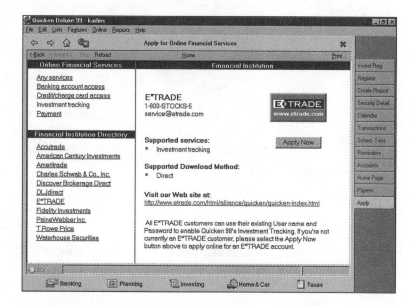

When you find your investment company, click the Apply Now button and apply for an online account with your financial institution.

Tracking Investments Online

To conduct online investment transactions, you must first enable online investment for the firm that conducts your transactions. To do this, right-click the company in the Account

List (Lists, Account). Select Edit from the shortcut menu, and click the Enable Online Investment check box for the selected financial institution. Click the Next button in the dialog box, and fill out required information about your online investment company.

Before you can specify a financial institution to conduct online investment transactions, you must have two things. You need an account with the company. You also need to apply for *online* an investment account with that company (see the previous section in this hour, "Applying for an Online Investment Account").

23

After you have signed up for an online trading account, you can conduct investment transactions over the Internet by selecting Online, Online Center from the main Quicken menu.

Select your investment company from the Financial Institution drop-down menu. Then, click the Trade button.

Depending on the financial institution, you are prompted for your name, account number, pass code, and information to complete your trade, as shown in Figure 23.12.

FIGURE 23.12

Making on online investment transaction with Quicken.

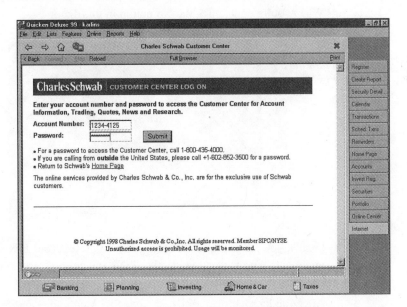

In Hour 24, "Accessing Online Information," you learn to research your investments and track stock prices using additional online investment tools in Quicken 99.

Using the PIN Vault

Quicken's PIN Vault allows you to store all the personal identification numbers (PINs) associated with all your online accounts in a file. You can then enter a single PIN created by Quicken, and use it to access all online accounts.

Does that sound a little scary? It probably should at least give you pause to consider how secure your computer files are. If you are comfortable that your single Quicken PIN is secure, you can save time and trouble by entering one PIN for all your online accounts. If you don't mind spending time entering a PIN for each account, you can avoid defining a single PIN. The choice is yours.

To Do: Define a PIN Vault Access Code

1. Select Online, Pin Vault, Setup.

2. Read the Welcome tab of the Pin Vault Setup dialog box, and click the Next button.

3. Select the first online account for which you define a PIN from the Financial Institution drop-down menu. Click the Next button.

4. Enter the PIN for your institution (once in each field), and click the Next button. The final dialog box asks whether you want to add another PIN, as shown in Figure 23.13. Click the Yes radio button, and click Next to continue to add new accounts. When you're done, click the No button in this dialog box.

FIGURE 23.13

Storing several PINs in Quicken's PIN Vault.

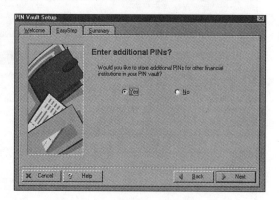

5. Finally, you are prompted to enter a PIN to protect your PIN Vault. This PIN is important! It protects all your other PINs and controls access to all the online accounts stored in the Vault.

6. After you have defined a PIN for your PIN Vault, you can log on to financial services using that PIN. You are still prompted for PINS assigned by the financial institution for any account that does not have a PIN stored in the Vault.

Summary

You can conduct almost all your financial transactions online with Quicken. First, you need to synchronize Quicken with your Internet Service Provider (ISP). Quicken helps by identifying your installed ISPs, and prompting you to select one to handle your Quicken transactions.

With your Internet connection defined, you need to sign up for online accounts with financial institutions that support Quicken 99. Then, you can use electronic payments, or other online transactions.

23

Q&A

Q What do I do if my bank is not on the list of available banks for online banking with Quicken?

A You can try to convince them to support Quicken, or you can sign up for an account with a financial institution on Quicken's list.

Q Are there fees associated with online banking with Quicken?

A Quicken doesn't charge online fees, but many financial institutions do. You need to carefully read and consider the online banking information provided by your financial institution.

HOUR 24

Accessing Online Information

This hour demonstrates the types of online information you can access from Quicken and how to download it to your Quicken system. You can retrieve security quotes, historical prices, and asset class information individually or use Quicken's one step procedure to download investment information and financial records from the Internet at the same time. You can also access detailed investment research and online credit reports as well as mortgage, insurance, and other financial information from the Quicken.com Web site.

The highlights of this hour include

- Where to access online quotes, news, and historical prices
- How to use the One Step Update
- What kinds of investment research Quicken provides
- How to use the Quicken.com Web site to access financial information
- How to check your credit online

Accessing Investment Information Online

Quicken provides several ways to update your portfolio and accounts with current information from the Internet. You can update information such as quotes and historical prices individually, or download all investment information and financial data at the same time.

Updating Your Portfolio

From within Portfolio View, you can update detailed investment information from the Internet. Figure 24.1 illustrates Portfolio View.

FIGURE 24.1

Update stock quotes from Portfolio View.

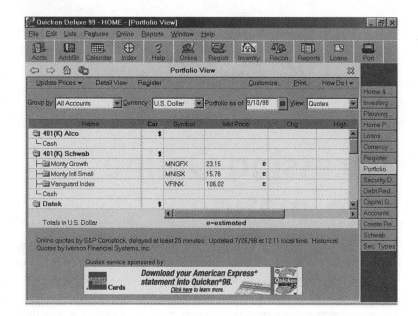

Quicken must be set up to connect to the Internet before you can download information. To do so, select Online, Internet Connection, Setup. Hour 23, "Using Online Financial Services," provides more information on connecting to the Internet.

To open Portfolio View, select Features, Investing, Portfolio View, or click the Port icon on the Iconbar.

Click Update Prices to display a menu of options. This menu includes the option to do the following:

- *Get Online Quotes Only.* Updates the quotes for the securities in your portfolio.
- *Get Online Quotes & News.* Displays the Quicken 99 Download Selection dialog box where you can choose what you want to download.

> Later this hour, you learn how to use the Quicken 99 Download Selection dialog box.

- *Get Asset Classes.* Displays the Download Security Asset Classes dialog box, shown in Figure 24.2.

FIGURE 24.2

Download the exact asset class of a particular security from the Internet.

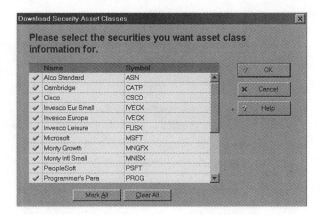

Select the securities for which you want to download asset classes and click OK to download.

> Downloading asset classes is particularly a good idea for mutual funds, because they usually contain a mix that is difficult to determine on your own. By downloading the exact mix, you're sure to have an accurate picture of your true asset allocation.

- *Get Historical Prices.* Displays the Get Historical Prices dialog box, shown in Figure 24.3.

FIGURE 24.3

Historical prices help you track the long-term performance of a security.

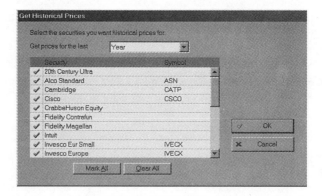

Select the securities for which you want to download historical prices, specify a time frame—from a month to five years, and click OK to proceed.

You can then view these historical prices in the Security Detail View for each selected security (see Figure 24.4).

FIGURE 24.4

Get a visual representation of historical price in Security Detail View.

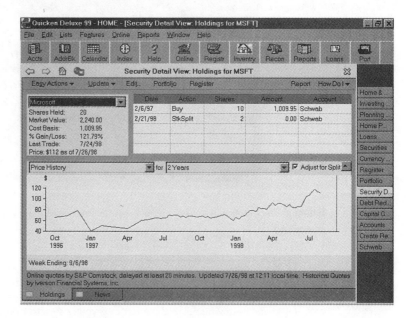

 You can also download quotes, news, asset classes, and historical prices from the Update menu in Security Detail View.

Using One Step Update

One Step Update is a new Quicken 99 feature that helps save time and money by connecting to the Internet just once to handle a variety of transactions.

One Step Update provides the capability to download multiple items from the Internet through selections you make in a single dialog box.

To Do: Use One Step Update

1. Select Online, One Step Update to display the Quicken 99 Download Selection dialog box, shown in Figure 24.5.

24

FIGURE 24.5

Choose the specific items you want to download.

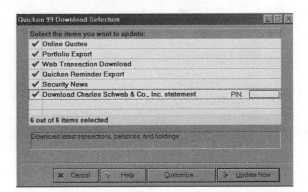

2. Select the items you want to update from the list. Options include the following:

- *Online quotes.* Downloads quotes for securities you select.

- *Portfolio export.* Exports your portfolio to the Quicken.com Web site where you can track its performance online.

- Web transaction download. Downloads portfolio transactions you make on the Web.

You must be registered with Quicken.com or Excite.com to use portfolio export or Web transaction download. If you're not registered, Quicken prompts you with information on how to register.

- *Quicken reminder export.* Exports your reminders to the Web so that you can see them when you access Quicken.com.

- *Security news.* Downloads news items for the securities you select.

- *Any account for which online access has been enabled.* For example, if you activated a brokerage account for online account access, it appears in this list. You must enter your PIN to gain access.

3. Click the Customize button to open the Customize Investment Download dialog box, shown in Figure 24.6.

FIGURE 24.6

Customize your downloads to include only certain securities.

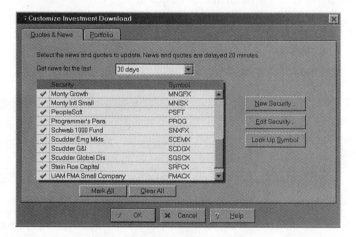

4. On the Quotes & News tab, select the time span for which to retrieve news items. Options include retrieving news for the last day, week, two weeks, or 30 days.

5. Select the securities for which you want to retrieve quotes and news from the list. A green check mark indicates that you want to get download information for this security.

> Click the Mark All button to select all securities. Click the Clear All to remove all check marks and start again.

> To add a new security to the download list, click the New Security button. Click Edit Security to modify an existing security in the list. And you can look up security symbols on the Internet by clicking the Look Up Symbol button.

Quicken only retrieves quotes and news for stocks/funds with an associated ticker symbol. If your items don't include the ticker, look it up before proceeding.

6. Click the Portfolio tab to move to the next step, illustrated in Figure 24.7.

FIGURE 24.7

You can track selected portfolios as well as your watch list.

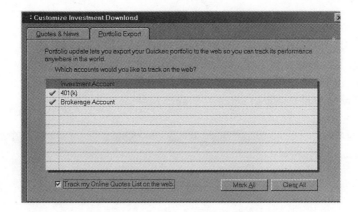

24

7. Select the portfolios you want to export to the Web from the list that displays.

8. Choose the Track My Online Quotes List on the Web check box to add these securities to your Web portfolio.

9. Click OK to return to the Quicken 99 Download Selection dialog box.

10. Click the Update Now button to connect to the Web and update the selected items.

11. When Quicken finishes downloading, the Quicken 99 Download Summary dialog box displays (see Figure 24.8).

FIGURE 24.8

This dialog box summarizes your downloads and warns you of any errors.

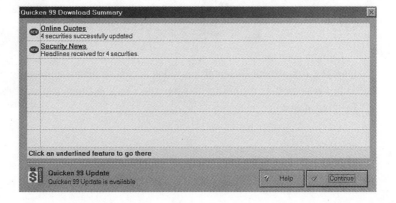

▼   This dialog box provides details on what Quicken updated for each item, whether it
        downloaded new information , any problems it encountered, and the date and time
        of the last download.

> You can look at this dialog box at any time by selecting Online, Download
> Summary.

▲

Performing Investment Research Online

Quicken provides online access to detailed investment information, research, and
analysis. Select Online, Quicken on the Web, Investment Research to open the Quicken
Investment Research window. Figure 24.9 illustrates this window.

FIGURE 24.9

*You can analyze both
stocks and mutual
funds in this window.*

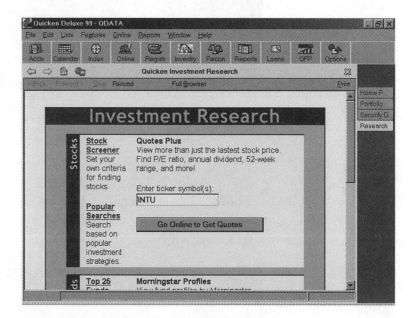

Quicken Investment Research provides access to information on specific stocks or mutual funds as well as the ability to screen stocks and funds to find those that are suitable
for your portfolio.

Getting Information on Specific Stocks and Mutual Funds

If you want to get information on a specific stock and know its ticker symbol, enter it in the Edit box under Quotes Plus and then click the Go Online to Get Quotes button. Quicken logs on to the Web and displays the Quotes Plus page, shown in Figure 24.10.

FIGURE 24.10

Get an analysis of a specific stock.

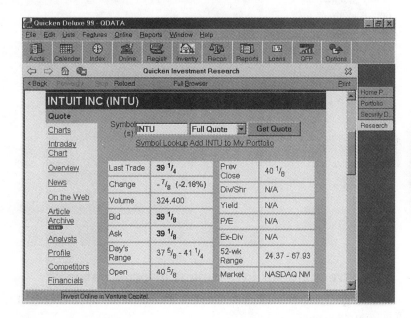

Quotes Plus also offers access to analyst recommendations, articles, news, charts, and security overviews.

If you want to retrieve either a Morningstar or Value Line report on a specific mutual fund, enter the fund's symbol in the appropriate box and click the Get Morningstar Profile Online or Get Value Line Profile Online button.

Morningstar and Value Line are well-known research firms that offer reports evaluating mutual fund performance.

Figure 24.11 displays a sample Morningstar report.

FIGURE 24.11

View a Morningstar report on a mutual fund you own or want to purchase.

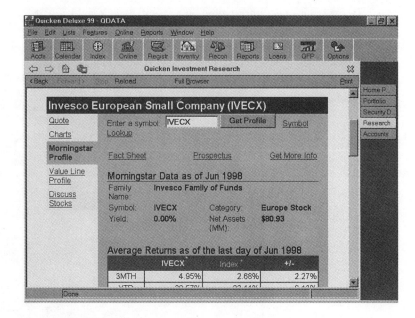

Screening for Investment Information

The Quicken Investment Research window also offers access to five special screening tools:

> To make the best use of Quicken's powerful investment research tools, you need to have a basic understanding of investment theory and terminology. If you don't, look at the Investments section on Quicken.com for detailed information that teaches you the basics of investing.

- *Stock Screener.* Displays the Stock Screener (see Figure 24.12) in which you answer five questions regarding the type of stock you are looking for— the industry, earnings ratio, growth rates, company size, and desired return.

  Click Submit Search and Quicken displays a list of stocks that match your criteria. Figure 24.13 illustrates a sample stock list.

FIGURE 24.12

Specify the type of stock you're looking for in the Stock Screener tab.

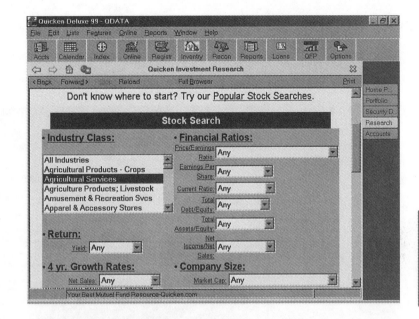

FIGURE 24.13

Quicken provides a list of stocks that you can further analyze.

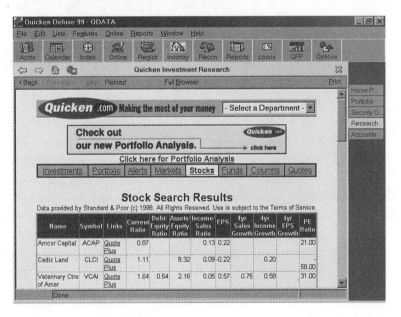

24

Click the Clear Form button to enter new search criteria.

- *Popular Searches.* Lets you search for potential stocks based on their growth, yield, earnings strength, and valuation (four popular criteria for selecting promising stocks). Quicken displays a list of stocks that match the search you selected, shown in Figure 24.14.

FIGURE 24.14

See a list of potential stocks based on popular stock screening criteria.

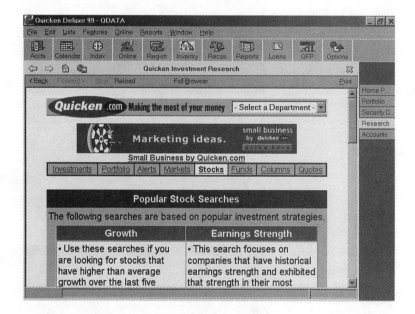

- *Top 25 Funds.* Displays the top 25 mutual funds based on the Morningstar category (similar to asset class) and time span you select, displayed in Figure 24.15.

- *Fund Family Directory.* Provides a list of many popular mutual fund families and lets you access their Web site from Quicken (see Figure 24.16).

- *Fund Finder.* Displays the Fund Finder in which you answer a number of questions regarding the type of fund you are looking for—Morningstar category, ratings, loads, expenses, returns, and so on. You can also specify how you want to sort the matching funds and how many funds to display (see Figure 24.17).

  Click the Show Results button for Quicken to provide a list of the funds that match your criteria.

FIGURE 24.15

You can see the top 25 funds in a variety of categories.

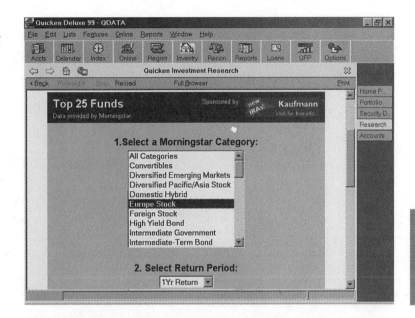

FIGURE 24.16

Access information on specific fund families.

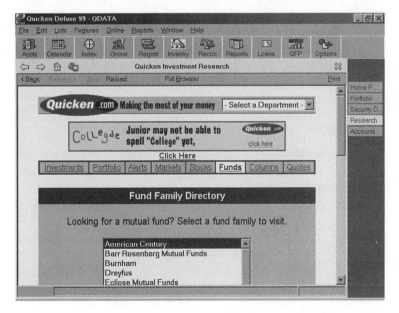

24

FIGURE 24.17

Search for mutual funds based on criteria you specify.

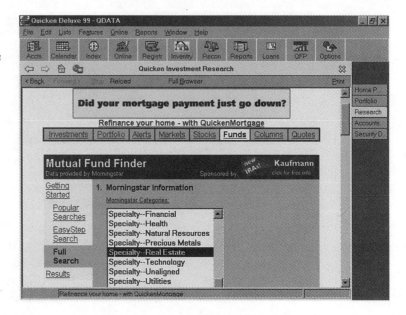

Accessing the Quicken.com Web Site

Quicken.com is a very useful Web site with detailed financial information for Quicken users. It includes online quotes, portfolio tracking, bank rates, investment research, and detailed articles on a variety of financial topics.

To access Quicken.com, select Online, Quicken on the Web, Quicken.com. Figure 24.18 displays this Web site.

The Departments on the right side of the screen include a wealth of information on topics such as investments, mortgages, insurance, small business, banking, retirement, and taxes.

Click Full Browser to open this Web site using Internet Explorer rather than Quicken's internal Web browser.

FIGURE 24.18

Use Quicken.com to learn more about your finances.

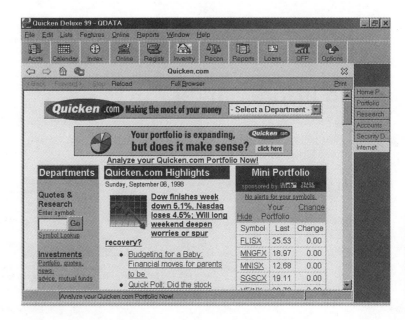

Using QuickenMortgage

QuickenMortgage offers advice on buying a house, applying for a mortgage, refinancing, and locating low loan rates. To access this online area, select Online, Quicken on the Web, Mortgage Center. Figure 24.19 displays the initial QuickenMortgage window.

FIGURE 24.19

QuickenMortgage simplifies looking for a mortgage loan.

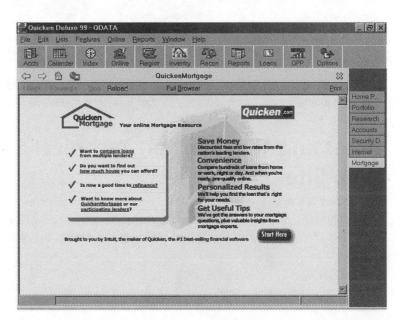

You can also apply for a loan online through participating lenders.

Using InsureMarket

Quicken's InsureMarket enables you to shop online for the best life, home, car and other types of insurance. Select Online, Quicken on the Web, InsureMarket to open the InsureMarket window (see Figure 24.20).

FIGURE 24.20

Use InusreMarket to determine your insurance needs.

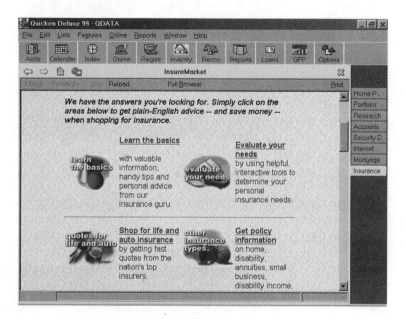

This Web site also offers basic insurance information and an interactive planner to help you evaluate how much and what kind of insurance you need.

Accessing the Quicken Technical Support Web Site

When you're having a problem with Quicken that you can't resolve, check the detailed technical support information Quicken provides on it Web site. To access this site, select Help, Product Support. Figure 24.21 displays the Product Support dialog box.

FIGURE 24.21

The Product Support dialog box offers several options for getting technical assistance.

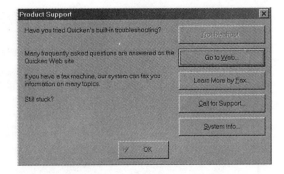

Click the Go to Web button to open the Quicken Technical Support Web site, illustrated in Figure 24.22.

24

FIGURE 24.22

You can find answers to many Quicken problems.

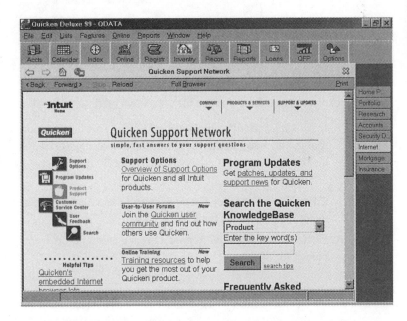

This Web site offers search capabilities, a list of frequently asked questions, and program updates.

Checking your Credit Online

To check your credit online, select Online, Quicken on the Web, Credit Check. Figure 24.23 displays the CreditCheck window that opens.

FIGURE 24.23

Quicken provides several options for getting a credit report—some free and some for a fee.

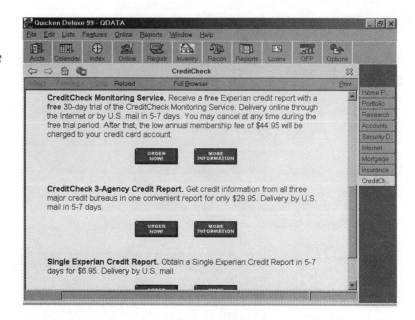

Quicken provides three options for ordering a credit report online:

- *CreditCheck Monitoring Service.* Offers a free credit report as well as a 30-day trial membership in the CreditCheck Monitoring Service. If you don't want to keep the service, you must cancel within those 30 days or you are charged an annual fee of $44.95.

- *CreditCheck 3-Agency Credit Report.* Offers a credit report from each of the three major credit bureaus for $29.95.

- *Single Experian Credit Report.* Offers a credit report from the Experian credit bureau for $6.95.

As a Quicken user you can get a free credit report by submitting a request in writing (not via the Internet). The CreditCheck window provides details on the information required and where to submit your request.

Summary

This hour explored the many ways you can use the Internet to enhance your use of Quicken. Use One Step Update to download both investment quotes and records from your financial institutions at the same time. You can download investment information individually as well, such as historic prices and asset class mixtures. Quicken also offers detailed investment research, an online credit report service, and access to Quicken.com, its own Web site that contains a wealth of financial information.

Now that you've completed 24 lessons on using Quicken, you should be equipped to handle all basic tasks and start to explore advanced capabilities in more detail.

Q&A

Q Do I need to set up anything before I start using One Step Update?

A You need to set up Quicken to connect to the Internet before you can use this feature. Also, if you want to download account information, you must sign up for online account access first. And to use the Web Transaction Download and Portfolio Export features you must be registered with Quicken.com.

Q How can I use the Web to help me select investments?

A First, go to the Quicken.com Web site to educate yourself on basic investing, types of investments, terminology, asset allocation, and so on. Using this background information, come up with a plan for how you want to allocate the money you have available to invest. From there, use the Quicken Investment Research window to help you select the investments that fit this plan.

24

APPENDIX **A**

Using Quicken Home & Business 99

Each of the 24 lessons you just completed covered Quicken features you'll find in both Quicken Deluxe 99 and Quicken Home & Business 99. The Home & Business version, however, also includes a number of features specifically targeted to using Quicken to manage small business finances. With Quicken Home & Business you can

- Create, track, and print custom invoices
- Track and record customer payments
- View unpaid invoices
- Track and record business bills you need to pay
- Issue and receive credits/refunds
- View and print business reports including profit and loss, balance sheet, and schedule C reports
- Track business-related taxes

Setting Up Accounts for Receivables and Payables

Quicken Home & Business 99 enables you to create two additional kinds of accounts—Invoices/Receivables and Bills/Payables. Figure A.1 illustrates the Create New Account dialog box in the Home & Business version, which includes these account types in the list of options.

FIGURE A.1

Using Quicken Home & Business you can create receivable and payable accounts.

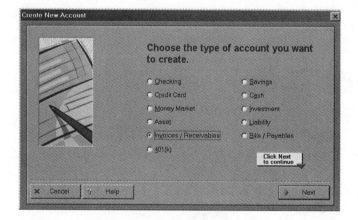

Setting up either of these types of accounts is similar to setting up any other account. You can either use the EasyStep approach for more detailed guidance or go directly to the Summary tab for faster setup. When you set up an invoice account, Quicken automatically creates a related sales tax account in which all sales tax is tracked and stored.

Using the Invoices/Receivables Register

Every invoices/receivables account you create has a corresponding invoices/receivables register. To display this register, click the Accts icon on the Iconbar and double-click the Invoice account you want to open. Figure A.2 shows a sample register used for a small business.

In this register you can enter

- Invoices
- Customer payments
- Credits
- Refunds
- Finance charges

FIGURE A.2

Use this register to enter invoices and customer payments.

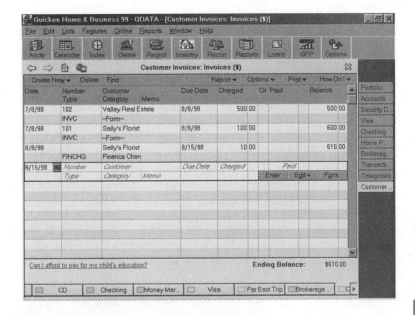

Quicken provides specific forms to enter each of these transactions. Click the Create New button to display a menu of options and choose the transaction you want to create.

Creating an Invoice

For example, if you want to invoice a customer, you can choose Invoice from the menu, which opens the Invoice form (see Figure A.3).

FIGURE A.3

Use the default invoice template or create one of your own.

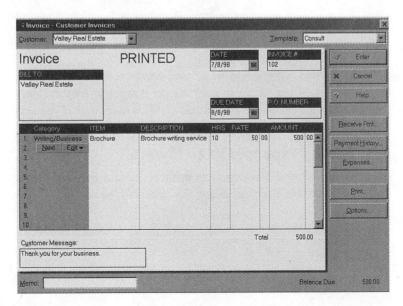

Select the customer you want to invoice, choose the appropriate invoice template, and then fill out the form. By specifying a category, you can properly record the payment when you receive it. When you finish the form, click the Enter button to record the transaction in the register.

> If an item is taxable, be sure to select the Tax column that displays the letter T. Quicken then calculates the tax based on the rate you enter on the form and records this taxable amount in the corresponding Sales Tax register.

Creating Invoice Items

In the Item column, enter a name for the particular item you're invoicing. If this is the first time you've entered an item, Quicken asks you if you want to create a new item with that name. Click Yes and the New Item dialog box appears (see Figure A.4).

FIGURE A.4

Creating invoice items helps reduce future data entry.

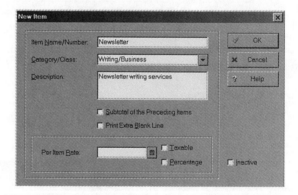

In this dialog box you enter a name, category, description, and other information about this item. Then when you need to enter it again on another invoice, Quicken recalls these details and enters them automatically. This saves time if you sell the same product or service over and over again to numerous customers.

Adding Expenses to an Invoice

To add external expenses to an invoice, click the Expenses button. The Choose Reimbursable Expenses dialog box appears as shown in Figure A.5.

FIGURE A.5

You can add expenses to an invoice.

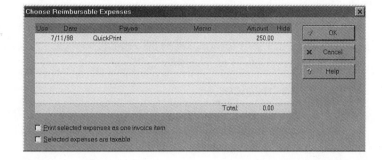

Select the Use column of the expense or expenses you want to attach to this invoice and click OK. Quicken displays the selected expenses as invoice line items.

Creating a New Invoice Template

You can customize an invoice to suit the needs of your business. To do so, select New from the Template drop-down list to open the New Template dialog box (see Figure A.6).

FIGURE A.6

You can add your company address to an invoice if you like.

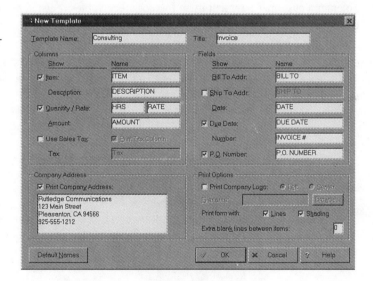

A

 Select Edit from the Template drop-down list to edit the template you're currently using.

In the New Template dialog box, you can choose and modify the fields and columns you want to display. For example, a consulting business may not need quantity or tax fields, but a business that sells artwork needs these fields. You can also choose to display your company address or logo on your invoices.

Printing an Invoice

To print an invoice, click the Print button from the Invoice form. The Print dialog box appears. Click the Preview button to preview the invoice or click OK to go ahead and print the invoice.

> You can print multiple invoices by selecting Features, Business, Print Invoices and choosing the invoices you want to print in the Print Invoices window.

Entering a Customer Payment

To enter a customer payment in an invoices/receivables register, select Create New, Customer Payment. The Payment form appears (see Figure A.7).

FIGURE A.7

When a customer pays you, record it in the Payment form.

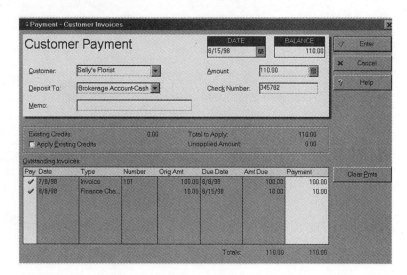

Select the Customer from the drop-down list and specify the account to which you want to deposit the payment. The lower portion of the form displays outstanding invoices; you can apply the payment to any of these. Quicken stores the payment information in both the invoices/receivables register and the register of the deposit account you selected in the form.

Entering Credits and Refunds

If a customer returns a product, you need to issue a credit. Select Create New, Credit to open the Credit form (see Figure A.8).

FIGURE A.8

You can quickly enter a customer credit using this form.

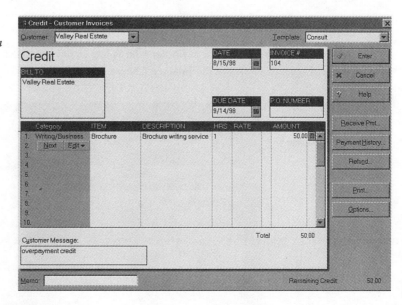

 You can also issue credits and refunds from the bills/payables register.

This form is similar to the invoice form and you create, enter, and print a customer credit as you would an invoice. If a customer has already paid and you need to refund money for some reason (a return, an overpayment, and so on), select Create New, Refund. The Refund form opens, as shown in Figure A.9.

FIGURE A.9

Enter a refund using the Refund form.

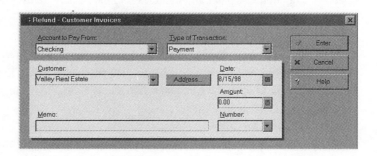

A

The refund form is similar to the Payment form. Select the Account to Pay From, the name of the Customer, and details about the refund. Quicken records the refund in both the invoices/receivables register and the register of the account from which you paid the refund.

Issuing a Finance Charge

To issue a finance charge to a customer who is late in paying, select Create New, Finance Charge. Figure A.10 shows the Finance Charge dialog box.

FIGURE A.10

You can issue finance charges to customers who pay late.

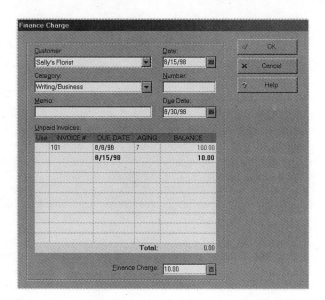

Select the Customer and Category to which this charge applies and enter a new Due Date. You can select the invoice to which you want to apply this charge from the Unpaid Invoices list. Finally, enter a specific Finance Charge and click OK. Quicken records the finance charge in the register and includes it in the next customer statement you issue.

Creating Customer Statements

You can create customer statements to remind customers about invoices, credit memos, payments received, and finance charges for late payments. Select Features, Business, Create Statement to open the Customer Statements dialog box, shown in Figure A.11.

FIGURE A.11

Customer statements enable you to notify customers of payments received as well as late payments.

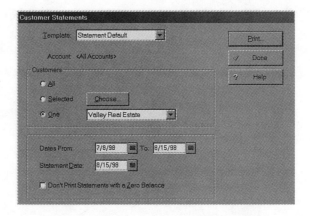

Specify the customers and dates you want to include in your statement and click the Print button. From the Print dialog box you can either click Preview to see what your statement looks like before printing or OK to print without previewing.

Select New or Edit from the Template drop-down list to create a new customer statement template or edit an existing one.

A

Using the Bills/Payables Register

The bills/payables register tracks your accounts payable—the bills you need to pay. To display this register, click the Accts icon on the Iconbar and double-click the Bill account you want to open. Figure A.12 illustrates a sample register.

In this register you can enter

- Bills
- Payments
- Credits
- Refunds

Quicken provides specific forms to enter each of these transactions. Click the Create New button to display a menu of options and choose the transaction you want to create.

FIGURE A.12

Track the bills you need to pay in this register.

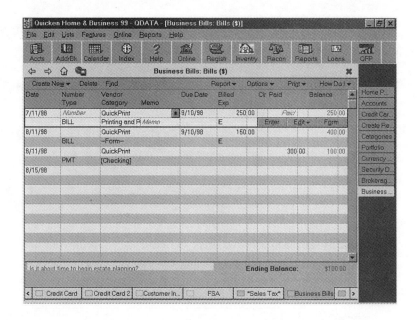

Entering a Bill

To enter a bill that you need to pay, select Create New, Bill. The Bill form appears (see Figure A.13).

FIGURE A.13

Enter a bill you want to record using this form.

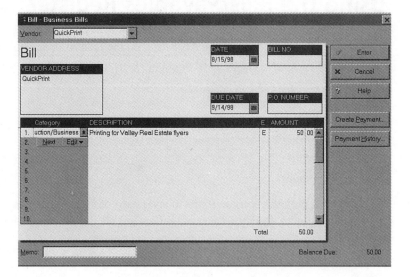

Select the appropriate Vendor from the drop-down list or enter a new one. Complete the rest of the form, paying particular attention to assigning an appropriate category to this bill.

If you want to be able to expense this item and attach to a customer invoice, select the E column. For example, if you create flyers for one of your customers, you might charge a design fee as well as expense the cost of printing the flyers. When you finish, click Enter to record the transaction.

Making a Vendor Payment

After you enter a bill, you need to enter a vendor payment when you pay it. Choose Create New, Payment to Vendor to display the Payment form (see Figure A.14).

FIGURE A.14

Specify the vendor to pay and the account from which to withdraw funds.

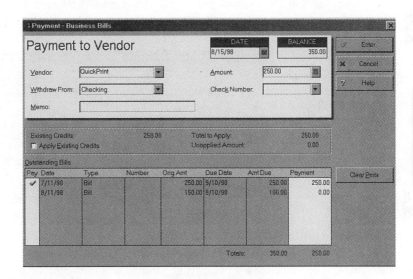

Select the appropriate Vendor and an account to Withdraw From. Any Outstanding Bills from that vendor appear in the lower portion of the form. You can specify which bill you want this payment to cover if there are multiple outstanding bills.

Quicken records the payment in the bills/payables register as well as in the register for the account from which you withdrew money.

Viewing Business Information in Quicken

Quicken enables you to print reports analyzing your business performance, display a Small Business Center with details of your business activities, as well as view a list of unpaid invoices.

Viewing Business Reports

Quicken Home & Business includes several reports that you can use to track and analyze your business income and expense. These include

- P&L Statement
- P&L Comparison
- Cash Flow
- A/P by Vendor
- A/R by Customer
- Job/Project

- Payroll
- Balance Sheet
- Missing Checks
- Comparison
- Tax Schedule
- Schedule C

Click the Reports icon and go to the Business tab in the Create Reports window to view these reports (see Figure A.15). They are also available with Quicken Deluxe.

FIGURE A.15

You can print a variety of business reports with Quicken Home & Business.

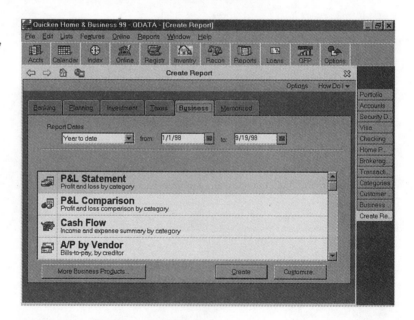

Viewing the Small Business Center

Quicken Home & Business includes an additional financial activity center—the Small Business Center. To open this center, select Features, Centers, Small Business Center (see Figure A.16).

This center displays unpaid invoices by customer, accounts payable bills due by vendor, as well as a bar chart illustrating your business income and expenses.

FIGURE A.16

The Small Business Center gives you an overall look at your small business finances.

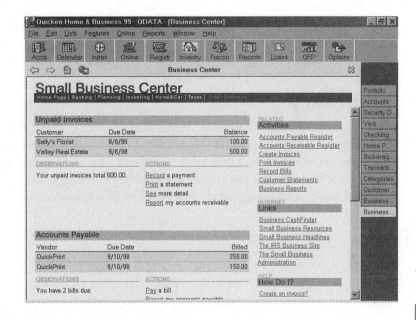

Viewing Unpaid Invoices

To see a list of unpaid invoices, select Features, Business, Unpaid Invoices (see Figure A.17).

FIGURE A.17

You can quickly see which customers still need to pay you.

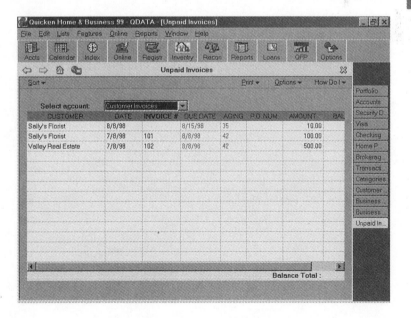

A

Select the account that contains the unpaid invoices. Quicken displays these invoices in the lower portion of the Unpaid Invoices window. Double-click an individual invoice item to open the complete invoice form.

Summary

This appendix showed you how to take advantage of the special features you'll find in the Home & Business version of Quicken 99. With this version, you can create and print invoices as well as track their related payments. You can also track and record the business-related bills that you need to pay. Finally, you can view and print a variety of reports that help you track and analyze your business performance, including tax implications.

INDEX

B

C

E

T

U